1988

W9-DAR-996

# CLARA BOW
## RUNNIN' WILD

The "It" Girl on her infamous made-to-order bed. Clara installed mirrors in its canopy. (Academy of Motion Picture Arts and Sciences).

# CLARA BOW
## RUNNIN' WILD

BY
## DAVID STENN

*95311*

**Doubleday**

NEW YORK LONDON TORONTO SYDNEY AUCKLAND

Photographs, recordings, and writings of Clara Bow, Rex Bell, Robert Bow, and Sarah Bow copyright © Rex A. Bell. All rights reserved. Used by permission.

Cover photograph courtesy of Beauregard Houston-Montgomery.

Published by Doubleday, a division of Bantam Doubleday Dell Publishing Group, Inc., 666 Fifth Avenue, New York, New York 10103

**Doubleday** and the portrayal of an anchor with a dolphin are trademarks of Doubleday, a division of Bantam Doubleday Dell Publishing Group, Inc.

Library of Congress Cataloging-in-Publication Data

Stenn, David.
Clara Bow: runnin' wild / by David Stenn. — 1st ed.
p. cm.
Bibliography: p.
Includes index.
1. Bow, Clara, 1905–1965.   2. Motion picture actors and actresses—
United States—Biography.   I. Title.
PN2287.B65S74   1988
791.43'028'0924—dc19
[B]        88-11896
CIP

ISBN 0-385-24125-9

BG

*For the movie pioneers
and film preservationists,
with gratitude and respect*

# AUTHOR'S NOTE

Teet Carle, Arthur Jacobson, and William Kaplan endured numerous interviews with grace and charm. Tui Lorraine Bow's concern about the expense of my trans-Pacific telephone calls led her to tape herself and mail the results, a treat for any listener. Daisy DeVoe broke fifty-five years of self-imposed silence to discuss "the blackest period of my life" in unsparing detail.

Jacqueline Onassis, my editor, and Owen Laster, my agent, believed in the project from its beginning. Their enthusiasm and encouragement meant more than they know.

Additional guidance and assistance was given by Karen Aderman, Rudy Behlmer, Kevin Brownlow, Kevin Jarre, Justine Kaplan, Sidney Kirkpatrick, Richard Lamparski, Dr. Jan Leestma, B. Ann Moorhouse, Barry Paris, Judy Sandman, David Shepard, Marc Wanamaker, Michael Yakaitis. And as always, forever, my family.

Finally, this book could not exist without the cooperation of Rex A. Bell, who, besides sharing his own memories, provided unrestricted access to his mother's psychiatric, medical, and financial records; professional and personal correspondence; and private photographs. I am beholden to and honored by his trust, friendship, and support.

# CONTENTS

# CLARA BOW
## RUNNIN' WILD

# PROLOGUE

I'm runnin' wild, lost control
Runnin' wild, mighty bold
Always goin', don't know where,
All alone, runnin' wild . . .

*– Runnin' Wild*

Anyone who went to the movies in the spring of 1927 knew who ran wildest, boldest, and beyond control. "She was the girl of the year," wrote F. Scott Fitzgerald, "the 'It' girl, the girl for whose services every studio was in violent competition. This girl was the real thing, someone to stir every pulse in the nation." She had a heart-shaped face, an hour-glass figure, and thick auburn hair dyed a flaming orange-red. She had "It," the most desirable attribute of the decade. She was twenty-one. Her name was Clara Bow.

Superficially there was nothing special about Clara, or so she thought. "Just a working girl," she said of herself. "Jest a woikin' goil," was how she sounded when she said it, her raucous Brooklynese a barbaric contrast to her beauty. But the world had not yet heard Clara talk, and in 1927 it was in no hurry to do so. For the moment her presence was plenty.

Fans and critics felt there had never been anyone like her. Where other women acted, she came to life, a three-dimensional being in a two-dimensional medium. There was an energy, a vitality, a restlessness within her that turned rival actresses into zombies. "Miss Van Cortland seems rather lacking in reserve," sniffs a haughty supporting character of Clara's heroine in *It,* her namesake hit that spring in 1927, and as one historian has noted, "it's one of the great, classic understatements." Of course it is. "The 'It' Girl" ran wild.

But there was more to Clara than "It," and occasionally she said so. "I smile, but my eyes never smile," she told reporters who considered her interchangeable with the carefree flapper she played. "I wish I were," sighed Clara. "She's much happier than I am." From the personification of frivolity this was heresy, not honesty. Her protests were ignored.

Ultimately Clara had the last word, and when she did, it was a haunting one. "All the time the flapper is laughin' and dancin', there's a feelin' of tragedy underneath," she said at the height of her career. "She's unhappy and disillusioned, and that's what people sense. That's what makes her different."

"The 'It' Girl" was running wild, all right. And running away. And running scared. Had she told anyone why—and she never, ever had—they would not have believed her. The truth was too incredible, tragic, and frightening. The truth revealed what made Clara run.

# 1

## Brooklyn Gothic

"Even now I can't trust life. It did too many awful things
t'me as a kid."

– Clara Bow (1928)

# 1

"Nobody wanted me t'be born in the first place."

She said it without self-pity, but with parents like Robert and Sarah Bow, pity is exactly what Clara deserved. Robert Bow was less than two years old when his mother died giving birth to her thirteenth child. He was raised without affection, attention, or care, and by adulthood his appearance and character showed it: all who knew him describe Robert Bow as puny in body and mind, "a stupid, ugly little guy" whom some were convinced was mentally retarded. They also remember his huge blackish-brown eyes, whose white rings around the iris gave them a dull and deadened expression.

Clara's father had one other remarkable feature, a rich baritone singing voice used to entertain fellow wastrels in the downtown Brooklyn dives he frequented after dropping out of grammar school. With their swinging doors, brass footrails, spittoons, and air made blue from cigar smoke (Robert himself was never seen without a stogie stuck in his mouth), these sleazy saloons substituted for the home he never had. Here Robert would make maudlin toasts, swap dirty jokes, and boast of his imminent success as a singing waiter at a swell New York restaurant. Few believed him, for although Robert had talent, he lacked drive. He was not just a big dreamer, but a big baby, a man stunted not just physically, but emotionally. Nowhere was this more apparent than in his attitude toward the female sex, whom he regarded as objects put into existence for the same reason as liquor: so he could abuse them.

There were plenty of brothels to service his needs. By 1898, the year Manhattan, Brooklyn, the Bronx, Queens, and Richmond (Staten Island) were incorporated into one joint entity known as New York City, there was so much whiskey and so many women for sale that one outraged reformer called the new metropolis "a modern Gomorrah" and an ecclesiastical council complained that the city harbored more whores than Methodists. In Brooklyn's notorious Navy Yard district, "tarts" in transparent shifts stood in windows, beckoning men inside for a dollar "lay" or a five-dollar, orgiastic "circus." The belle of the Navy Yard was a whore with a mouth of gold nicknamed "Submarine Mary" for the way she went down.

Here Robert Bow bought the bodies of underage girls while dreaming of an ideal one. He found her in Sarah Gordon, one of six children of florist Frederick Gordon. With her knee-length flaxen braids, fair skin, blue eyes, and regal profile, Sarah's beauty belied her slum background. Her life did not, for Frederick Gordon was a father who ruled his family with an iron will and clenched fist. His two favorite pastimes seem to have been drinking and wifebeating, and as she watched her emotionally unstable mother pummeled mercilessly, Sarah swore she would never let a man subdue her the same way.

She almost didn't live that long. At sixteen, Sarah fell headfirst from a second-story window while plucking grapes off a vine for her brother. After hovering near death, she was sent to an uncle's farm in Richmond to convalesce from what was diagnosed as "serious anemia."

Sarah loved country life and had no wish to leave it, but soon she had recovered sufficiently to return to Brooklyn, where her family was leading an even more marginal existence. By 1898 Brooklyn boasted one million inhabitants, many of them Eastern and Southern Europeans willing to work longer hours for lower wages than English and Scotch-Irish immigrants like the Bows and Gordons, who had arrived in America a generation earlier. With salaries cut and jobs scarce, flowers were a luxury few could afford. Frederick Gordon lost his job.

When Sarah came back to Brooklyn, her father had not worked for six months. Instead Frederick Gordon passed his days drinking "chain lightning" whiskey and battering his wife, who soon lost her mind. Since insanity was considered even more shameful than illegitimate pregnancy or cancer, Frederick Gordon commanded his children to keep their mother's condition secret, and when a federal census was conducted in 1900, he locked his wife in a closet and told the census taker he was a widower. Better dead than mad, ran the prevailing wisdom of the time, and Frederick Gordon firmly believed it.

It was a grotesque situation from which Sarah was desperate to escape. But as beautiful as she was, a destitute woman with an alcoholic father and insane mother (Frederick Gordon could fool a census taker, but not his neighbors) was hardly besieged by suitors. In fact, there was only Robert Bow, who lived a block away and had been infatuated with her since childhood. Back then she had scorned his attentions, but now she encouraged them. Apparently she was so encouraging that by the time Sarah married Robert Bow on November 26, 1902, she was already pregnant.

The union of a hypersexed loser like Robert to an asexual wretch like Sarah was a match made in hell, so it was grimly appropriate that reformers referred to the tenement neighborhood into which the newlyweds moved as "hell on earth." Unrestricted by building regulations or fire, health, and sanitation codes, tenements crammed a maximum of tenants into a minimum of space. Apartments were closets, with no ventilation, windows, or sunlight ("in the tenements," it was said, "the sun is ashamed to shine"). Two dozen residents shared a single toilet, whose rotten drains filled hallways with the overpowering stench of excrement. Roaches and rats feasted on waste dumped from windows.

Not surprisingly, the most common event of tenement life was death. Wooden fire-escape ladders went up in flames and trapped residents were burned alive. Tuberculosis was so prevalent that tenement neighborhoods were designated "lung blocks." Epidemics of cholera, diptheria, scarlet fever, and smallpox decimated entire families. Common childhood diseases like diarrhea, influenza, measles, and pneumonia became lethal. Infant mortality was so common that six-foot high stacks of tiny pine coffins often stood outside slum buildings, awaiting delivery to the nearest potter's field.

The Brooklyn tenement into which the Bows moved was located at 160 Sands Street. Rivaling only Manhattan's Bowery and San Francisco's Barbary Coast as the roughest area in America, Sands Street was pockmarked with pawnshops, gambling dives, pothouse bars, flophouses, and fleabag hotels which rented by the hour. Its denizens included prostitutes, pimps, homosexual hustlers, dope peddlers, white slavers, thieves, and killers for hire.

In the greasy restaurant where he worked as a busboy, twenty-seven year-old Robert Bow served them all. His miserable wife stayed home, and sometime during the summer of 1903, she gave birth to a daughter who died two days later. Instead of a burial, Sarah Bow threw her unnamed, unbaptized baby into the trash.

A few months later she was pregnant again, and on May 13, 1904, a second daughter was born prematurely. She was dead within two hours. Since a doctor had been present and a death certificate filed, Sarah could not dispose of this daughter like her last. A technicality necessitated Emily Bow's burial in an unmarked mass grave.

Sarah almost died during Emily's birth, and the attending doctor warned that further pregnancy would prove fatal for both mother and child. Yet that fall, with two strikes already against her, Sarah conceived for the third time. It was a perverse form of suicide, but suited to her purpose: forced to bear children she did not want by a man she did not love, Sarah had decided to die trying.

Robert did not object. He was sick of Sarah nagging him about money and his inability to earn it. She also mocked his dream of success as a singing waiter, reminding Robert that he was a lowly busboy in a disgusting restaurant. Rather than face the truth, he left her.

Abandoned and pregnant, Sarah had no choice but to return to her father's tenement apartment above a storefront Baptist Church at 697 Bergen Street. Since she had only married to flee her family, the homecoming was doubly humiliating, and although it did not seem possible, living conditions were worse than ever. That July, as temperatures inside tenements hit 115 degrees, the Board of Health dispatched "summer doctors" in a futile attempt to combat an infant mortality rate estimated at eighty percent.

Amidst the heat wave, Sarah went into labor. Regarding death as deliverance and believing this birth would bring it, she did not bother to summon a doctor. Instead her insane mother served as midwife when Sarah gave birth to a third daughter on Saturday, July 29, 1905. To her relief, the baby seemed dead.

Then a sudden miracle occurred: as Sarah's mother shook the lifeless newborn, it emitted a feeble cry. A twist of fate had let both mother and child live.

Apprised of this, Robert returned to his wife and named their daughter after his sister-in-law. Still, so certain was he (and so hopeful was Sarah) of the baby's imminent death that no birth certificate was ever obtained. Already Clara Bow was unloved and unwanted, and it would not be long before she knew it.

# 2

Clara was a robust child with auburn hair, high cheekbones, translucent coloring, and blackish-brown eyes as alive and expressive as her father's were deadened and dull. But health did not guarantee happiness, and Clara's life remained grim. A few weeks after her first birthday, her grandfather Frederick Gordon committed his wife to an asylum for the terminally insane, where she died a year later. Afterwards Sarah Bow hated her father more than ever, but since her own husband had taken to disappearing for weeks at a time, she had no alternative but to let Frederick Gordon move in with her and Clara. Amazingly, he treated his granddaughter with kindness and affection and even built a swing for her inside their single room. Ignored by her parents, Clara grew devoted to her grandfather.

Her delight was short-lived. On January 20, 1909, sixty-three-year-old Frederick Gordon was stricken by an apoplectic fit while pushing Clara on her swing. The child's terrified screams brought Sarah, who had been on a crying jag all day anyway, from the pot-bellied stove where she had been burning coal to keep warm. When Frederick Gordon died the next day, Sarah told Clara she wished it had been her instead.

Nonetheless Clara worshipped her mother, creating what one psychiatrist would call "very much a dream existence" and placing Sarah on a pedestal at its center. Clara thought of Sarah in fairy-tale terms, idealizing her aloofness as appropriate for "a princess. It must be true," she insisted years later, "that she had good blood in her." Actually it was just the opposite: descended from poverty, madness, death, and despair, Sarah seemed destined to return to her roots, and an incident in 1911 hastened her descent. Clara was told that her mother "fell" down a rickety tenement staircase, but given Sarah's state of mind, a suicide attempt seems more likely. Whether intentional or not, Sarah's fall reopened the head wound she had suffered at age sixteen, and with rural convalescence no longer feasible, stitches had to suffice.

After her head injury, Sarah began to suffer from a mysterious malady that struck without warning. Clara described the symptoms only once, and then vaguely, as neither "fits" nor "regular faintin' spells," but seizures whose onset would cause Sarah to look at her daughter pathetically, "like a woman caught in some trap. Then her eyes'd grow glassy an' she'd start t'gasp for breath just like she was bein' strangled." Often Sarah's seizures would occur three times a day, then vanish for weeks. When they returned, Clara would watch in horror, powerless to prevent or control them. All she could do was massage her mother's throat until the tormented woman breathed freely again.

Clara rarely spoke of her early years, unwilling to exploit them for publicity (Marilyn Monroe, on the other hand, often told fictitious tales of childhood traumas to elicit sympathy). When Clara did discuss her youth, her tone was terse: "I have known hunger, believe me," she told one journalist. Asked by another for further detail, she told the truth: "We just lived, and that's about all."

Just living was tough enough. The Bows were ghetto nomads, moving from tenement to tenement and appealing for aid from relatives who wanted nothing to do with them. Most of the time Clara and her mother were left to fend for themselves, but that was better than when Robert Bow returned home. Family reunions created a destructive and violent dynamic, with Sarah goading her husband about his failure and Robert relieving his frustration by beating Clara. His favorite form of discipline was both senseless and brutal: while arguing with Sarah, Robert would suddenly turn upon Clara and snarl, "Don't look at me in that tone of voice!", then slap her face so hard that she was thrown to the floor. He also whipped her with his leather razor strop.

Clara developed into a lonely, hypersensitive child, acutely self-conscious of a slight speech impediment which caused her to "hang up" on a word and haltingly stammer its first letter—"H-h-h-h-hello"—until her mind caught up with her mouth. Her stammer was a source of constant amusement to other girls at P.S. 111, who mimicked the way Clara talked and mocked the clothes she wore, which were made from Sarah's tattered shirtwaists. Scorned " 'cause I was the worst-lookin' kid on the street," Clara became a tomboy, roving streets where packs of teenage ruffians fought neighboring gangs with knives, bricks, or stones hauled in onion sacks. Eye-gouging, facial disfigurement, and fatal beatings were business as usual in the Brooklyn tenements, but Clara's favorite weapon was her fists. "I could lick any boy my size," she recalled with pride. "My right was famous." When boys organized stickball games in the streets, she was chosen first.

Her only real friend, however, was a younger boy named Johnny who lived in the same tenement. Johnny was her imaginary kid brother, the fantasy sibling Clara could play with and protect. Any boy who bullied him got a beating from her.

As if her grandfather's death, her mother's attacks, and her father's abuse weren't enough, Clara now saw her best friend burned alive. In her tenement one afternoon, she suddenly heard bloodcurdling screams coming from Johnny's apartment. Clara rushed downstairs and found him on fire, howling her name in agony. She rolled him in a carpet. He died in her arms.

Johnny's grisly death left Clara alone once again. She was nine years old.

In 1916 a cousin allowed the Bows to occupy a single room in her Prospect Place whitestone and Clara transferred from P.S. 111 to P.S. 9, where she finished fifth grade. "I never opened a book and the teachers was always down on me," she would claim. "I don't blame 'em." Actually she had a B+ average and a perfect record for classroom conduct, yet so low was Clara's self-esteem that all she remembered about her schooling was her stammer and the cruelty it provoked from female classmates. "They was always hurtin' my feelin's, and I thought they was silly anyway," said Clara. "I never had no use for girls and their games." Instead she found refuge and comfort from a special source: "In this lonesome time, when I wasn't much of nothin' and didn't have nobody, [there was] one place I could go and forget the misery of home and heartache of school.

"That was the motion pictures."

Whether it was slapstick comedian Roscoe "Fatty" Arbuckle, "America's Sweetheart" Mary Pickford, dashing swashbuckler Douglas Fairbanks, or impossibly handsome Wallace Reid on screen did not matter: Clara adored movies and spent all her spare time attending them. "We'd go to the Carlton or Bunny Theater and see whatever was showing," recalls John Bennett, her friend and fellow movie fan. Like his predecessor, this Johnny was a neighbor four years younger than Clara. "I was the only one who would listen to her little tales of fantasy, her dreams. She wasn't loved at home, and nobody in the neighborhood bothered with her, so she would confide in me." On Sunday afternoons Johnny kept Clara company as she sat on the stoop of her cousin's whitestone, surrounded by movie magazines and fantasizing about how someday she would appear in them. "She told me that she was going to be a great movie star," he says. "Of course, I didn't believe her."

Sarah Bow forbid any such ambition. In her opinion actresses and prostitutes were interchangeable, and the heavy makeup worn by both as they walked the streets (though the movie industry was based in Hollywood, many studios still operated in New York City) confirmed it. "You ain't goin' inta pictures," she ranted. "You ain't gonna be no *hoor.*"

By now Sarah had confined herself to bed due to her strange and uncontrollable "spells." But just because she led the life of an invalid did not mean she possessed the temperament of one. Manipulative and antimaternal, she treated Clara not as a daughter, but as a domestic. The child was her mother's nurse, maid, companion, and confidante, and to maintain her tyranny, Sarah kept Clara in a state of nervous anxiety that would last the rest of her life.

The basic topic of Sarah's tirades was her mortal enemy: man. Sarah taught Clara little about sex but much about men; all of it negative. Using her ne'er-do-well husband as a bitter example, Sarah hammered into Clara that men limit, disappoint, humiliate, and abandon their mates. When a woman gives herself up to a man, she loses her power. Man is the master and thus the enemy. Woman must control him any way she can.

What Sarah did not realize and what her daughter could not verbalize was that unlike her mother, Clara did not seek independence. What she needed was more basic, and after she sensed that her parents would not provide it, she assumed a film career would. For just like the rest of her generation, Clara was not only fascinated by the brand-new medium of movies, but brainwashed to believe that stardom in them would provide fame, adulation, and, most elusive and important of all, love.

In 1918 an epidemic of Spanish influenza turned tenements into morgues, with as many as 4,500 fatalities a week for six months. This was too much for even Robert Bow, who, in a rare display of responsibility and concern, moved his wife and daughter to Sheepshead Bay at the opposite end of Brooklyn. From their bayfront apartment on Emmons Avenue Sarah could inhale the sea breezes, while Clara, now a sixth-grade student at P.S. 98, had the most famous amusement park in the world for a neighbor: Coney Island.

Fronting a six-mile beach, Coney Island was "the Empire of the Nickel," the sum that admitted patrons to a spectacular array of bathhouses, carousels, dance halls, Ferris wheels, freak shows, fun houses, penny arcades, roller coasters, shooting galleries, waxworks, restaurants, tearooms, chop suey parlors, custard counters, and hot dog stands. Also within Coney Island was Luna Park, an imitation city of Bagdad, and Dreamland, the nation's largest ballroom. When not in class or at the movies, Clara spent her time exploring the park where her father was a busboy.

Finally Robert was earning enough to support his family, and for a year his wife was, according to Clara, "almost herself." Sarah even showed an interest in her daughter's appearance, curling Clara's hair and sewing her a new dress that did not come from her own ragged ones. Mistaking her mother's remission for recovery, Clara again shared her dream of stardom with Sarah, who promptly ridiculed her daughter for entertaining such a notion. Not only was Clara "the ugliest little mutt in the family," sneered Sarah, but she was utterly devoid of talent.

The child listened to her mother's taunts and believed them.

A grammar-school teacher did not, and to Clara's amazement she was chosen to play Priscilla in the P.S. 98 production of *Miles Standish.* She prepared for the role by reciting her lines over and over, until the stammer which plagued her in moments of stress disappeared. Now Clara awaited her modest stage debut with confidence.

As usual, reality intervened in gruesome fashion. Not only did Sarah's "spells" return, but now they were preceded by episodes of bizarre and hostile behavior. In February of 1919 Sarah's disapproval of her daughter's upcoming performance reached an extreme. As Clara stood on the back porch of their apartment scrubbing clothes in a washtub, Sarah crept up behind her. "I think I'll kill ya," she hissed in her daughter's ear. "This is a terrible world. You'd be better off dead." A "spell" followed. Afterward Sarah had no recollection of the incident.

Clara could not forget it, and when she told her father what had happened, Robert Bow took Sarah to a charity clinic. There he was informed that his wife suffered from "a nervous disease" for which nothing could be done.

Sarah was not safe alone and Clara was not safe with Sarah, so the Bows left Sheepshead Bay and returned to their cousin's Prospect Place whitestone. Yanked out of school, Clara was ordered to find work. She never finished eighth grade. She never played Priscilla.

A thirteen-year-old girl with a seventh-grade education was not in great demand by legitimate professions, but finally Clara was hired to slice buns at Nathan's, a Coney Island hot dog stand. A year later she left Nathan's to answer the telephone for a doctor in Manhattan. Apparently her abrupt departure was due to the discovery that he was an abortionist.

Through it all, the movies and fan magazines provided the form and content of Clara's reveries. Her favorite publication was *Motion Picture,* a monthly publication which cost a quarter and was filled with portraits and stories about the stars. When Wallace Reid appeared at a local theater, Clara waited outside for eight hours to catch a glimpse of him. She also wrote letters to *Motion Picture*'s

Answer Man about Reid and Mary Pickford, whom she imitated in front of a mirror when her mother wasn't looking.

Sarah's fanatical disapproval kept Clara from discussing the Fame and Fortune Contest announced by *Motion Picture* in January 1921. Sponsored by Brewster Publications, a Brooklyn-based company which published *Motion Picture, Motion Picture Classic,* and *Shadowland,* the Fame and Fortune Contest had begun a year earlier and Mary Pickford had been its judge. The panel for 1921 would be comprised of Howard Chandler Christy, Harrison Fisher, and Neysa McMein, the country's most famous commercial artists. "Thru the portal of the Fame and Fortune Contest you may enter the kingdom of the screen," proclaimed the entry form in each Brewster publication. It was not a casual promise. The contest's first prize was a part in a motion picture.

It was the only chance a nobody like Clara would get, and she was desperate to seize it. But she could not enter the contest without two photographs of herself, and she did not have the money to obtain them. As a last resort Clara went to her father, and to her eternal gratitude, Robert Bow took her to a cheap photographer's studio in Coney Island and paid a dollar for two portraits. When Clara saw them, she was crestfallen. Both looked "terrible."

She proceeded anyway. Behind her mother's back but with her father's consent, Clara took the streetcar to the Brewster offices in downtown Brooklyn and delivered her pictures to the Fame and Fortune Contest manager. It was a wise move: unbeknownst to Clara, the manager wrote "Called in person—very pretty" across the bottom of her photos.

The comment would have astonished Clara, who felt foolish for even entering the contest. "It was silly t'even dream of it," she said later. "There wasn't no one who knew me who wouldn'ta laughed loud and long at the idea." Her confidence crumbled further with the monthly appearance of a nationwide Honor Roll of contestants whose portraits were published as a consolation prize. Clara could see for herself how good-looking these competitors were, and how superior the quality of their pictures were compared to hers. "What chance'd I have?" she wondered. "I could see what I looked like in a mirror."

Evidently a mirror did not do for Clara what a camera could, for on Friday, September 2, she and dozens of other contestants took a chartered bus to Eugene Brewster's Long Island home for screen tests. A week later a letter from Brewster Publications invited her to its office for further tests with other finalists.

Clara's longing to share the stupendous news with her mother was precluded by the Arbuckle case, which made headlines that same day. It was the first instance of the cruel timing that would plague her, for this scandal gave Sarah Bow damning proof of Hollywood depravity. During a drunken Labor Day party hosted by 266-pound "Fatty," a sometime actress named Virginia Rappe had become gravely ill, then died four days later from a ruptured bladder. As lurid rumors circulated ("Fatty" had purportedly violated his victim with a champagne bottle), the baby-faced comedian was brought to trial in a kangaroo court dominated by a corrupt district attorney. Meanwhile Rappe's reputation as a "party girl" suffering from both alcoholism and gonorrhea surfaced. Her untimely death, it now appeared, was due not to "Fatty," but a botched abortion.

Though "Fatty" Arbuckle was innocent of the charges against him, the case supported Sarah Bow's conviction that actresses were "hoors." Her denunciations of them grew more vehement than ever, so Clara kept her status as a Fame and Fortune Contest finalist a secret between herself and her father.

Her arrival at the Brewster office for further tests was greeted with snickers from other finalists, and Clara knew why: "I was wearin' the one and only thing I owned: a little plaid dress, a sweater, and a red tam." What would the judges think of her threadbare appearance? "I hadn't thoughta that angle," she realized miserably. "I'd only looked at my face, and that was disappointin' enough."

The finalists were made up, then instructed to walk into camera range, pick up a telephone, laugh, look worried, then terrified. Nine contestants fought to go first; the tenth waited in a corner, not saying a word. "I sat through every one of those tests," recalled Clara later, "watchin' everythin' that was done, everythin' they was told, every mistake they made." For a sixteen-year-old with little education and no acting experience, her verdict was canny: "The trouble was, I thought, that they was all tryin' t'do it like somebody they'd seen on the screen, not the way they'd do it themselves." Instinctively Clara had grasped the essence of stardom: individuality. The girl who spent hours imitating Mary Pickford sensed that to be special, she must be *herself,* an artistic credo that Clara maintained for the rest of her career. Now she was ready. "When it came my turn, I did it the way I'd do it myself."

More tests were made during the following weeks. Clara wore her one dress to them all, fully expecting to be eliminated after each round. The judges, however, were spellbound. "The rapidity of her improvement is scarcely credible," they noted. "She is plastic, quick, alert, young, and lovely . . . her features are photographically excellent." Finally only Clara and a statuesque blonde from San Antonio, Texas named Lula Hubbard remained. After one last test of each, Clara went home. So far it seemed too good to be true.

It was. When she arrived that afternoon, she found her mother hunched over a chair, her face ashen, her eyes glazed. "Where ya been?" Sarah demanded in what her daughter described later as "a cold, awful tone."

Clara told the truth. "I told her where I been and what I done. I told her it looked like I hadda chanceta win this contest, and if I did it meant a job in pictures and a chanceta make good and I could do lotsa things for her."

Hearing this, Sarah toppled from her chair in a dead faint. Clara rushed to revive her but couldn't. She shook Sarah, patted her face, and threw water on it. Nothing worked. Clara was frantic. She was sure she had killed her mother.

Then Sarah awoke. "You're goin' straighta hell," she cursed Clara tonelessly. "I'd rather see ya dead." Then she stared at her daughter "with those awful, burnin' eyes, and her face so white and still." Blaming herself for her mother's condition, Clara burst into tears and swore she would abandon all thoughts of an acting career.

Three days later, Brewster Publications announced its 1921 Fame and Fortune Contest winner: Clara Bow.

# 3

Her Fame and Fortune Contest victory was Clara's chance of a lifetime, and she could not renounce it despite her mother's damnations. Meanwhile the Brewster organization whisked her to the Greenwich Village studio of Nickolas Muray for a portrait to replace the cheap photos she had submitted. Muray shot Clara in two standard ingenue "attitudes": playful, with her thumb hooked jauntily beneath the rim of her red tam, and pensive, gazing off camera with an arm draped modestly over her breasts. Dissatisfied, Muray ordered an additional setup. This time his subject stared directly into the camera, her hair swept across her forehead, her lips locked together, her face half-shadowed, and her eyes haunted. Here was the real Clara, and though she had never looked as lovely, the image is harrowing.

It was hardly what the Brewster organization wanted, so the January, 1922 issue of *Motion Picture Classic* featured the photo of Clara and her tam. The article announcing her victory was entitled "A Dream Come True."

At this point it hadn't, and unless someone spruced Clara up, it wouldn't. Ultimately funds allocated to travel (which Clara, a local resident, did not need) were used to buy her a decent outfit: one crepe dress trimmed with monkey fur, a pair of "Sally pumps," and a velvet hat to replace her tam. The effect, concluded *Motion Picture Classic* with editorial bias, "made a 'still' worth any producer's attention."

But neither attention nor work was forthcoming, and Clara felt her "dream come true" slipping from her grasp. "Panic was drivin' me crazy," she recalled of this period. "After all I'd been through, was this gonna be a failure?" If so, her defiance of her mother had been pointless, and since Sarah's "spells" were occurring with increasing frequency, Clara felt guiltier than ever. She had made her mother sicker, and she had nothing to show for it.

Finally a movie role materialized. *Beyond the Rainbow* starred
Ziegfeld Follies showgirl Billie Dove, already one of the most celebrated beauties of the decade. Beside "the Dove," Clara was a
chubby nobody, and director Christy Cabanne wasted no time
telling her so. "Don't tell me *she* won a beauty contest," hooted
Cabanne to an assistant when Clara entered his office. Instead of
reminding him that the Fame and Fortune Contest had been based
on ability, not beauty, a devastated Clara fled his office in tears.
Afterward the Brewster organization persuaded Cabanne to hire
her by promising free publicity for his film in its publications. The
part of a lead character's little sister was written for Clara. She
would receive fifty dollars for one week's work.

There was, of course, a catch: Clara was expected to furnish
four dresses from her own wardrobe. Since all she owned was the
new dress bought by the Brewster organization and the old one
she had worn to all her screen tests, Clara appealed to Clara Bow,
her wealthy aunt. The fifty-nine-year-old woman listened in silence
to her niece and namesake's plea for a loan, then threw Clara out of
her house.

While her aunt wrote her father that Clara had disgraced the
family, a cousin loaned her eighty dollars. The next day she reported for work on *Beyond the Rainbow* and received a rude awaken-
ing to her new profession. Four other actresses were in the dressing room when Clara arrived. Since she had never used makeup,
she asked them to help her apply it. All four refused. "Find out for
yourself the way we did," they told her. Clara did, and when she
appeared on the set for her first scene, Cabanne swore in disgust.
So much greasepaint caked Clara's face that she looked like a
clown.

It was the second disastrous encounter between Cabanne and
Clara, but this time she redeemed herself. In her first scene, the
director wanted her to cry but assumed she couldn't. Instantly
Clara shed tears. Surprised and impressed, Cabanne wondered
where she had learned to cry on cue. Clara knew but kept the truth
to herself: "It was easy for me t'cry," she admitted later. "All I
hadda do was think of home."

So far Sarah Bow's violent opposition to her daughter's career had been limited to verbal threats, but after Clara finished work on *Beyond the Rainbow,* Sarah turned her words into deeds. Awaking one night from a sound sleep, Clara was startled by the sight of her mother hovering over her, a butcher knife in one hand. "I'm gonna kill ya, Clara," said Sarah as she pinned her daughter's hands to the bed. "It'll be better." Sarah raised the knife to Clara's throat. Then she fainted.

The next morning Sarah had no memory of the incident. Clara could not forget it, and that night marked the beginning of her lifelong, losing battle against insomnia. Soon fans familiar with her sleepless existence would consider Clara a metabolic marvel whose private restlessness suited her public image. Still traumatized by the truth, she did not discourage the fallacy.

On February 1, 1922, director William Desmond Taylor was slain in his Hollywood bungalow. The case was never officially solved, but the careers of two actresses implicated in it, Mary Miles Minter and Mabel Normand, were ruined by revelations that their virtue was a figment of their audience's imagination. It was more fodder for Sarah Bow's tirades, which increased as the release of Clara's first movie approached. Sarah's death threats against her daughter were constant. Clara was sick with fear.

*Beyond the Rainbow* opened on February 19, 1922. That day Clara invited two girls from grammar school to accompany her to it, certain that the sight of herself on screen would avenge their cruelty. Instead her strategy brought further ridicule, for the film contained not a single shot of Clara. With sixteen major characters complicating its plot and slowing its pace, Christy Cabanne had cut several actors from *Beyond the Rainbow.* Clara was among them.

Subsequent to her stardom, *Beyond the Rainbow* would be reissued with her scenes restored and her billing above Billie Dove's. But Clara could not foresee the future, and the present disappointment was crushing. The knowledge that she had been excised from the film did not appease her mother either, and a few days after *Beyond the Rainbow*'s opening, Sarah decided it was her "duty" to kill her daughter before she made another movie. This time she chased Clara around their flat with a butcher knife, then banished her to the streets with all the other "hoors." For two days Clara wandered around Coney Island in a daze. Finally Robert Bow found her and brought her home.

Robert had no intention of caring for his wife and could not let his daughter do so, even though Clara defended her mother. "She wasn't insane," said Clara of Sarah. "She could answer any question, talk, be calm . . . then these spells came on." Robert did not realize that his daughter preferred a homicidal parent to no parent at all, and since he had abandoned Clara long ago, Sarah was all she had.

It didn't matter. Robert Bow refused to assume responsibility for his wife, so on Friday, February 24, 1922, less than a week after *Beyond the Rainbow*'s release, he committed Sarah to an asylum. Sixteen years earlier Sarah's father had incarcerated her mother in the same facility.

Later Clara would claim she suffered some sort of breakdown during this period, though her memory of it was mercifully vague. Prior to intensive psychotherapy, all she could recall were two facts: she and her father moved into an apartment in the Bay Ridge section of Brooklyn, and her efforts to find film work continued. By now Clara was convinced that "winnin' the contest hadn't seemed t'mean a thing. I wore myself out goin' from studio t'studio, from agency t'agency, applyin' for every possible part. But there was always somethin'. I was too young, too little, or too fat. Usually I was too fat."

She was ideal for director Elmer Clifton, who was casting a low-budget whaling saga called *Down to the Sea in Ships*. In need of cheap talent, Clifton noticed the Fame and Fortune Contest winner in *Motion Picture Classic*, liked her youthful look, and summoned her for an interview. When Clara arrived, Clifton couldn't believe his eyes: where was the merry girl from the magazine photo? In a misguided attempt to anticipate his needs, Clara had borrowed a dress and worn heavy makeup. Clifton took one look at her and said she was too old for the part.

Clara was frantic. "I'm only sixteen!" she cried. The director smiled and shook his head. He did not believe her.

Clara rushed home and returned to Clifton's office in her shabby clothing and a scrubbed face. Her gumption and unadorned appeal led the director to hire her for a two-week trial period at a salary of thirty-five dollars a week.

On location in New Bedford, Massachusetts, the two weeks stretched into thirteen as Clifton, impressed by Clara's instinctive talent, padded her role as Dot Morgan, the bland heroine's tomboyish kid sister. Dot was a character Clara could relate to: the spunky, chunky girl who beats up boys her age, then masquerades as one when stowing away on a whaler to escape her repressive Quaker family. Her role also provided the stodgy film with welcome comic relief.

Since *Down to the Sea in Ships* was more concerned with whaling than acting, Clara was left to fend for herself amidst a cast of veteran players. Alone and friendless, away from home for the first time, and fearful that this role would be her last if she did not distinguish herself, Clara's thirteen weeks in New Bedford consisted of arduous days and sleepless nights. When she did doze off, she would dream of Sarah Bow with a butcher knife and wake up crying.

She returned to Brooklyn in a state of exhaustion but went straight to the asylum, where Sarah Bow ordered her daughter to secure her release. So powerful was Sarah's hold on Clara that she overlooked her mother's attempts on her life and begged Robert Bow to bring her home. He refused. Desperate, Clara appealed to the cousin who owned the whitestone where her family had once lived. This relative was sympathetic but unwilling to take a madwoman back into her home.

Sarah's malady was still a mystery, yet that October she was discharged from the asylum and listed as "Recovered." Clara rented a furnished room for them, and when Johnny Bennett visited her there, she told him that her mother had been on location with her in New Bedford. No mention of an asylum was made.

After her release, Sarah dealt with her daughter's career by ignoring it. *Down to the Sea in Ships* had not opened, so Clara made the rounds of studios and agencies without results until late 1922, when William Randolph Hearst's Cosmopolitan Pictures hired her as an unbilled extra for *Enemies of Women.* One day her mother demanded to accompany her to the studio. Clara declined.

Sarah acted hurt. "You're ashameda me," she accused Clara. "Ya think I'm crazy." Her daughter's guilt turned to horror when Sarah lapsed into a catatonic state interrupted only by spells which left her gasping for breath. Days passed with Sarah lying silent and rigid on a couch, her face devoid of expression.

Confused and terrified, Clara kept her mother's condition secret and continued to work. *Enemies of Women* juvenile lead William Collier, Jr., met her on the set, thought her "scared to death," and attributed her fear to youth and inexperience. Only Clara knew the truth and its irony: "In the picture I danced on a table. All the time I hadda be laughin', rompin', displayin' joy of life . . . I'd cry my eyes out when I left my mama in the mornin'—and then go dance on a table."

On New Year's Eve, Sarah was taken back to the asylum and pronounced terminally insane. Robert Bow authorized her transfer to the same state mental institution where her mother had died in 1907.

On the day before her transfer, Sarah Bow died. It was Friday, January 5, 1923. Robert Bow went to the studio where Clara was working—*dancing*—to tell her.

Clara did not cry during the funeral service, nor aboard the ferry to Staten Island, where Sarah was buried beside her parents. But when her mother's coffin was lowered into the ground, she "came to life and went crazy. I triedta jump in after her." Certain that her film career had aggravated Sarah's illness, Clara blamed herself for her mother's death. "I was dancin' on a table with just a few clothes on when she left me for good," she would sob years later, still tormented by the thought. "I disappointed her. I went against her wishes."

Insight into Sarah Bow requires an understanding of the disease that destroyed her. On her death certificate, the primary cause is listed as "chronic myocarditis," an umbrella term of the time for heart disease. The forty-three-year-old Sarah had no history of heart trouble; if her death was caused by cardiac arrest, some other factor must have instigated it. That factor was noted by an asylum physician, who listed it as a secondary cause: "psychoses due to epilepsy."

Sarah Bow was epileptic, a result of the head injuries she suffered in 1895 and 1911. Although her condition was complicated by mental illness inherited from her mother, "temporal lobe epilepsy," the most common adult epileptic type, corresponds to Sarah's symptoms: psychotic episodes characterized by an intensified emphasis on morality, verbal violence and brandishing of knives, and a diminished sex drive. Seizures over a prolonged period may lead to catatonia, then death.

During Sarah's lifetime, epilepsy was classified as a nervous disorder caused by masturbation and sunstroke. Doctors prescribed enemas or emetics and seizures were endured in shame, creating a classic epileptic dilemma: the greater Sarah's frustration, the more frequent her psychoses. Invariably her daughter was their target.

Sarah's death made Robert Bow the only person left in Clara's life. When she vowed to obey her mother's last wish and leave acting, he dissuaded her. Since her salary exceeded his, the encouragement was less altruistic than economic.

Two months later *Down to the Sea in Ships* was released. Elmer Clifton's whaling saga harpooned audiences for a remarkable twenty-two-week New York run, and though critics loathed the movie, they loved Clara's performance in it. Watching *Down to the Sea in Ships* today, it's easy to see why: her work is wholly natural, lacking the mannered style of other actors. There's a jolt of vitality when she appears on screen, a quality that would contribute heavily to her appeal.

Success came at a crucial moment for Clara, assuaging her guilt and despair over her mother's death. In its wake arrived another emotional boost. Clara fell in love.

# 4

Arthur Jacobson will never forget the day Clara walked into an Astoria film studio and into his life. Six feet tall and sturdily built, with thick brown hair, piercing blue eyes, and a gentle nature beneath his rugged veneer, Jacobson was the twenty-one-year-old second cameraman for the Film Guild, a group of Ivy League graduates making independently financed movies on miniscule budgets. Film Guild founders delegated their responsibilities according to talent: Townsend Martin (Princeton) and Osgood Perkins (Harvard) acted, James Ashmore Creelman and Frank Tuttle (both Yale) wrote and directed, and non–Ivy Leaguer Fred Waller manned the main camera. Waller hired the Jewish, Bronx-born Jacobson to shoot a second negative (hence his designation as second cameraman) for foreign distribution.

For the Film Guild's fourth release, Townsend Martin commissioned college chum F. Scott Fitzgerald to devise a story. Fitzgerald responded with *Grit,* a tough if uninspired tale of cowardice and revenge set on New York's Lower East Side, and was paid $2,000 for his efforts. The rest of the company received two thirds of their salary in cash and the remainder in Film Guild stock.

Glenn Hunter would play *Grit*'s hero, but his romantic interest, a sexy street urchin named Orchid McGonigle, remained uncast. Actresses under consideration were summoned to an Astoria studio for screen tests. Clara, whose work in *Down to the Sea in Ships* was now well known, was among them.

Arthur Jacobson shot every test. When Clara's was screened, he thought it "horrible. I didn't light it properly. I overlit one side and underlit the other." Technical flaws aside, the test left one indelible impression: Clara Bow. "She just jumped right off the screen," Jacobson recalls. "And her *eyes*—all she had to do was lift those lids and she was flirting." He was smitten and so was the Film

Guild, who immediately cast Clara as Orchid. She approached Jacobson to express her gratitude. Days later they were in love.

Their dates shared the same routine: each Saturday at dusk, Clara and "Artie" would leave Long Island City's Pyramid Studios and take the elevated train to downtown Brooklyn for a feast of Chinese food, their favorite. A little money went a long way in a chop suey parlor on Fulton Street, and the couple would sit for hours "just looking at each other and eating . . . God, we must've been dopey." When the restaurant closed, they would return to the Flatbush section of Brooklyn, where Clara and her father had found an apartment after Sarah's death. On their first date Jacobson called a cab; Clara never let him do so again, insisting the "el" suited her fine.

Once outside her home, they would sit on the stoop, "necking" until tolling church bells told them it was dawn. So began Jacobson's trek from lower Brooklyn to his upper Bronx home by local train. After a few hours sleep, he would return to Brooklyn and spend Sunday with Clara in Prospect Park or Brighton Beach, where they would stroll hand in hand along the crowded boardwalk to Coney Island for a hot dog at Nathan's and a Ferris wheel ride.

Raised by poor but loving parents, Jacobson was shocked by Clara's terse references to her mother's madness and mystified by her father's combination of vigilance and neglect. Robert Bow seemed overprotective of his daughter around other men but oblivious to her at all other times. "There's no describing him," says Jacobson, "because no matter how you tell it, it's detrimental. Clara came from a very *odd* group of people." It is, of course, a colossal understatement.

As their relationship grew more intimate, Jacobson schemed to escape Robert's watchful eye. Finally he persuaded his cousin to include Clara's father in a regular Saturday night pinochle game. Now the couple had her apartment to themselves and a foolproof method of preventing detection: as soon as Robert left his pinochle game, Jacobson's cousin would phone Clara and warn that her father was en route. By the time he arrived, the lovers were back on the stoop outside, above suspicion or reproach.

*Grit* gave Clara her best role to date, and she seized it with gusto. Once again she saw her screen character as herself: "a little roughneck and a tomboy [like] I was." But it was her talent that impressed Frank Tuttle, whose unpublished memoirs spare no superlatives. "This dynamic and erratic whirlwind was a joy to her director," he declared, "one of the most arresting personalities the screen has ever known." From the start Tuttle marveled at Clara's ability to express emotion without apparent concentration or advance preparation. A typical example: "One day during the shooting, she'd been clowning around just before a take. I ran through the scene with her. She parked her chewing gum and said, 'Ya want me t'cry?' I nodded. 'Let's shoot it,' she said. Seconds later the tears were streaming down her cheeks."

"Oh, that happened all the time," affirms Jacobson. "Never had to use glycerine to make *her* eyes water. Clara could turn 'em on and off like a faucet."

Though no prints of *Grit* survive, accounts at the time indicate that its quality was as low as its budget. "Christ!" wrote Scott Fitzgerald to a friend in disgust. "You should have seen [the Film Guild's] last two pictures—one from my story." Charging that "the whole picture is sordid, showing disgusting scenes of immorality and crime," New York censors refused to permit its exhibition unless cuts were made (they were). Once again Clara emerged unscathed. *Variety* panned the movie but noted who stole it from the star: "Glenn Hunter gives an interpretation of the 'fright child' . . . but it is Clara Bow that lingers in the eye after the picture has gone."

By then she was two thousand miles away and one step closer to stardom. Her "discovery" had occurred when a man named Jack Bachman showed up on the *Grit* set and introduced himself to Clara as an officer of Preferred Pictures, an independent production and distribution company based in Hollywood. Bachman said he had heard about Clara, seen *Down to the Sea in Ships,* and convinced West Coast partner B. P. Schulberg to offer her trainfare to California for a three-month trial period at fifty dollars a week. The salary was low and the term was short, but that didn't matter. "Money never meant much to Clara," explains Artie Jacobson, who witnessed both Bachman's offer and her reaction. "The fact that somebody *wanted* her is what thrilled her."

Bachman appointed Maxine Alton, a beautiful blonde with minimal experience, as Clara's agent. Alton's sole responsibility was to accompany the seventeen-year-old minor to California. Since Robert Bow could not afford trainfare, father and daughter would separate for at least three months.

After a secondary role in a third-rate quickie, *The Daring Years,* Clara departed. Robert escorted her to Manhattan's Grand Central Station, where Maxine Alton awaited her. Alton had assumed that the prospect of traveling by train across America would thrill her client. She was wrong. "Clara was going into a new world," she discovered, "and yet she took it as a savage would: fearlessly, naively. She was going to be a movie star! That was all." The farewell from father to daughter also struck Alton as remarkable, for Robert Bow seemed determined to make it a "parting peculiarly lacking in sentiment. He said nothing, just nothing at all. Not a sign of tenderness passed between them." Alton barely knew the Bows, but what she saw led her to conclude that "neither Robert nor Clara, completely ignorant of the world as they were, knew that words were expected." Again she was mistaken. Clara knew words were expected and craved to hear them. Her father knew but did not care.

Even the Twentieth-Century Limited could not arouse Clara's curiosity. That she was traveling first class on a world-famous train meant nothing; that she was bound for Hollywood, everything. She did not look like she belonged in either, for aside from the shabby sweater and pleated skirt she wore, her sole possessions were a papier-mâché satchel, a portable phonograph, and one 78-r.p.m. record, "The Parade of the Wooden Soldiers," which she played at full blast until Alton finally ordered her to shut it off. Clara obeyed but grew restless and began paying uninvited visits to other compartments. "By the time two hundred miles had been ticked off by the wheels," her agent noted with newfound admiration, "Clara knew everybody on the train—conductors, porters, millionaires, and children." The son of one millionaire was so smitten that "when he swung off the train at his destination, he held her somewhat grimy little hand and looked into her large, emotional eyes until his family dragged him away. Ten minutes later Clara had forgotten him.

"Clara's first trip to the dining car was an experience I shall never forget," continued Alton. "She could read, but the menu was Abyssinian to her." Clara solved the problem by ordering one of everything, and during a stopover in Chicago she made Alton take her to a chop suey parlor. When Alton showed her a salad fork and explained its function, Clara thought she was being teased. "Aw, g'wan," she scoffed to show that she had "caught on" to the gag. "Why d'ya wanna dirty up another fork when one'll do for everythin'?"

Clara worried about when the conductor slept, since the train never stopped long enough for him to take a nap. The process of sending flowers by wire also bewildered her. When Alton received a bouquet in Chicago from a friend in New York, Clara could not understand it. "Howda they stay fresh so long and get here so quick?" she wondered.

The Santa Fe Chief carried the two women from Chicago to California, but neither the Southwest scenery, with its sagebrush, cacti, and real-life cowboys and Indians, nor the Mojave Desert, littered with skulls of oxen bleached white by the sun, interested Clara. Over and over she danced to "The Parade of the Wooden Soldiers" as the train left the desert, passing miles of orange groves and vineyards until it reached its final stop, the stucco train station in downtown Los Angeles.

At last Clara looked out the window, and as she did, Alton looked at Clara. "She wore the same sweater. There was not a crease left in the one pleated skirt. Her hair stood on end." About to disembark, the agent spotted reporters who routinely met arriving trains and froze: what if B. P. Schulberg had announced the arrival of his new "find" and this dishevelled urchin emerged? Taking no chances, Alton bribed a porter and whisked her charge out a rear exit.

The back-door route was beside the point: Clara was in Hollywood.

# II

# Hollywood Flapper

Oh, come my love and join with me
    The oldest infant industry.
Come seek the bourne of palm and pearl,
    The lovely land of boy-meets-girl.
Come grace this lotus-laden shore,
    The isle of Do-What's-Done-Before.
Come curb the new and watch
    the old win,
Out where the streets are paved
    with Goldwyn.

                                  – Dorothy Parker

# 5

Clara's arrival in Hollywood (which had incorporated itself into the city of Los Angeles following a catastrophic 1919 drought) coincided with a postwar boom that was transforming it into a major American metropolis. By mid-1923 the population of Los Angeles had reached one million, its buildings were valued at $200 million, 150 miles of new streets were under construction, and the city's harbor was the nation's largest oil terminal. The greatest growth factor of all was the film industry, which staked a $750 million investment in local real estate, studios, and equipment. Four out of every five films made worldwide came from Hollywood, and its economy reflected the monopoly.

A slew of scandals jeopardized it. The Arbuckle-Rappe "rape" and William Desmond Taylor's murder were the most notorious, but others preceded and succeeded them. In 1920 tabloids blamed starlet Olive Thomas's suicide on husband Jack Pickford (Mary's wastrel brother), whose drug habit had allegedly driven her to it. Narcotics also felled Wallace Reid, the matinee idol of Clara's childhood. After injuring his head in a train wreck, Reid's studio provided him with morphine to alleviate the pain and avoid a delay on his latest picture. Soon the actor was hooked, and two weeks after Sarah Bow's funeral, Reid died during an agonizing, "cold-turkey" withdrawal in a sanitarium. His widow testified at a narcotics conference in Washington, then financed and starred in two antidrug movies condemning off-camera debaucheries in Hollywood. Meanwhile thirty-five million people attended movies each week.

Civic and church groups were outraged. Not only did real-life Hollywood revel in depravity, they charged, but violence and sex were becoming staples of the movies one third of the nation went to see. With government intervention a grim possibility, Hollywood moguls like ex–penny arcade proprietor William Fox, exfurrier Samuel Goldwyn *(né* Goldfish), and ex–glove salesman Adolph Zukor established a self-imposed censorship board and hired teetotaling Postmaster General Will Hays to run it. The moguls believed they had scored a strategic hat trick: now they had Hays on their side, the federal judiciary off their backs, and continued control over their product.

The plan backfired when Hays, though hired as a figurehead, turned the Motion Picture Producers and Distributors Association into a powerful force which policed Hollywood's behavior both on and off screen for the next three decades. The Hays Office regulated the subject and content of every American movie. If its rules were broken, the offending film was denied an M.P.P.D.A. seal of approval, ensuring its ban by religious groups, women's clubs, and local censorship boards, and thus its commercial failure.

It was easier to control a film than its cast, but the Hays Office found a solution for this, too: "the morals clause," a new paragraph inserted into every actor's contract. Paramount, the studio which had literally worked Wallace Reid to death, worded their morals clause this way: "The Artist agrees to maintain a standard of conduct with due respect to public conventions and morals, and agrees not to do any act which will tend to degrade the Artist in society, or bring the Artist into public disrepute, or subject the Artist to scorn or ridicule, or that will tend to offend the public sense of decency, or prejudice the Corporation or the motion picture industry in general." With their private conduct contractually stipulated by "public conventions," actors became virtual slaves to their studios, and although a newcomer like Clara paid no attention to the phenomenon in 1923, she would learn an expensive lesson from it five years later.

All that mattered upon her arrival in Hollywood was the promise of work and fifty dollars a week. After Maxine Alton had whisked Clara from the Santa Fe Chief through a rear exit, she placed a phone call to B. P. Schulberg. "What happened?" he shouted. "My men say you weren't on the train. I had planned a good publicity break."

"You'll understand," Alton replied, "when you see Clara."

A half hour later he did. Agent and client took a taxi to the

Preferred Pictures studio, where Clara's bedraggled appearance made Alton's point more eloquently than words. Schulberg studied his new contractee silently, then turned to Alton. "Is this a joke?" he demanded.

At the time he posed the question, thirty-one-year-old Benjamin Percival Schulberg represented a new breed of budding mogul. An American-born Jew with a college education, Schulberg was an intellectual cut above immigrant competitors like Fox, Goldwyn, and Zukor. While they ran penny arcades or peddled furs and gloves, he apprenticed as a magazine editor, screenwriter, and publicist. Eventually Schulberg rose to the exalted position of Paramount production head, only to be fired during an internecine power struggle. Shunned by the studios, he retaliated by launching his own. He was not yet thirty.

Preferred Pictures featured a small roster of minor stars and shoestring budgets. Since his company had no distribution arm, Schulberg "state-righted" each movie separately, selling distribution rights state by state in advance of production. He had hoped Clara could replace beautiful Katherine MacDonald, whose popularity was on the wane, but the sight of this grubby Brooklyn girl left him aghast. She hardly seemed like star material.

Maxine Alton "pleaded and cajoled" with Schulberg, who finally agreed to give Clara a screen test. The three walked from his office to an adjoining shooting stage. Unwilling to waste company time on Clara, Schulberg decided to direct the test himself.

What happened next amazed Alton. Here was the head of the studio putting her client through the emotional paces less than an hour after her arrival, and here was Clara, taking it all in stride. "It was the most brutal experience a girl could have had," recalled Alton. "An ordinary person would have been petrified with fear. She would have known that her future hung in the balance, and an unjust balance at that."

Not Clara. As Schulberg barked commands, she complied with ease. He told her to laugh. She did, joy flooding her face. He snapped his fingers and ordered Clara to cry. Tears ran down her cheeks.

"She was an emotional machine," marveled Alton.

Flabbergasted, Schulberg gave Clara the second lead in *Maytime*, his latest movie. She was on her way.

Clara felt she had found a friend, protector, and, although she was in her twenties, a surrogate mother in Maxine Alton. No one had ever lavished as much attention and encouragement upon her, and Clara idolized the sophisticated agent and relied on her for professional and personal guidance. It was Alton who rented them an apartment on the corner of Hollywood Boulevard and Hudson Avenue and Alton who drove Clara to the Preferred studio each morning, then picked her up at night. Since Schulberg controlled her career, this was the extent of Alton's duties, but Clara did not complain. Her agent's companionship was worth her commission.

Back in New York, Artie Jacobson was miserable. The days following Clara's departure stretched into "the longest weeks of my life," he recalls. "I was so in love I couldn't see." Within two months Jacobson had withdrawn his savings and come to California. Clara was delighted, but Alton, "who protected Clara like a mother cub," disapproved of his presence. "She tried to shunt everything away from Clara," Jacobson discovered. *"Nothing"* was to interfere with her."

Just as he had diverted Robert Bow with a pinochle game, Jacobson found an excuse to escape Clara's new chaperone: driving lessons. In the sports car Alton drove (and Clara paid for), he took her to nearby Magnetic Hill to "practice." From the start Clara had no patience for low speeds or red lights, and her reckless driving would soon become as renowned as her generosity. When the threesome went out for Chinese food, Clara always picked up the check. "I'd try to pay, but Clara wouldn't let me," says Jacobson. "She'd say, 'Maxine, *you* pay for it. Artie don't got that kinda money.' " Since Alton's cash, like her car, came from Clara anyway, she made no objection.

At the time of Jacobson's arrival, Clara had just completed work on *Maytime*. Schulberg had no other project nearing production, so he began looking for a "loan-out," a common practice between independent producers and movie studios. In theory, a loan-out was mutually beneficial to all parties: a studio borrowed an actor for a movie, the producer was remunerated for the actor's services, and the actor earned another screen credit. Since exposure and experience were of critical importance to an unknown like Clara and Schulberg could not afford to give it to her, he sought parts at studios like First National, which was bringing the bestselling novel *Black Oxen* to the screen. Director Frank Lloyd was looking for a vivacious type to play Janet Oglethorpe, a key supporting role similar to Clara's character in *Maytime.* But unlike her inconsequential Preferred debut, *Black Oxen* boasted a top studio, big budget, and famous star, Corinne Griffith. Its plot concerned the new science of plastic surgery and featured Griffith as Countess Zattiany, a fifty-eight-year-old woman rejuvenated by an X-ray operation into the beauty she once was decades earlier. Following her transformation, the countess bewitches a man half her age but renounces him after revealing the truth. Her admirer finds solace in the arms of Janet Oglethorpe, a jazz baby his own age.

Schulberg suggested his new find to Frank Lloyd and sent her to the director's office. Clara never forgot Lloyd's reception: "He didn't try t'make me think I didn't have no chance an' that he was doin' me a favor lettin' me work in his picture. When I came inta his office, a big smile came over his face. He told me I was just what he wanted."

Lloyd didn't regret his decision. Clara's work in *Black Oxen* was so impressive that First National requested her for another important movie, *Painted People.* Schulberg quadrupled her salary to $200 a week, enabling her and Alton to move into a bungalow off Sunset Boulevard. Clara wanted Artie Jacobson, who was living in a $5-a-week furnished room nearby, to join them. Alton refused.

*Painted People* producer John McCormick was married to its star, Colleen Moore. Earlier that year Moore had made *Flaming Youth,* the movie that popularized the flapper with the public. Discarding her mother's cotton underwear, ankle-length skirts, tight corsets, black cotton stockings, and high-button shoes, the flapper bobbed her hair, rouged her face, rolled her silk stockings, and raised her hemlines. She smoked, drank, danced, and threw petting parties. She read Freud, advocated free love, and enjoyed "makin' whoopee." And although Colleen Moore's flapper character in *Flaming Youth* was as pure as any Victorian virgin, she was an acknowledged influence on later, sexier incarnations like Clara. Their teaming in *Painted People* presented intriguing possibilities.

It also set off fireworks. "Two days was all Clara could take," claims Moore. "She said to me, 'I don't like my part. I wanna play yours.' And Clara was right, she *was* miscast. So she quit."

Actually, Clara worked on *Painted People* for three weeks, until the day she and Colleen Moore performed a scene together. After the two-shot of both actresses, director Clarence Badger shot Moore's close-ups, then ordered some of Clara.

Colleen Moore objected. "You don't need that close-up," the movie's star and producer's wife commanded Badger, who instantly agreed.

Clara couldn't believe it. "You're a big star," she pleaded to Moore in front of the entire company. "Ya don't need close-ups like I do. Every close-up I get helps me. Why d'ya haveta stop 'em?"

Whether or not Clara realized it, her question was rhetorical. Moore was not about to let a supporting player steal a scene from her. No close-up of Clara was shot.

That night Clara came home seething. During dinner she regaled Alton and Jacobson with an account of the incident, then suddenly stormed out of the bungalow.

Hours passed and she did not return. Jacobson went out looking for her but returned alone and frantic. Finally at one A.M. Clara came home, her face swathed in bandages. "She'd gone straight to a doctor about a sinus condition she had and said, '*Now*. I want that operation *right now*,'" says Jacobson. Obviously Clara could not continue working on *Painted People,* so McCormick and Moore had no choice but to replace her with another actress, rebuild the sets, rehire the extras, and reshoot three weeks of footage. Not only had Clara extricated herself from *Painted People,* but she put Moore's movie over budget and behind schedule. "She made that bitch pay," chuckles Jacobson. "That's what Clara could do when she got mad."

For several months Clara had begged Maxine Alton to send for her father, but the agent always dissuaded her, warning that

Robert Bow's interference "would make the bosses sore." Alton also undermined her client's confidence: "She kept tryin' t'make me think I wasn't makin' good," recalled Clara, "an' that they was goin' t'send me back to New York soon. I worried all the time and gave her more and more authority and power, 'cause I thought she might keep 'em from doin' that." Trusting by nature and insulated by work, Clara never doubted Alton's dire forecast, even though she played a lead role in Preferred's *Poisoned Paradise,* then was loaned-out to Principal Pictures for *Daughters of Pleasure.* The facts did not allay her fears. What Alton said, Clara believed.

Her faith was shattered when she accidentally discovered Schulberg and Alton having sex. Since she had regarded her agent as a parent and her boss as a benefactor, the betrayal was double, and Clara was devastated by it. She had worshipped Schulberg, convinced that without him, her career would cease to exist. Amidst Alton's browbeating, the slightest supportive gesture by Schulberg had been cause for joy. "The first Christmas we were in Hollywood," remembers Jacobson, "he gave her a beaded bag as a Christmas gift. Well, Clara was beside herself. It was the most beautiful thing that had ever happened to her, that 'Mr. Schulberg' would give her a beaded bag. This wasn't being stupid, this was being *naive.*"

Seeing Schulberg and Alton together made Clara less so. Her agent had maintained that only her intervention lay between Clara and a one-way ticket back to Brooklyn, but now Clara realized that Alton needed her more than she needed Alton. She insisted that Schulberg fire Alton and bring her father to Hollywood. "Clara was the sweetest kid in the world," explains Jacobson, "but you didn't cross her, and you didn't do her wrong."

It was an obvious dichotomy and a necessary one, for the stardom Clara sought required not only talent, but emotional fortitude. She had not been born with both.

# 6

*Black Oxen* premiered in December 1923. Billed fifth, Clara stole star Corinne Griffith's thunder. "She ran away with it," declares Artie Jacobson, who saw a sneak preview with Clara. As usual, critics singled her out. "A horrid little flapper [is] adorably played by Mary [sic] Bow," noted *Variety.* The New York *Times* called her character "quite well played" but confused Clara with Kate Lester, the actress who portrayed her mother.

The Hollywood community made no such mistakes, and its reaction to Clara in *Black Oxen* surpassed B. P. Schulberg's greatest expectations. Upon her arrival, he had deemed her prospects "impossible;" now, just months later, she was considered one of the industry's most promising young actresses, a ranking confirmed by her citation as a WAMPAS Baby Star of 1924. An acronym for the Western Association of Motion Picture Advertisers, WAMPAS compiled an annual list of thirteen Baby Stars "who during the past year have shown the most talent and promise for eventual stardom." Winners received as much national attention as Academy Award nominees do today, culminating with the WAMPAS Frolic, a party held in the grand ballroom of the Ambassador Hotel. There Baby Stars were presented to prominent actors, directors, and producers.

The year Clara was cited, Los Angeles police proscribed dancing after midnight, so the Frolic was held in San Francisco instead. That January the Baby Stars, their parents, agents, publicists, and assorted celebrity guests boarded a special train chartered for the occasion. At Clara's insistence (and at her expense) Robert Bow had been brought to Hollywood, and although he demanded to accompany his daughter and attend the Frolic, WAMPAS officials refused. "He was a drunk and a disgrace," recalls Baby Star Ruth Hiatt. "They wouldn't allow him on the train." Betrayed by her agent and forcibly separated from her father, Clara was left to make the trip alone, and the fourteen-year-old Hiatt befriended her.

Her memories of Clara aboard the train reveal a confused, lonely, and love-hungry girl who searched for support and affection from virtual strangers. "Clara *clung* to my mother," remembers Hiatt. "She never left her side, and my publicity man wasn't happy about it." The Baby Stars were instructed to circulate among the celebrities and "get acquainted." While others did, Clara sat on the floor, staring in awe at the stars in her midst.

Before a camera she could exude personality. Newsreel footage shows Clara among the Baby Stars, her unruly hair blowing in the wind while others wear chic cloche hats. Grinning impishly, she blows a kiss to the camera, as natural as the rest are formal. The moment is charming, but misleading: Clara was not the carefree Baby Star she seemed, and the distinction between her public and private selves did not pass unnoticed. "She was peppy and vivacious in front of people, but when you talked to her one on one, she was serious and sad," says Hiatt.

"I liked her, but I didn't get to know her well," admits Dorothy Mackaill, another Baby Star aboard the train. "Nobody did. She was away from the crowd, a loner."

"Clara was an awfully sweet girl," concludes Hiatt, "but a very *lonesome* sweet girl."

Back in Hollywood there was little time to dwell on loneliness. As the demand for his Baby Star rose, Schulberg began loaning her out for $500 a week, out of which he paid Clara $200 and pocketed the difference. It was a lucrative situation which Schulberg took to an extreme: excluding *Poisoned Paradise* (which was shot in 1923 anyway), not one of Clara's eight 1924 releases was a Preferred Picture.

Not one was of merit, either. *Wine,* a Universal quickie, featured Clara as a bootlegger's daughter who reforms when her mother goes temporarily blind from bad booze. She died at the beginning of *Empty Hearts,* a Banner Production. Warner Brothers' *This Woman* cast her in a minor role for which the New York *Times* again miscredited her, this time as "Clare Bow." Her leading man in Gotham Productions' *Black Lightning* was Thunder the Dog.

*Helen's Babies,* a Principal Pictures release, used Clara and character actor Edward Everett Horton as foils for its star, six-year-old Baby Peggy. During shooting her behavior baffled the child star and vexed everyone else. "She'd change her hairstyle and color at whim," recalls Baby Peggy, "coming to work one day with a hennaed straight bob and the next in blonde curls." It was not Clara's whim, but Schulberg's greed which was at fault, for his scheduling forced her to work on several films simultaneously. Often she played a blonde at one studio in the morning and a redhead at another that afternoon and was somehow expected to transform herself in between. On *Helen's Babies,* Baby Peggy grew accustomed to the sight of "the script girl trying to tell Clara that if she was walking in one door and out another in different shots from the same scene, she couldn't have different hairstyles and coloring. Clara would just shrug her shoulders." The gesture indicated her frustration at supporting canines and children in films that wound up on the bottom half of double bills, disliked by critics and audiences alike. Other producers treated promising contract players as valuable assets and chose their loan-outs carefully. Schulberg pimped Clara for profit.

While shuttling unhappily from studio to studio, Clara rented a three-bedroom house at 7576 Hollywood Boulevard for herself, her father, and Artie Jacobson. He and Clara shared one bedroom, her father had another, and the third was occupied by a dog. It was Clara's first pet and she adored it, so when the dog caught distemper, she was frantic. Jacobson suggested she keep it inside at night, but since Clara never did anything halfway, her dog soon had a room of its own that looked and smelled like an untended kennel.

Clara found a solution for this, too. To Jacobson's amazement, "She had somebody come in during the day when I wasn't there and put dirt all over the bedroom floor for the dog! We argued like hell about it." Despite his opposition, Clara adamantly refused to let her dog live outside.

When Los Angeles *Times* columnist Grace Kingsley arrived to interview Clara in her home, she cocked a curious eyebrow at Jacobson, whom Clara introduced by name but not his relationship to her. The columnist also overlooked the unsightly presence of

Robert Bow's spittoon, which was on prominent display in the living room.

After the interview Clara asked Kingsley to stay for dinner and the columnist accepted, unaware that, as usual, the bill of fare *chez* Bow would be Robert's one and only specialty: macaroni. Before anyone could begin eating, Clara and her father began quarreling and throwing their meal at each other. Much of the macaroni missed its mark and hit the columnist, who was escorted, stunned and bespattered, to the door by an amused Artie Jacobson.

Robert Bow's migration to Hollywood had not made him any less strange or shiftless. In the weeks, then months, following his arrival, Robert made no effort to find work, preferring to give his occupation as Clara's business manager. Wherever she worked, he loitered, trying to pick up extra girls. "I'm Clara Bow's father!" Robert would boast by way of introduction, then offer his prey a ride home in the Stutz Bearcat his daughter had bought him.

For some reason Robert did not object to her living with Artie Jacobson, but the thought of Clara with any other man made him violently paranoid. One night Jacobson casually mentioned to Robert that Clara was visiting a director who lived across town. Enraged, Robert grabbed his gun, jumped into his car, and vowed to kill the director if he found Clara there. Envisioning a scandal similar to the mysterious death of William Desmond Taylor, Jacobson borrowed Clara's car, took a shortcut, and spirited her from the director's home moments before Robert arrived.

On July 9, 1924, Robert went down the block for a soda and returned with a wife. Ella Mowery listened to his pick-up line and said she was a twenty-three-year-old orphan from Paris. Robert proposed, Ella accepted, and the two were wed at the Hollywood Episcopal Church. On the marriage certificate Robert listed his age as thirty-eight. He was actually forty-nine.

The bride and groom returned to his home, where their wedded bliss ended "about an hour and a half after it began," cracks Jacobson. "Bob brought her over and Clara threw her out."

Robert Bow's "kissless romance," as the press derisively called it, landed in divorce court one month later. Under oath Ella Bow admitted her true age (eighteen, the same as Clara) and revealed that she was hardly an orphan; in fact, her husband had given her $1,000 to transport her large family from New York to California. Ella said she had left Robert after five days because each time she refused to kiss him, he spanked her. Claiming financial dependence on his daughter, Robert was nonetheless ordered to pay $15 a month in alimony. Ella Bow's own mother, a "Mrs. Dick," testified that her daughter was a "wild harum-scarum child," while the presiding judge called Clara's new stepmother "the most colossal golddigger I have ever heard of." With court costs, alimony payments, and the groom's thousand-dollar wedding gift to his bride, Robert's short-lived second marriage cost Clara more than six weeks' salary.

At the time she was considering matrimony herself. Clara wanted stability and love, and Artie Jacobson seemed eager to provide them. Since Robert refused to surrender his daughter to any man, the couple planned a secret ceremony in Santa Ana, where advance preparations were not necessary. One day they drove there but bickered and turned back. By the end of the year their romance had cooled into close friendship, and Jacobson found an apartment of his own.

Meanwhile Schulberg brought Clara back to Preferred for *Capital Punishment*. To exploit a controversial newspaper campaign to abolish the death penalty, he devised a story of a man condemned to die for a murder he didn't commit. The producer's clumsy plot reached its predictable climax with the innocent hero saved at the eleventh hour by a reticent eyewitness (Clara) who reveals the real killer's identity. Schulberg figured *Capital Punishment*'s title alone would sell tickets, and it did despite scathing reviews. "The pivotal idea in this picture is better suited to comedy than melodrama," sneered the New York *Times*.

But Schulberg had state-righted *Capital Punishment* in advance, and its widespread exhibition did more for Clara's career than her last half dozen movies put together. It also led to her biggest break since *Black Oxen*.

Director Ernst Lubitsch was renowned for "the Lubitsch Touch," a singular approach to sexual material that stymied the

Hays Office censors. Lubitsch used an audience's imagination, not a movie's images, to make his suggestive point, and his films remain as titillating today as they did at the time.

Lubitsch met Clara at Warner Brothers, where she was on loan-out for *Eve's Lover* and he was casting *Kiss Me Again*. During her screen test she spied Lubitsch smacking his lips off-camera, mistook his nervous tic for a taunt, and smacked her own lips back at him. The director turned crimson and called Clara "a damned fresh kid," but her test was too impressive to ignore. Lubitsch cast Clara as Grizette, a sexy Parisian secretary who bewitches her married boss.

Clara would later refer to Lubitsch as "a godsend," and after the schlock Schulberg stuck her in, *Kiss Me Again* must have seemed like one. The movie was a success and a delight, and according to critics, so was she. "Clara Bow absolutely triumphs in the role of a lawyer's steno," announced *Variety*. It was her most distinguished achievement yet.

A rave review in a hit movie led Clara to expect better parts in better productions; instead, Schulberg relegated her to low-budget loan-outs once again. The grind resumed with *The Scarlet West,* a cowboys-and-Indians shoot-'em-up for Frank J. Carroll Productions. "Joseph P. Kennedy presents Clara Bow in her greatest emotional triumph!" proclaimed the preview for the Film Booking Office's *The Keeper of the Bees* (the Boston tycoon was FBO's owner), but *Variety* disagreed: "Clara Bow acts all over the lot and aside from weeping and swirling around, does little." The self-described plot for Associated Exhibitors' *The Adventurous Sex* was typical of the tripe forced upon her: "When a man spends too much time tinkering with his airplane, his sweetheart gives him the air and begins to enjoy the wild life, taking up with a lecherous charmer. This adventurer forces his way into her hotel room and then calls to his buddies to come on in, badly compromising the girl's reputation. Highly distraught, she jumps into the river above Niagara Falls, over which she is about to be swept to her death when she is spotted by her former sweetheart. He swims out to her, and they climb to safety up a rope ladder hanging from the airplane. The boy and girl are reconciled, and the charmer is socked in the face."

Not surprisingly, *The Adventurous Sex* and her next loan-out, Arrow's *The Primrose Path,* didn't last two days in New York. Films like this were classified as "daily changes," a pejorative term for movies that played one day, then moved on to another theater in another town. Subjecting Clara to them demoralized her but accomplished Schulberg's aim: with characteristic shrewdness, he had signed a neophyte, then made other studios pay him to give her exposure. Though Clara learned more from one encounter with Ernst Lubitsch than a dozen low-budget loan-outs, her time was Schulberg's money, so he sacrificed quality for quantity and put her in sixteen movies in eighteen months. What he regarded as experience, she resented as exploitation, and each view had merit. Overworked and underpaid as Clara was, Schulberg's strategy had been successful: in less than two years, he had established her as a minor star and made money in the process. In June, 1925 *Motion Picture Classic* put her on its cover—Clara's first—and ran a story ("The Kid Who Sassed Lubitsch") analyzing her appeal. "The truth is," it concluded, "little Clara Bow shows alarming symptoms of becoming the sensation of the year in Hollywood. There is something vital and compelling in her presence. She is the spirit of youth. She is Young America rampant, the symbol of flapperdom."

With Clara's name and face increasingly familiar to moviegoers, Schulberg switched tactics and made her exclusive to Preferred Pictures. His production schedule was simple and brutal: from six A.M. on Monday morning until midnight the following Saturday, the company worked on a rented stage at the Robertson-Cole studios. No Preferred production exceeded its rock-bottom $35,000 budget, and if one was behind schedule and unfinished by Saturday night, production manager Sam Jaffe would nonetheless order the crew to "wrap it up" and the movie would be released anyway.

It was a relentless and unrewarding routine, and a vivid portrayal of Clara during it comes from Schulberg's son. Budd Schulberg was a painfully shy, sensitive, stammering ten-year-old when he met Clara in his father's office, and the introduction left an indelible impression. "She was wearing a tight cotton dress, and her Cupid's bow of a mouth was constantly moving in the act of chewing gum," recalls Budd in his memoirs. "Is this ya little junior, Mr. Schulberg?" she asked. "Gee, he's cute as a button!"

Clara ran her fingers through the boy's hair. "Mmmmm. Howja liketa drive upta Arrowhead this weekend, Buddy? Just the two of uz!"

"Now Clara," chided Schulberg, "he's just a little boy."

"Okay, maybe we'll hafta wait a few years," Clara pouted. As she fingered her spit curl, Budd Schulberg felt that she "seemed to be openly flirting—with both of us."

The boy was accustomed to ambitious actresses fussing over him in front of his father, and superficially this coarse teenage girl seemed no different. But she was, and Budd knew it from their first meeting. "Even then, I think I sensed that she communicated sexually because she had no other vocabulary," he realized. "She had to flirt with me, as she did with everyone, because she simply didn't know anything else to do."

When Budd visited her on the set of her next Preferred picture, Clara ran to greet him and announced that he was her secret boyfriend. Then she prepared herself for the movie's big dramatic scene, a typically trite moment where the unfairly compromised heroine mourns her abandonment by her true love. As usual, Clara transcended her material, and Budd never forgot the process: "the assistant director gave the cue for the [off-camera] three-piece orchestra to begin. They played a tender, schmaltzy version of 'Rock-a-bye, Baby.' Clara, now in front of the camera, was listening intently. '. . . on a tree top . . . when the wind blows . . . the cradle will rock . . .'

"Clara Bow, the tough little jazz baby, began to rock a little. No longer did her face look happy and full of the devil as it had at our first meeting. She was pressing her lips together and her big round eyes were blinking. 'When the bough breaks . . . the cradle will fall . . .' A little shudder passed through Clara Bow. Tiny clouds of mist began to float across her eyes. 'Down will come cradle . . .' Photogenic tears welled in the eyes of Clara Bow, gathered like waves in miniature and began rolling down her cheeks. 'Baby and all . . .'

"Clara Bow was crying. Crying beautifully. Crying like a real

actress. And when the director triumphantly called 'Cut!' Clara
went on crying."

Budd Schulberg wasn't the only one watching in awe. "She
could cry at the drop of a hat, and you'd *believe* her," remembers
Preferred prop man William Kaplan. "A beautiful actress, just
beautiful. And I often wondered to myself, 'Where did this young
girl get all this knowledge, this understanding, this *feeling?*'"

Only nineteen himself, Billy Kaplan kept his crush on Clara
hidden. So did the rest of the Preferred crew. "We *all* loved her,"
confesses Kaplan. "The electricians, the grips, the painters . . .
everyone loved Clara." With their working-class background and
no-bullshit style, these men were grown-up versions of her childhood playmates, and around them Clara felt comfortable. In turn,
they treated her like one of the boys. "Clara was always a good guy
on the set," says Kaplan. "Very professional, always on time. And if
anything was wrong, she came to us and said, 'Can we do something else for about an hour?' And because she was special to us,
we always found something else to do."

Crews loved Clara because she had the talent but not the
temperament of a star. She liked them because they protected her,
prohibiting mention of her mother or ridicule of her father, whose
presence was as unwelcome as it was ubiquitous. "As long as she
was working and making the money, he was happy," recalls Kaplan
of Robert Bow. Women in Preferred's steno pool were less generous, snidely referring to Robert's shabby clothing as his "Bar Mitzvah suit, because it looked like he hadn't taken it off since then,"
says Gertrude Cohn. "He was filthy." Meanwhile Henrietta Cohn,
Gertrude's sister and fellow secretary, sent an anonymous letter to
Adeline Schulberg "alerting her to the B.P.-Bow situation," a tip-
off which, says Budd, "my mother accepted philosophically."

Given her husband's reputation, Ad Schulberg's attitude was
not surprising. "His organization was the cheapest, and his reputation for the sexual abuse of young actresses who worked for him
was the worst in Hollywood," wrote Louise Brooks, a stunning
showgirl who would soon work for Schulberg herself. "Consequently, coming from the Brooklyn slums to work for Ben automatically labeled Clara a 'cheap little whore.'" Today Schulberg's

son admits as much. "My impression of my father and Clara was that he knew she was a gullible know-nothing," says Budd. "And as for Henrietta Cohn's warning, I'm inclined to think it was true."

It wouldn't have been unusual if it were. Producers like Schulberg were the rule, not the exception in Hollywood, and after twenty films in two years, Clara was desperate. She was not loaned-out any longer, but Preferred pictures like *My Lady's Lips, Lawful Cheaters,* and *Parisian Love* were no improvement. Nor were working conditions, for by now the combination of Clara and cheap movies had proven so surefire that Schulberg accelerated the shooting schedule for *Free to Love* from three weeks to two. Clara deserved better and could have bartered her body to obtain it when Schulberg made his position clear, which he definitely did. "He wanted her," confirms Artie Jacobson. "But he couldn't get to first base with her. I know this for a fact because she told it to me. She knew that he wanted to get her in the hay, so she used to tease him. 'Ben, darlin',' she'd say, 'd'ya know what happened last night? I slept with the prop man. Oh boy, was he *great.*' "

Although Clara managed to keep "Ben" (as she had indeed begun calling him) Schulberg at bay, Sam Jaffe, Preferred's production manager and Schulberg's brother-in-law, exploited her sexually and emotionally. Six decades later Jaffe remains unapologetic about their affair. "She was scared of all the people in the business, but she trusted me," he shrugs. "She was in love with me and wanted to marry me, but I couldn't think of marrying her." Why not? "She came from *Brooklyn.* She looked cheap. Men wanted to screw her."

Taking no chances, Ad Schulberg imported a "nice Jewish girl" from New York for her brother, who promptly married her. Clara, known contemptuously within the Schulberg family as a *"meshuganah shiksa"* (Yiddish for "crazy Gentile girl"), was alone again.

This time neither her solitude nor servitude would last long. One movie heralded the change. Shot in the summer of 1925, it brought Clara both a groundbreaking new image and an ardent lover to go with it.

## 7

Percy Marks was a Dartmouth professor and popular novelist whose fiction chronicled his students, the sheiks and flappers who danced to the "jungle rhythm" of jazz, drank from silver flasks, and debated whether to "go the limit." In *The Plastic Age,* published in 1922, Marks portrayed a rite of passage gone wrong: freshman Hugh Carver's exposure to hard-drinking, fast-living students of Sanford College endangers his moral character and athletic career. After escaping a road house raid and almost succumbing to temptation with "hotsy-totsy" classmate Cynthia Day, Hugh reforms and leads his teammates to victory in the big football game. He is rewarded with self-respect, parental pride, and a chastened Cynthia's love.

School, sports, and sex: *The Plastic Age* had three commercial topics, and Ben Schulberg knew it. Convinced that a movie adaptation would establish Preferred Pictures and catapult Clara to major stardom, Schulberg bought the rights to the novel. Obviously Clara would play Cynthia, and as the rivals for her affections, Schulberg cast contractees Donald Keith as Hugh Carver and Luis Antonio Damaso de Alonso as his roommate, Carl Peters. Like Clara, both actors were barely twenty. Keith, a slight, bland juvenile lead, had already appeared opposite her in *Parisian Love* and *Free to Love,* while the Mexican-born Alonso had no experience except extra work. But Alonso was tall, dark, and, with his lustrous black hair and emerald eyes, strikingly handsome, so Schulberg signed him anyway and changed his name into an amalgam of two matinee idols, John Gilbert and Ronald Colman. For his acting debut in *The Plastic Age,* Luis Antonio Damaso de Alonso became Gilbert Roland.

*The Plastic Age* boasted a bigger budget and better director, Wesley Ruggles, than any prior Preferred production, and the impact of Clara's performance in it was already palpable during shooting. As usual, Schulberg had rented a stage at Joseph P. Kennedy's FBO Studios (formerly Robertson-Cole) in Hollywood, and though Clara had worked on many prior movies there, never before had her set been so popular: now actors and technicians from neighboring productions gravitated to *The Plastic Age* stage as if drawn by its star's sexually magnetic force. When the company traveled to Pomona College in Claremont for location shooting, male extras (one of whom was a young hopeful called Clark Gable) would greet Clara's appearance each morning with wolf whistles. "They all bristled up when she walked on the set," recalled actor David Butler. "She was a *very* sexy-looking girl."

The sexy-looking girl sought companionship from eleven-year-old Budd Schulberg, who had come to Claremont chaperoned by prop man Billy Kaplan. While Kaplan bolstered the confidence of Gilbert Roland, whose English was as limited as his acting experience ("Am I doing all right? *Bee*-ly, you must help me," Roland would plead in his heavy accent), Budd attached himself to Clara, who had promoted him, she told everyone, from her boyfriend to "steady fella." Between shots the twosome sat in her red roadster, chewing gum and trading confidences. She listened sympathetically to his stories about stammering in school, confessing that she had suffered through the same humiliating ordeal. He asked about her grief-stricken reaction to "Rock-a-bye, Baby," and she told him about Johnny, the best friend burned alive before her eyes. Johnny's mother always sang him to sleep with the song, explained Clara. Now whenever she heard "Rock-a-bye, Baby," she cried like one.

Budd also served as an unwitting go-between for what Clara would soon call "my first really big love experience." While she acted and he watched, Gilbert Roland approached shyly, handed Budd a folded note, and asked him to give it to Clara. "I don't know what was in the note," wrote Budd, "because I was too conscientious to read it, especially when I could feel his strong Latin eyes drilling into my back as I caught up with Clara and delivered it. She mumbled, 'Oh, thanks, Buddy, sweet of ya,' and took a quick glance over her shoulder at the young bullfighter turned actor."

"That evening they came into the local hotel dining room together, two head-turning twenty-year-olds whom my father had put together from such totally different worlds—Chihuahua and Brooklyn."

They were better-suited than Budd realized. Like Artie Jacobson, Roland was simultaneously rugged and gentle, sensitive yet macho. Men liked him and women wanted him, and both nicknamed Roland "Amigo," a sobriquet that has endured for six decades. Though Roland was as jealous as he was ardent, a lonely girl like "Clarita" (his pet name for her) found this trait thrilling. The couple also shared the same social insecurities, his from a language barrier, hers from a lack of self-esteem. Still, they had each other, and for now it was enough. "We was real happy," Clara told an interviewer, "sorta like two youngsters that didn't know what [life] was all about and was scared t'death of it."

Robert Bow despised his daughter's new lover, whose roots and religion provoked his bigotry (curiously, Artie Jacobson's Jewishness had not). Clara, ranted Robert, was forbidden to marry a Catholic, especially a "greasy Mexican" like Roland.

Love made loan-outs bearable. After *The Plastic Age* Schulberg again sold Clara's services to the highest bidder, and though there was no dearth of offers, there were no worthwhile ones, either. She was miscast as a frontier gal in Fox's *The Best Bad Man,* a vehicle for cowboy star Tom Mix. Audiences jeered *The Ancient Mariner,* Fox's fey modernization of the Samuel Taylor Coleridge poem. Arrow's intermittently enjoyable *My Lady of Whims* featured Clara as a flapper heiress who shares a Greenwich Village loft with a butch sculptress until hero Donald Keith intervenes. Two for Associated Exhibitors, *The Shadow of the Law* and *Two Can Play,* disappeared on the daily-change circuit.

By now Schulberg's loan-out racket was well known within Hollywood. "B. P. Schulberg is probably getting the best break of any producer on the Coast so far as renting stars are concerned," editorialized *Variety.* "Schulberg several years ago placed Clara Bow under contract, and ever since that time has been renting her out at sums which have netted him as much as 500 percent profit for her services. At present Schulberg is paying her $750 a week and providing her wardrobe, but finds little difficulty in disposing of her services for over $3,000 a week." With so much money at stake, not a moment was wasted, and by the end of 1925 Clara had appeared in fourteen movies in twelve months. The exposure made her name familiar; *The Plastic Age,* her fifteenth and final film of 1925, made it famous. Promoted as "the hottest jazz baby in films," Clara caused such a sensation that even the staid New York *Times* lost its stylized restraint. "She has eyes that would drag any youngster away from his books," its reviewer gushed, "and she knows how to use eyes, shoulders, and all the rest of her tiny self in the most effective manner. She radiates an elfin sensuousness."

Schulberg had guessed right: *The Plastic Age* was Preferred's biggest hit yet.

Paramount's Adolph Zukor paid close attention to the triumph. Since Schulberg's enforced exit from his studio seven years earlier, Zukor had turned Paramount into the major of majors, with an annual $5 million-plus profit that doubled Fox's, tripled Universal's, and quintupled Warner Brothers'. Paramount also controlled six hundred theaters across the country, which played its product under a "block-booking" system. The method was simple and monopolistic: at its annual convention, the studio presented exhibitors with a "program" of upcoming releases. No exhibitor could play one movie and not another; if one was wanted, the rest had to be booked, too. The result ensured Paramount that its theaters would play only its movies.

But in order to maintain exhibitor allegiance, Paramount had to provide desirable product, and by 1925 they had few stars to do so. "Fatty" Arbuckle and Wallace Reid had both been under contract to Paramount. So had Rudolph Valentino and Gloria Swanson, who had just defected from Paramount to United Artists, a studio formed six years earlier by Mary Pickford, Douglas Fairbanks, Charlie Chaplin, and D. W. Griffith. Not only was Paramount short on talent, but its ramshackle Vine Street studios were in immediate need of renovation. Finally Adolph Zukor feared Metro-Goldwyn-Mayer, a studio formed the previous year that already posed a greater threat to Paramount than its established rivals.

In early November, Zukor contacted Schulberg. Since they had not spoken in seven years, the meeting was momentous, and in it Zukor swallowed his pride and made Schulberg an offer he couldn't refuse: to rejoin Paramount as associate producer and bring his entire company with him. In return Paramount would swallow Preferred whole, permit Schulberg to make any movie he wanted, and distribute it in the studio's six hundred theaters. Schulberg's revenge was sweetened further by the knowledge that Clara could now become an even more valuable property at Paramount's expense. He would make the studio pay him for her services but supervise her films himself, selecting the best roles, leading men, directors, and crews for them. Technically Clara was on loan-out to Paramount, and from the start Schulberg realized that his value to the studio depended upon her success there.

One week after Zukor's offer, Clara was given the second lead in *Dancing Mothers,* an adaptation of a Broadway play which Paramount had bought for $45,000, more than the entire budget of a Preferred picture. The studio had originally cast Betty Bronson, boyish star of Paramount's *Peter Pan,* in the role. Bronson was a charming but sexless actress; as one frustrated director discovered, "When she tried to be sexy, she looked like a little girl that wanted to go to the bathroom." Evidently Paramount agreed: at a convention in Chicago, "the inadvisability of having Miss Bronson appear in this type of a role was discussed," and Clara was deemed an ideal replacement.

On November 19, 1925, she arrived in New York for shooting at Paramount's Astoria studios. No sooner had she left Hollywood than newspapers printed rumors of her romance, then engagement to Donald Keith, who had also come east for *Dancing Mothers.* Clara ignored the stories (and wired Gilbert Roland to do the same) until they had spread so far, so fast that she felt compelled to issue a denial. "If I read this in a paper once more," she told *Photoplay* magazine, "I'll believe it myself." Typically, the item was planted by Schulberg, who still had all three sides of the "triangle" under personal contract. It was Clara's first taste of the insatiable public appetite for details, either factual or fabricated, of her private life.

*Dancing Mothers'* title reflected its Jazz Age theme. Ethel Westcourt (Alice Joyce), a still-beautiful society matron, languishes at home while her philandering husband Hugh and flapper daughter Kittens frequent nightclubs and speakeasies. Both regard Ethel as a moral fossil until she follows their example and entices the "rotter" trifling with Kittens. The film's conclusion lacks a comforting resolution: Ethel sails to Europe, leaving her husband and daughter to reflect upon their selfish natures. When she does, audiences are supposed to side with Ethel not only in principle, but out of sympathy.

Clara's startling performance prevented this. Before shooting she saw the play and instinctively reinterpreted her role. "I saw that the girl got no sympathy 'cause she played her drinkin' and smokin' scenes with a sorta 'This is my business—I gotta right t'do what I like and I'll do it' air," she told an interviewer. "I played her as a girl out for havin' fun. When I said mean things, I tried t'put over the idea with a look after I'd said the thing: 'Oh, why'd I say that? I didn't really mean it.' " As a result, Kittens steals the film from its nominal heroine.

Critic Pauline Kael's contrast between the "languidly patrician" Joyce and the "alarmingly active" Clara indicates how the coup happened. From her first close-up (also the first of the film, indicating how far Clara had come since Colleen Moore and *Painted People*), she infuses *Dancing Mothers* with overwhelming vitality. When Kittens invades her lover's lair, she storms past his butler, makes a beeline for the bar, snatches a silver cocktail shaker, leaps onto a divan, pours herself a stiff drink, guzzles it, traces the liquor's trail down her gullet delightedly, then hurls her cloche hat over her shoulder with one hand while rumpling her bangs with the other. Her energy undiminished, Kittens lights a cigarette, inhales ravenously, emits chimney stack-sized puffs of smoke, then fidgets, eyeing the elderly butler flirtatiously. The madcap sequence energizes a movie stale with stiff-upper-lip sentiment, and though one wonders what genetic mutation made Ethel bear Kittens, audience sympathy shifts from mother to daughter.

Clara also gave Kittens a depth the role did not have onstage. When her lover rejects her for her mother, Kittens is supposed to throw a tantrum of self-absorption; instead Clara's tears of be-trayal suggest a hidden sensitivity beneath Kittens's superficial facade. The effect was not lost upon critics or contemporaries, all of whom realized that, once again, Clara had stolen a movie from its stars. "She was absolutely a sensation in *Dancing Mothers*," re-members Louise Brooks. "Everybody forgot Alice Joyce, because Clara was so marvelous; she just swept the country! I thought she was oh, so wonderful; *everybody* did. She became a star overnight with nobody's help."

Clara's Paramount debut was so successful that the studio awarded her a cameo appearance—as Clara Bow, *movie star*—in *Fascinating Youth,* then rushed her back to Hollywood for *The Run-away.* Afterward Paramount spent nearly six weeks preparing Clara's next project, a period equal to the shooting time of two Preferred pictures. Since the studio paid her salary, Schulberg made no objection.

During her hiatus Clara bought a chow dog the same shade as her recently hennaed hair. The sight of her speeding down Sunset Boulevard in her red roadster, red hair blowing in the wind and red puppy perched on the seat beside her, became a familiar one in Hollywood.

That April, Paramount ranked Clara thirty-eighth in its Galaxy of Stars. One year later she would be beyond numerical rating. The ascent began with *Mantrap,* the film that brought fame, fortune, and Victor Fleming into her life.

# 8

"Every dame he ever worked with fell on her ass for him," declared director Henry Hathaway. "Norma Shearer. Clara Bow. Ingrid Bergman."

"Oh, honey, you name any gal, and he had a thing with her," says Helene Rosson. "Women just fell all over themselves to get at him, he was so attractive: six feet tall and perfectly proportioned, with steel-gray eyes, salt-and-pepper hair, a deep voice, and conservative but beautiful style . . . I was his stepdaughter, and *I* was in love with him."

"A tough guy," recalled director Edward Sutherland. "A great, big, strong fellow."

"Oh, yeah, he was a tough guy," agrees Artie Jacobson. "He had balls. He had guts. He was a *man*. He was the guy that replaced George Cukor on *Gone with the Wind.* Because after a few weeks, Clark Gable said, 'Look, this picture calls for a *man.*' And Cukor, although he was an excellent director, was a flaming—— And Gable said, 'I want Fleming.' "

"Gable owes everything he was, his personality, to Vic," stated producer Arthur Freed. "He modeled himself on him."

"I was responsible for getting Vic Fleming to direct *The Wizard of Oz,* " Freed continued. "No one had ever thought of using Fleming for a musical before. He was this strange fellow who was part Indian and had this *feeling* . . . one of the great unsung men of this business. Someday someone's going to bring up what Victor Fleming meant to movies."

Victor Fleming remains an unjustly neglected figure in film history. How many movies are as beloved as 1939's *Gone with the Wind* and *The Wizard of Oz?* What other director made two commensurate classics in a single year?

Such laurels lay ahead of Fleming when *Mantrap* began shoot-

ing on April 7, 1926. At the time he was forty-three years old and
had directed eighteen films, none of particular distinction or success. Indeed, Fleming's background was more interesting than his
movies: born and raised in San Dimas, California, he had parlayed
a daredevil personality and mastery of auto mechanics into a position as Douglas Fairbanks's chauffeur. One day Fleming walked
into the Triangle Studios and boasted of his expertise with movie
cameras (he hadn't any) and was soon promoted to the studio's
director of photography. He shot several of Fairbanks's films, then
directed two and joined Paramount. A 1924 affair with Norma
Shearer publicized his sexual prowess, but by the time he made
*Mantrap* and met Clara, Fleming was more concerned with his
career than his cocksmanship, and though his sensitivity rarely
surfaced in person, its presence was increasingly apparent on film.

   *Mantrap* offered Fleming his best opportunity yet. Playing Sinclair Lewis's solemn tale of backwoods adultery for laughs, Fleming and title writer George Marion, Jr., transformed protagonist
Joe Easter (Ernest Torrence), proprietor of the Mantrap River
Trading Company in the Canadian wilderness, from a noble savage
to a comic oaf. "My last thrill was in 1906, when I seen a girl's
ankle," complains Joe to a visitor. A pleasure trip to Minneapolis is
prescribed despite the disapproval of Mrs. McGavity, Joe's
hatchet-faced neighbor. "Them free-and-easy city hussies will get
you, Joe Easter," she warns. "They're so free and you're so easy."

   Indeed, no sooner does Joe arrive in Minneapolis than he
meets Alverna (Clara), a manicurist who impulsively accepts the
smitten hick's proposal. Trading her silk gowns for gingham
frocks, Alverna returns with her husband to Mantrap, where her
domestic bliss disappears with the arrival of Ralph Prescott (Percy
Marmont), a divorce lawyer who has fled New York to escape
predatory types exactly like her. Ralph's presence at Mantrap reminds Alverna of the life and men she's left behind, and her former
restlessness returns. "I thought I'd get a kick out of life up here,"
she sighs, "but gee, I'd like to go back. It's fierce to be dead before
you die." Gazing into her eyes, Ralph cannot resist feeling sympathetic.

   Finally Alverna loses patience with Ralph's gentlemanly conduct and makes a very forward pass. To her astonishment, he blocks it: "I'll *never* kiss you," Ralph pledges, then leaves Mantrap. Alverna follows, promising to behave and proving her mettle after their Indian guide absconds with their food and canoe. Impressed by her grit, Ralph breaks his vow and kisses her. Suddenly an aquaplane appears on the horizon. As Ralph waves it down, Alverna grabs her compact and powder puff, her wiles returning with Pavlovian alacrity. The plane lands, but Ralph cannot convince its pilot to part with his rations until a freshly rouged Alverna peeks out from behind him. "Aw, major, have a heart," she pouts. Moments later they have a meal, but Ralph is furious. "And I thought you were through flirting!" he grumbles.

"Don't be sill," says Alverna. "I only flirted because it was *necessary.*"

Joe catches up with the eloping couple, and instead of a duel he and Ralph debate Alverna's future. Ralph believes "Continental culture—New York, Paris, Monte Carlo," the best solution, while Joe favors exiling her to his aunt in Minneapolis. Outraged, Alverna interrupts them: "I'm my own boss from now on!" she announces, then jumps into Joe's motorboat and leaves her husband and lover stranded.

"Remember, you still bear my name!" Joe shouts after her.

"So does your old man!" retorts Alverna, laughing victoriously as she heads toward civilization.

Ralph returns to New York, relieved to deal with divorcees whose snares pale beside the mantrap at Mantrap. Alverna returns to Joe, who wraps her in his ursine arms with an all-forgiving embrace as a strapping mountie enters. Still holding onto her husband, Alverna gives the stranger a brazen once-over. "Hang on to me, Joe," she warns, eyeing her prospective prey. "I'm slipping just a little . . ." The movie ends with Joe maintaining his grip, fully prepared for the struggle.

The *Mantrap* company shot interiors at Paramount's dilapidated Vine Street studios, then traveled to Lake Arrowhead for location work. Though Fleming was involved with actress Alice White and Clara was concentrating on her role (assistant director Henry Hathaway remembers her as " 'on' all day and alone at night"), it didn't take long for life to imitate art. Fleming was too much of a gentleman to mention it, but prop man Billy Kaplan "knew that there was something going on between the two of them, even though Vic still had Alice White. You could see there was a relationship there."

Clara had never experienced one like it. Her new lover was more than twice her age and treated her as a talent of limitless potential. "A temperament that responded like a great violin," he told a friend with uncharacteristic flourish. "Touch her and she answered with genius." It was heady praise for a twenty-year-old whom one film historian has called "the most undereducated aspirant to stardom ever to make the grade, Marilyn Monroe not excepted," and Clara was awed by the attention. No man of Fleming's stature had shown her respect or kindness, let alone love; overwhelmed with gratitude, she gave him the only thing she felt she could offer in return: herself. It was typical of Fleming that he never let their affair preclude his paternal role; nor was the stability and security he gave Clara contingent upon her sexual submission. And it was typical of Clara that, convinced her true self had no worth, she incorporated aspects of Alverna into it. Her director-lover had created more than just a movie character.

With advance word on *Mantrap* building, Schulberg suggested that Paramount executives trick Clara into signing an extension of her Preferred contract without renegotiating its terms. This way her Paramount salary would remain as it was at Preferred: $750 a week, a pitiful sum considering that the previous year, before *Dancing Mothers* and *Mantrap,* Schulberg had loaned her out for four times that amount.

While she was on location in Lake Arrowhead the studio contacted Robert Bow, who went to Paramount and agreed to all its terms. It was robbery: Clara would earn $750 a week through 1926, $925 a week in 1927, and $1,500 a week in 1928. To add treachery to trickery, Jack Bachman, Schulberg's former partner and the man who had urged him to bring Clara to Hollywood, was cut out of the deal.

Paramount executives thought the Bows fools and enjoyed

belittling them in interoffice correspondence. An exchange between studio attorneys Bernard Campe and Henry Herzbrun is
typical:

July 16, 1926

Dear Bernie:

    Pursuant to your wires I have procured the enclosed consents to
the use of Clara Bow's name and photograph in connection with
special exploitation of *Mantrap,* all of them duly signed by her.
    Don't let the position of Clara's signature annoy you [Clara had
not signed the document on the designated "dotted line"]. The
remarkable thing is that she did not sign on the back or at the
bottom.
    The first two consents were delayed several days because Clara
was on location and her father was carrying them around in his
pocket for trading purposes; he gets several cigars every time he
comes here.

Henry

After *Mantrap* finished shooting, Clara rented actress Bessie
Love's log cabin at 261 West Canyon Drive, resumed her relationship with Gilbert Roland, continued her affair with Victor Fleming,
and met Tui Lorraine, her first close female friend. Born Tui Lorraine Leigh, the blonde, five-foot, nineteen-year-old New Zealand
native came from a circus family. "I'd been in show business since
age five and a kid star before I came to California," she explains,
"so I was not overly impressed by movies. They were just another
job to me." It was Clara, however, who had achieved stardom while
Tui worked sporadically in unbilled roles.

    They were introduced at a party in Laurel Canyon. Clara gave
Tui her telephone number, Tui called a few days later, and Clara
invited her over for a drink. Any professional envy on Tui's part
vanished when Clara confessed her loneliness. "I couldn't believe
she would ever be blue," says Tui. "I'd never met such a bubbling,
friendly, natural person anywhere, especially in Hollywood." Her
hostess felt likewise. Tui was no phony, and Clara befriended her
because of it.

    Their conversation was interrupted by Gilbert Roland, who
stormed into Clara's cabin and demanded in his heavy accent,

"Where is he? I know he's here. I'll fix him. I'll fight a duel with him!" The threat didn't impress Tui, but Clara seemed delighted; apparently Roland's melodramatics appealed to her as much as Victor Fleming's maturity (since she was involved with both men, the "he" Roland referred to was presumably Fleming). Tui also found the display absurd, for no one was present but she and Clara, who considered herself informally engaged to Roland anyway.

Nonetheless his fears were justified. Though Fleming was Roland's only real rival, Clara basked in the attention of other admirers—"and they came, my dear, in droves," states Tui flatly. To someone so love-starved, stardom was akin to winning an emotional lottery, and Clara suddenly found herself surrounded by "people who'd never paid no attention t'me comin' 'round t'tell me how 'wonderful' I was." For the first time in her life, she could seek steadying counsel: "Victor Fleming steered me straight."

But Fleming's paternal guidance, like Roland's romantic passion, wasn't enough for Clara, so less than a month later a *third* party entered the picture. What he did for her love made headlines, turned her private life into public property, and confirmed her mantrapping talent.

# 9

Robert Savage was the black-sheep son of a blue-blooded Connecticut family. Subsequent headlines to the contrary, he was not a Yale football hero, though he did play on the school's scrub team during his one-year college career (Savage's name has since been expunged from university records). When the twenty-five-year-old ne'er-do-well came to Hollywood in May, 1926, he had already wooed Geneva Mitchell, the "Pogo Girl" of the Ziegfeld Follies, and was determined to win Clara Bow. Within three days of his arrival Savage had wangled an introduction to her through a mutual acquaintance who called Clara "and said he hadda friend from Yale who was just crazy t'meet me."

An athletic new admirer with an Ivy League pedigree suited her fine, so Clara invited Savage to her Canyon Drive cabin. "We talked for a long time that afternoon," she recalled, "but Mr. Savage was real nice and didn't tryta make love t'me. I told him 'bout my success on the screen and he told me 'bout his career as a newspaperman and poet [Savage had dabbled in each]. He's a wonderful talker, 'cept he talks too much 'bout hisself and his family," she concluded.

Self-proclaimed Yale alumnus and Savage chum Gus Patterson told a juicier version. According to Patterson, he and Savage attended a party at Clara's cabin that evening. Savage remained on the porch while Clara socialized, returning periodically to kiss him and pronounce him her "poet lover."

"Never mind my fiancé," Patterson heard Clara assure Savage. "He's justa conceited Spaniard."

"She bit his lips until they bled," Patterson added. "He said they ached for two days."

"I didn't bite his lip," countered Clara angrily. "He musta gone home an' cut it."

Savage's boast put a premature end to the romance. Spurned, he had a friend warn Clara that he was contemplating suicide.

"Don't worry, he won't kill himself," she retorted. "He thinks too mucha himself." After several days of abject pleas, Clara allowed Savage to pick her up from a lunch at the Ambassador Hotel. "I thought it'd be safeta ride home with him," she testified later. "He promised it'd be the last time he'd bother me."

Savage arrived at the Ambassador on Friday, June 4. Once Clara was in his car, he told her that instead of returning to Canyon Drive, he was taking her to obtain a marriage license. "He said, 'I'm gonna marry ya. In a few hours you'll be Mrs. Robert Savage, or I'm gonna waste my life away in Alaska.' "

" 'Don't be sill,' I told him. 'I don't love ya. I don't even *lik* ya.' "

Undaunted, Savage drove to an attorney's office. Clara decided to go along with the gag until she realized it wasn't one. "If we get a license, do we haveta go on an' get married?" she asked the lawyer anxiously. "Is that the same as gettin' really, truly married?" Luckily the couple was caught in rush-hour traffic and arrived at the Marriage License Bureau five minutes too late.

Clara's relief gave way to rage. "Take me home or I'll walk back," she snapped. Savage did, then shared the story with reporters.

Accounts of Clara's foiled elopement enraged Gilbert Roland, who considered himself her fiancé. So did she: "I am engaged to Gilbert Roland," Clara announced the next day. "I don't love Bob Savage. This whole thing is ridiculous."

Savage was devastated. "I thought she returned my love," he testified later, "but I guess she didn't. She threw me down cold. I wrote her notes, begged for interviews, called on the phone, but to no avail. Finally I went out to her home in Laurel Canyon. Her father came to the door and told me Clara wasn't in.

"That was absolutely the last straw, and it was then I decided to stage something desperate."

Savage carried out his threat that night. First, one last poem was composed to commemorate his love:

> A haunting voice comes in the twilight
> Whispering soft and low,

> Telling of a beautiful creature,
> Telling of Clara Bow.
> And I lie in my bed by the window,
> To happily, happily scan
> The heavens so star-filled above me,
> Grateful, indeed, I'm a man.
>
> I know of the rules, and I'll gamble,
> No matter the score in the end.
> I know of the prize, and it's worth it,
> I'll pray for Good Luck as my friend.
> So on with the game, I am ready;
> Clara, you'd better beware.
> Muster your wiles for protection,
> This warns you, young lady—prepare!

After dropping broad hints to friends of his intention "to end it all," Savage sat on a couch, set a photograph of Clara beside him, and slashed his wrists. When the police arrived (as Savage anticipated, his friends had alerted his landlady, who called them), they found him stretched out on one side, smoking a cigarette and staring at Clara's picture. He had positioned himself so the blood from his superficial wounds would trickle atop her image.

Savage was taken to General Hospital's receiving room, bandaged, and transferred to the psychopathic ward. He demanded to meet the press, who gave the story front-page coverage. Mortified, the Savage family spirited its prodigal son to a private sanitarium, but they could not prevent a local "Lunacy Commission" hearing the following week to determine his sanity. As usual, Savage did most of the talking. "Say listen, Judge," he began, "I never wanted to die in the first place. I never had any intention of killing myself. I was just pulling some theatrical stuff to make an effect on her." Was Savage still smitten by Clara Bow? "Sure, I love her, and I'll get her yet. Just watch my smoke." The gales of laughter which greeted his boast caused Clara, subpoenaed against her will as a witness, to blush "the color of her hair." The Lunacy Commission threw Savage's case out of court.

Furious at Savage for exploiting their one-day dalliance into two weeks of headlines, Clara called a press conference of her own and spoke with characteristically quotable candor. "Mr. Savage is just an episode in my young life," she declared. "He says he triedta commit suicide 'cause I turned him down—'gave him the gate,' he calls it.

"Well, lemme tell ya this," said Clara with sudden, scornful authority on the subject, "when a man attempts suicide over a woman, he don't cut his wrists with a safety razor blade, then drape himself over a couch with a cigarette between his lips. No, they don't do it that way. They use *pistols*."

Paramount publicists couldn't have written a better exit line, and if they had, they wouldn't have dared use it. Five years earlier a stunt like Savage's could have ruined an actress's career, but by 1926 the incident merely tickled America's fancy. A titillated public assumed Clara's screen persona was identical to herself, and though nothing could have been further from the truth, she did not discourage the misrepresentation. Lacking an identity of her own, Clara tailored herself to her persona, becoming even more of a mantrap than the movie and Victor Fleming had already made her. If that was who was wanted, then that was who she would be.

In the end Clara had made headlines and emerged unscathed from them, a virtual miracle for a movie star. Only the Savage clan and Gilbert Roland were unamused by the episode, and his lovers' tiff with her ended in a broken engagement, followed by a front-page reconciliation a week later. Now a chastened "Clarita" promised Roland she would elope to Mexico with him after her next movie, *Kid Boots,* finished shooting. She loved Roland and intended to defy her father and marry him, but the message was clear: her career came first.

*Kid Boots* seemed likely to further it. Paramount bought the Broadway musical-comedy for $75,000, then spent another $275,000 shooting it, a budget *ten* times that of any Preferred Picture. "Banjo-eyed" comedian Eddie Cantor was hired to re-create his Kid Boots role on screen; to ensure audience identification between the heroine and Clara, her character's name was changed from Jane Martin to Clara McCoy—Clara Bow, "the real McCoy"—and described as "responsible for many accidents by making men look where they're not going." So notorious was

Clara's new reputation that studio gossip instantly linked her with Lawrence Gray, *Kid Boots'* handsome straight man. "She took Larry Gray home with her," recalls one executive secretary, "and when he came out, he could barely stand up!" Rumor also paired Clara with Cantor, even though she considered marriage sacrosanct and would never have threatened his.

Clara and Cantor developed an immediate rapport, based on their similar backgrounds: born in a New York City ghetto and orphaned in early childhood, Cantor began entertaining professionally at age fourteen and was once a singing waiter at Coney Island, a job Robert Bow craved but was too incompetent to attain. Like Clara, Cantor's fame had not enlarged his ego, and *Kid Boots'* cast and crew were often treated to songs and comedy routines between shots. Cantor also helped Clara with her comic timing, and in return she taught him how to play the camera. "She told me, 'Be yourself,' " the comedian wrote. "She is. She is never camera-conscious and acts on the set as she would in her home." One scene in *Kid Boots* called for Clara to squabble with Cantor, and to his astonishment she simultaneously expressed anger and offered encouragement: "While the camera ground away and caught all her pretty frowns, she was really saying, 'Eddie, ya doin' fine! Just flash them banjo eyes and there ain't nothin' to it!' "

A silent-film adaptation of a Broadway musical comedy seems a dubious prospect, yet the dual appeal of Cantor's comic bumbling and Clara's "captivating, heart-snatching heroine" made *Kid Boots* an immediate success. On opening day Manhattan police were needed to control crowds.

While *Kid Boots* was still shooting, *Mantrap* opened. Clara's first starring role at Paramount was her first smash hit, and *Variety*'s exclamatory review gave her sole credit for it:

Clara Bow! And how! What a "mantrap" she is!
    And how this picture is going to make her! It should do as much for this corking little ingenue lead as *Flaming Youth* did for Colleen Moore.
    Bow just walks away with the picture from the moment she steps into camera range. Every minute that she is in it, she steals it from troupers Ernest Torrence and Percy Marmont. Any time a girl can do

that, she is going some. In this particular role she is fitted just like a glove . . . and boy, how she vamps with her lamps! And how they fall!

That same week, Ben Schulberg arranged for *The Plastic Age,* which had gradually worked its state-righted way across the country, to premiere in New York. With two hits in theaters at the same time, Clara shot from sudden to established star overnight. "Clara Bow has taken everyone by storm," reported *Motion Picture Magazine,* adding that "the innocent cause of all this excitement is on her way to New York to play opposite Adolphe Menjou in *The Ace of Cads.*" Actually Clara never left Los Angeles, nor did she appear in a movie with Menjou. Instead Paramount gave her a month's vacation between *Kid Boots* and *Wings,* an aviation saga in preproduction. Naturally the magnanimous gesture had an ulterior motive: studio owner Adolph Zukor wanted to replace Clara's current contract with a newer, longer one. Zukor believed the craze for Clara was just beginning, and he also sensed why: "She danced even when her feet were not moving. Some part of her was always in motion, if only her great rolling eyes. It was an elemental magnetism, an animal vitality, that made her the center of attraction in any company." Since *Dancing Mothers, Mantrap,* and *Kid Boots* had already showcased Clara's magnetism and vitality and made huge profits in the process, Zukor ordered studio attorney Henry Herzbrun to draft a new contract for her.

Herzbrun considered her a pushover, but with the aid of Victor Fleming, Clara stalled negotiations, then announced that she would wait until her current contract expired before signing a new one.

This was dire news. With Gloria Swanson gone to United Artists and European import Pola Negri proving a box-office disappointment, Paramount desperately needed a new female star, and Clara had given them three hits in the last half-year alone. There was no choice, Zukor told Herzbrun, but to meet whatever demands she made.

Herzbrun drafted a revised version of Clara's contract with terms that bore no resemblance to her existing one: by 1931 she would earn $5,000 a week, a four hundred percent increase from the $1,250 Paramount had originally offered. Robert Bow said she would come to the studio the next day and sign it.

When she did, she wasn't alone. Besides her father, Clara was accompanied by attorney Neil McCarthy, who informed Herzbrun that, contrary to what Paramount might think, his client's deal was nowhere near closed. Zukor wanted Clara under contract, so what McCarthy demanded, Paramount granted: a ceiling on the amount of movies she would make each year (six in 1927, then four per year through 1931); no loan-out clause; no morals clause; guaranteed star billing; a specially designed wardrobe for each film; first-class train travel to all locations for Clara and a maid; eight weeks' paid sick leave; $100 a week for Robert Bow in his capacity as "Special Adviser" (needless to say, Robert wanted six months' salary in advance); and $25,000 for Clara if Paramount failed to exercise its option prior to the contract's expiration in 1931.

These were not casual concessions. Paramount had even relinquished its nonnegotiable morals clause, and though Neil McCarthy deserves credit for insisting the studio do so, it was Clara who hired him. Four months earlier she could not even sign a document correctly; now she had panicked her studio and put herself in a powerful negotiating position. Clara had beaten the studio at its own game.

The absence of a morals clause in her contract caused Paramount to search for a substitute, and their worries were understandable. "She could flirt with a grizzly bear," observed the New York *Times* of Clara in *Mantrap,* and as Paramount knew, her sexual provocation was not limited to her screen characters. A month earlier she had celebrated her twenty-first birthday, and already her name had been publicly linked with Roland and Savage, while her affair with Fleming was well known within Hollywood. If anyone needed a morals clause, it was Clara. Ironically, she was the only star at Paramount without one.

The problem was finally solved by making Clara's $25,000 cash bonus contingent upon her conduct. To ensure it, Paramount would establish a trust fund with itself as trustor, its bank as trustee, and Clara as sole beneficiary. Each week for the first year of her contract, the studio would deposit $500 into the trust fund, with Clara receiving its contents upon her contract's expiration, unless she became "involved in a public scandal or subjected herself to public scorn or ridicule, or tended to offend the public sense of decency to an extent that in the opinion of Mr. Will Hays . . . [it] warrants the dismissal of the Artist by the Corporation."

Though its wording was interchangeable with Paramount's regular morals clause, its ramifications were not. Unlike any other actor at the studio, scandal would deprive Clara of her $25,000 bonus *but not her contract.* As long as she was guaranteed employment (and she was literally the sole star at Paramount who was), nothing else mattered to Clara, for in her mind the money was Paramount's anyway: she had no access to the trust's funds, and its $500 weekly increments would be deposited by the studio, not deducted from her salary. Clara felt she couldn't lose what she never had, so while Paramount opened Trust PT-487 in September of 1926, its nominal beneficiary prepared for her departure to San Antonio, Texas, where *Wings* was shooting and Victor Fleming was directing *The Rough Riders,* another Paramount production. Traveling to a remote location for a new film and a reunion with Fleming excited Clara; haggling over a trust fund which wasn't even hers did not.

Two years later and two years too late, she would wish she had paid closer attention.

# 10

*Wings,* an homage to World War I combat pilots, was Paramount's most ambitious movie yet. A $2 million budget was entrusted to twenty-nine-year-old William Wellman, the only director in Hollywood with combat flying experience. Nicknamed "Wild Bill" Wellman for his foul mouth, short temper, and fast marriages, Wellman was a director of sensitivity and dedication. Like Clara, he had come to Paramount with Ben Schulberg, who kept him under personal contract at the typically paltry salary of $250 a week.

For Wellman, *Wings* was an ex–combat flyer's dream and a director's nightmare. Scenes requiring hundreds of extras were simple compared to aerial battles requiring ideal weather, and the *Wings* company once waited eighteen straight days for clouds to part in the San Antonio sky. As shooting dragged on from month to month (most films were made in four weeks), the predominantly male cast and crews of *Wings* and Fleming's *The Rough Riders* were left with too much idle time and nowhere to waste it. Mischief was inevitable, and soon "San Antonio became the Armageddon of a magnificent sexual Donnybrook," wrote Wellman in his memoirs. "We stayed at the Saint Anthony Hotel and were there for nine months. I know that was the correct time because the elevator operators were girls, and they all became pregnant.

"A motion picture company lives hard and plays hard, and they better or they will go nuts," Wellman continued, then divulged who played hardest: "To begin with, all the young actors in *The Rough Riders* and *Wings* fell in love with Clara Bow, and if you had known her, you could understand why.

"This presented a problem to both Vic Fleming and me, but a far greater problem to Miss Bow. She took care of it—how I will never know. She kept Rogers, Arlen, Cooper, Mack, a couple of pursuit pilots, and a panting writer all in line. They were handled like chessmen, never running into one another, never suspecting that there was any other man in the whole world that meant a thing to this gorgeous little sexpot—and all this expert maneuvering in a hotel where most of the flame was burning."

Though Wellman's version of Clara's "maneuvering" is considered authoritative, the facts tell a different story. On September 16, 1926, a day after her arrival in San Antonio, Clara and Victor Fleming announced their engagement. She had grown increasingly dependent on Fleming for guidance and support, and his aid in her contractual negotiations clinched it. Now Clara told reporters that she and "Vickie" (her new pet name for him) would marry the following February, and photos taken of the couple show a dazzling grin on the director's normally dour face. But although Fleming had fallen hard, he was still no pushover. Before their engagement he had accepted Clara's freedom and enjoyed his own. Once she made a commitment, he expected her to honor it.

By all accounts except Wellman's, she did. Charles "Buddy" Rogers, her leading man in *Wings,* had met Clara in the Paramount commissary where, bucking the caste system of stardom, she always ate with "the boys" in the cast and crew. One of them was Rogers, a twenty-two-year-old Kansan who came from such a sheltered background that before Wellman plied him with champagne for *Wings'* Paris bistro sequence, he had never even tasted liquor. In the film his intoxication is not acting.

Rogers adored Clara. "She was so cute, vivacious, thoughtful, and sweet," he recalls, refuting Wellman's insinuation of something more: "That's not true. We were *pals.* I had a little flirtation with her one night, but I was too scared to do anything about it." Why? "Vic Fleming was a *tough* guy, rough and tough. I was scared to death of him."

He needn't have worried. "Aw, jeez," groaned Clara when Tui Lorraine teased her about her screen romance with Rogers, "I hate them love scenes. It's like kissin' ya *brother.*"

"She wasn't fooling around," adds Tui. "Flirting, maybe; we *all* did that."

Contrary to Wellman's contention, not every man's eye was on Clara. Second male lead Richard Arlen fell in love with second female lead Jobyna Ralston and married her when *Wings* finished shooting. Finally, there is no indication that Clara even met the man Wellman refers to as "Cooper," an unknown actor who had just changed his first name from Frank to Gary.

She probably didn't have time. Most of Clara's scenes in *Wings* were shot not in San Antonio, but in the Los Angeles suburb of Pasadena or on a stage at Paramount's brand-new, million-dollar Marathon Street studios. In fact, she stayed in San Antonio only three days, during which "the weather was so hot that I was whipped."

Another reason Clara disliked working in San Antonio was her role as girl-next-door Mary Preston. In Clara's incarnation, the character was sexier than any Parisian floozy, yet *Wings* had Buddy Rogers treating Mary like a buddy until the fade-out. Star billing or not, Clara had a superfluous part in a war picture and resented it. Her wardrobe had become a battleground as well: eager to flaunt, not hide, her hour-glass figure, Clara enraged Paramount designer Travis Banton by discarding his froufrous and exposing her flesh. "She slit his necklines and cut off his sleeves," laughs Louise Brooks. "Clara was quite beyond Banton, and quite right." Since the *Wings* wardrobe consisted mainly of military uniforms, Banton assigned one of his apprentices to it, and five decades and eight Oscars later Edith Head described the experience: "Clara loathed the uniform and I couldn't blame her," said Head. "She would sneak around and try to belt it. I'd have to be on the set every minute to snatch it off her. I think she thought I was out to get her, to make her look less sexy. Now, granted, it's pretty hard to look sexy in a U.S. Army uniform, but Clara managed.

"Putting Clara in a drab uniform was like bridling an untamed horse. She loved wild colors, the wilder the better. They reflected her vibrant personality." It was a personality which Head found coarse but charming, and though Clara hated her costumes, she liked their designer. After *Wings,* the first of several movies on which the two women worked together, Clara gave Head a signed portrait of herself. FOR EDITH, she wrote, ONE OF THE BEST, AND BY THE WAY, WHY DON'T YOU WEAR YOUR BELT HIGHER, YOU BIG —— ? CLARA. For the rest of her life Head treasured the photograph and delighted in its inscription.

One scene in *Wings* required no wardrobe at all. In it, two soldiers burst into Mary Preston's room as she changes clothing, and before she has a chance to cover herself, her topless torso is briefly displayed. "I saw more of Clara in that scene than I ever saw in real life," declares Buddy Rogers. So did the rest of America, and the shot not only caused a sensation, but set a precedent for Clara's subsequent movies: the less clothing she wore, the larger her audience.

Production on *Wings* was followed by the most momentous film of Clara's career. Based on one pronoun, it would transform her from movie star to historic symbol. Afterward—after *It*—nothing would ever be the same.

# III

## The "It" Girl

"I was seventeen, an office boy—a messenger is what I was hired for. Clara Bow had just made *Wings,* and I thought she was sensational. She dashed into the office one day, and the publicity department just stopped dead. She was just flying around—she was just happiness personified. I've never taken dope, but it was like a shot of dope when you looked at this girl."

– John Engstead

# 11

"If Hollywood hadn't existed, Elinor Glyn would have had to invent it," screenwriter Anita Loos once observed. Since it did, Elinor Glyn concentrated on her greatest invention: herself. From scandal of Edwardian England to sovereign of twenties Hollywood, this woman used her genius for self-promotion to obtain riches and renown. Whether she deserved them was beside the point: Elinor foisted herself upon a community of frauds and outfoxed them all. She did not invent Hollywood, but she definitely belonged there.

Elinor caused her first commotion with *Three Weeks*, a 1907 novel that featured a tryst on a tiger-skin rug between the heroine and her dashing lover. "They were on the tiger by now," wrote Elinor in her oblique yet, for her era, daring and explicit style, "and she undulated round and all over him, feeling his coat, and his face, and his hair, as a blind person might, till at last it seemed as if she were twined about him like a serpent." Though quaint today, an unmarried couple undulating on a carpet was sensational at the time, and Elinor was branded as sinful as her heroine. An anonymous verse that followed the publication of *Three Weeks* asked:

> Would you like to sin
> With Elinor Glyn
> On a tiger skin?
> Or would you prefer
> To err with her
> On some other fur?

Even more notorious than the novel's sex was its dynamic, for intentionally or not, Elinor had inverted the sexual power structure by making *Three Weeks'* heroine an aggressor and its hero her prey. She gave her generation a preview of behavior its flapper daughters would take for granted.

By 1920 Elinor's career and capital were in decline, so an offer to write scenarios in Hollywood was accepted with alacrity (the fact that she had never actually *seen* a movie did not faze her). She arrived to find a community reeling from scandal and searching for a grandiose dowager type to deem it respectable. So what if so-called "Hollywood society" was comprised of shanty Irish, *shtetl* Jews, Italian peasants, and native pariahs? If her benediction of these yokels advanced her career in their industry, Elinor was more than willing to bestow it, and soon "Madame Glyn" had become the last word in matters of taste and refinement. Despite her squinty eyes, crude dentures, hair dyed the color of red ink, and comically false eyelashes, Madame ruled over Hollywood's inner-most social circle, which revolved around two residences: Pickfair, the baronial estate of Mary Pickford and Douglas Fairbanks; and San Simeon, the coastal castle shared by William Randolph Hearst and his mistress, actress Marion Davies. Hearst also built Davies a 110-room "beach house" in Santa Monica where Elinor Glyn was guest of honor.

Prior to her arrival in Hollywood, Elinor had considered movies a cheap and vulgar diversion of common folk, but once she actually saw one, she changed her mind. "You don't realize yet what has happened," she told actress Gloria Swanson, for whom she had been assigned to write a scenario. "Motion pictures are going to change everything. They are the most important thing that's come along since the printing press. What woman can dream about a prince anymore when she's seen one up close in a news-reel? She'd rather dream about Wallace Reid. People don't care about royalty anymore. They're much more interested in queens of the screen like you, dear."

Like the rest of the Hollywood elite, Swanson was a hoax, a screen queen whose ancestry, abortions, and affairs made her no different or better than most other movie actresses. Swanson was simply more successful, and in Hollywood success was grounds for social superiority. Sixty years later she would mock herself for groveling to Elinor Glyn, but at the time Swanson worshipped her.

"Her British dignity was devastating," she recalled with lingering awe. "She took over Hollywood. She went everywhere and passed her fearsome verdicts on everything. 'This is glamorous,' she would say. 'This is hideous,' she would say, as she baby-stepped through this or that dining room or garden party. People moved aside for her as if she were a sorceress on fire or a giant sting ray."

The feeling was hardly mutual. "It is a pity Miss Swanson is such a marionette and so common, but the public adore her," Elinor wrote her mother. "You will loathe her."

It took one hustler to recognize another, and in this sense mogul Samuel Goldwyn paid Elinor the supreme compliment. "I believe she plans her personality as carefully as her stories," he noted. "I once said of her that she was a great showman, and when she heard my comment, she was exceedingly gratified." Of course she was. Showmanship had made Elinor a bestselling authoress, then a social empress. Now, courtesy of Clara Bow, it would make her world-famous.

In 1926 Ben Schulberg read Elinor's latest novelette, a turgid study of sex appeal called *It* ("It, hell; she had Those," sneered Dorothy Parker of *It*'s heroine), and thought of an exploitable idea based upon it. A year earlier he had promoted Clara Bow as "the Brooklyn Bonfire," but the slogan had not stuck. Perhaps "the 'It' Girl" would.

Madame Glyn was game. She was a snob but no fool, and since flappers like Clara were fast replacing genteelwomen like Gloria Swanson, she agreed to proclaim Clara and "It" synonymous—for a price. When Schulberg agreed, Elinor wasted no time. "Of all the lovely young ladies I've met in Hollywood," announced *It*'s authoress and hence its authority, "Clara Bow has 'It.' " Her endorsement cost Paramount $50,000.

Now Schulberg arranged for *It*'s arbiter to meet its embodiment, who had recently returned from her three-day stay in San Antonio, where Gilbert Roland had sent her a sarcastic congratulatory telegram after her engagement to Victor Fleming. Clara wired Roland assuring him it wasn't true (it was). "When I got back, I hadda tough time convincin' Gilbert I loved him more than anybody," she admitted, sounding more and more like her screen characters than herself. "He finally said it was all right I didn't see no other men." With Fleming still in San Antonio, Clara could keep her promise while *It* shot. But first she had to meet Madame Glyn.

The introduction took place in late September of 1926, when Clara dropped by Schulberg's office during a lull in shooting on *Wings* and was greeted by the sight of a sixty-two-year-old redhead swathed in purple chiffon veils (worn, though Elinor would not admit it, to hide the healing process of a recent facelift). "So this is Clara Bow," she said, approaching Clara with mincing steps. Once she reached her, Elinor placed both hands upon Clara's head as if it were a crystal ball. "You are my medium, child," she informed Clara gravely. "You are to portray the leading role in my story." Schulberg explained that henceforth she would be known as "the 'It' Girl," and Elinor explained the title to her. " 'It' is an inner magic, an animal magnetism," she said. "Valentino possessed this certain magic. So do John Gilbert and Rex." Elinor's second and third choices were, respectively, another actor and a stallion.

"I was awful confused about the horse," recalled Clara, "but if she thought he had 'It,' then I figured he must be quite an animal." On that note, the meeting ended.

Though Elinor received a "story and adaptation" credit on *It,* Schulberg ordered Louis Lighton and Hope Loring, a husband-and-wife team he had brought from Preferred, to junk her tale and devise one for Clara incorporating the "It" concept. When Antonio Moreno was cast as the film's leading man, Elinor dropped Valentino, John Gilbert, Rex, and her latest addition, the doorman at the Ambassador Hotel, from her "It" list and declared that only Moreno possessed the quality.

Ultimately Moreno did not matter, for *It* was based so heavily on Clara that its plot might have been her life had she stayed in Brooklyn. The movie opens inside Waltham's, "the world's largest department store," where heroine Betty Lou Spence sells silk teddies she wishes she could afford. Despite the cheap fake cherries on her hat and the slang in her sentences, Betty Lou clearly has oodles of "It," as does Cyrus Waltham (Moreno), handsome son of the

store's owner. "Hot socks—the new boss!" sighs a fellow salesgirl
as Cyrus passes the lingerie counter.

Betty Lou's response is more direct. "Sweet Santa Claus,
gimme *him!*" Coming from her, it's less a wish than a command.

It was also the first instance during shooting when Clara con-
founded, then astounded director Clarence Badger, whom she had
nicknamed "Santa" for his jolly manner and apple cheeks. Though
Badger found Clara "a pleasure to direct," the way she played her
first scene startled him. "Following my directions, Clara gazed at
[Moreno] with an expression of lingering, calflike longing in her
pretty face: perfectly all right if she had stopped there.

"But she did not. Continuing on, the camera still grinding
away, her doll-like tantalizing eyes suddenly became inflamed with
unwholesome passion. Then the young rascal suddenly changed
her expression again, this time to one of virtuous, innocent appeal."

Badger angrily called "Cut!" and confronted Clara. "And
what was that all about?" he demanded.

"Well, Santa," explained Clara, "if ya knew your onions like ya
was supposedta, you'd know the first look was for the lovesick
dames in the audience, and the second look, that passionate stuff,
was for the boys an' their poppas, and the *third* look . . . well, just
about the time all them old ladies're shocked an' scandalized by the
passionate part, they suddenly see that third look, change their
minds 'bout me havin' naughty ideas, an' go home thinkin' how
pure an' innocent I was. An' havin' got me mixed up with this girl
I'm playin', they'll come again when my next picture shows up."

At a loss against such logic, Badger called "Action!" and continued shooting. In the movie, Clara's triple-take appears exactly
as described.

*It* continues as Betty Lou, who has just commanded Santa
Claus to give her Cyrus Waltham for Christmas, decides not to wait
that long. Instead she catches his eye that night at the Ritz, where
Elinor Glyn makes a cameo appearance as—who else?—herself,
announcing that " 'It' is self-confidence and indifference to
whether you are pleasing or not, and something in you that gives
the impression that you are not all cold." At that moment Cyrus

spots Betty Lou across the restaurant and ogles her brazenly. "Cyrus, do you believe in 'It'?" his oblivious fiancée inquires.

Cyrus snaps out of his trance, then gives Betty Lou a sidelong glance. "I certainly do!" he declares.

The next day Cyrus asks Betty Lou for a date. She accepts on one condition: "Let's go t'the beach an' do it up right!" No more foreign foods in fancy restaurants; instead, Betty Lou takes Cyrus to Coney Island and introduces him to the proletarian pleasures of Ferris wheels and roller coasters, of hot dogs and cotton candy. By the end of the evening Cyrus is so infatuated that he loses control and pounces. Betty Lou slaps his face. "So you're one of them minute men—the minute ya know a girl, ya think ya can kiss her!" she huffs, then scurries into her tenement flat. As Cyrus sits in his car rubbing his sore cheek, she peeks out a window and watches, pleased by her progress.

By now Clarence Badger had learned that the best way to direct Clara was to "set up the camera, explain the scene to her, and just let her go." His approach encouraged her inspired, improvised moments, one of which occurred at this point in the movie: after Betty Lou spies on Cyrus from her window, she hugs the stuffed animal he won for her at Coney Island, then suddenly turns it around, lifts its tail, examines its rear, and spanks it mischievously. It was a silly but adorable gesture that also mitigated Clara's carnality with her childlike innocence, and Badger knew better than to object. "When I start to direct her," he confessed to Louise Brooks, "I get mad because she's doing all these things. And then I run them, and they're wonderful."

After their date, Cyrus is led to believe that Betty Lou is the mother of a fatherless child (she, of course, was only protecting a girlfriend from welfare workers trying to take the baby away). Assuming her a woman already fallen, he makes a proposition that includes everything except matrimony. Betty Lou is shocked, humiliated, and hurt. "What're ya tryin' t'do?" she cries. "Offer me one of those 'left-handed arrangements'?"

Mistress versus marriage: will Betty Lou settle for the former? Absolutely not. Because she has "It," she quits her job and resolves to forget Cyrus. Because he has "It," this proves impossible,

Left, Sarah Gordon, age sixteen.
She did not love her husband
and she did not want children.

Below, three-year-old Clara and her
grandfather, Frederick Gordon,
in 1908.
A few months later
he dropped dead at her feet.

Nickolas Murray shot this stunning portrait of 1921's Fame and Fortune Contest winner. Clara was sixteen. Her mother had just tried to kill her. (IMP/Eastman House)

With Artie Jacobson at Brighton Beach, 1923. They fell in love in Brooklyn, then lived together in Hollywood.

Left, B. P. Schulberg
engineered Clara's rise and fall.
(Marc Wanamaker/Bison Archives)

Below, welcoming Robert Bow
to Hollywood in 1924.

ui Lorraine. Clara's best friend became her
epmother. (Academy of Motion Picture Arts
d Sciences)

On the *Mantrap* set. Left to right: Ernest Torrence, Percy Marmont, Clara, Victor Fleming,
James Wong Howe, and camera operator Rex Wimpy.

# BOW BEAUX

1925: Gilbert Roland called her "Clarita." She called him "my first really big love experience."

1926: Clara and Victor Fleming announce their engagement. Weeks later she would leave him for Gary Cooper. (Museum of Modern Art/Film Stills Archive)

927: "'It' Boy" Gary Cooper. Clara described im in graphic detail. (Phototeque)

1928: Clara's affair with Earl Pearson caused a scandal and cost her $56,000.

1929: Harry Richman slips the ring on Clara's finger. It was her fifth engagement in four years. (Museum of Modern Art/Film Stills Archive)

"Bow plus Glyn equals underwear": *Red Hair* stuck to formula and made a fortune. (Museum of Modern Art/Film Stills Archive)

and when Betty Lou learns what presumption led to Cyrus's proposition, she is even more insulted. "An' he wouldn't even gimme
the benefit of the doubt!" she fumes. Cyrus must learn his lesson,
and Betty Lou, "It"-laden hoyden that she is, vows to teach it to
him.

As usual, she wastes no time. Cyrus hosts a yachting party and
Betty Lou crashes it, masquerading as a "Miss Van Cortland" and
becoming the rowdiest guest aboard. "Miss Van Cortland seems
rather lacking in reserve," sneers his fiancée. "Personally, I think
she has *plenty* in reserve!" counters Cyrus, who corners Betty Lou,
apologizes, and proposes marriage. "I'd rather marry your office
boy!" she replies, her mission accomplished but her heart broken.
Fortunately the yacht crashes, allowing Betty Lou to rescue Cyrus's
fiancée (when the drowning socialite struggles, our heroine
coldcocks her), then clinch with him on the hoisted anchor of the
cruiser *Itola*. In *It*'s final shot only the ship's first two letters are
visible, and as Cyrus kisses her passionately, Betty Lou presses her
palm against his cheek and pivots it in a spontaneous, caressing
motion both innocently playful and boldly erotic. As predicted, she
really does have "plenty in reserve."

Her peers felt likewise about Clara. While directors marveled
at her intuitive, extraordinary talent, cameramen considered her
inexhaustible energy as awesome as it was aggravating. "She was
difficult to follow with the camera because she was a free soul on
the set," explains Artie Jacobson, now a second-cameraman at
Paramount himself. "She'd fly all over the place, which was part of
her charm. Complete abandonment." To cope with it, cameramen
would beg Clara to give them an idea of where she would be, then
light the set accordingly. If she deviated from her intended destination, a close-up of her was cut into the scene.

Clara couldn't lose: if her hyperactivity made a master-shot
unusable, she earned an extra close-up. However, she never
hogged the privilege as Colleen Moore had in *Painted People*. Re-
membering her own misery in loan-outs, Clara treated actresses in
a similar position with kindness and consideration. In *It*, Priscilla
Bonner played the mother of the baby Cyrus mistakes for Betty
Lou's. It was a deglamorized supporting role that Bonner hated,

though Clara did all she could to help. "Clara always 'gave' to me in a scene," says Bonner. "She worked with the other actor, and she worked hard. Always on time, very businesslike, and absolutely no 'star temperament.' " Bonner also recalls the day Elinor Glyn was "presented" to the *It* cast, still swathed in purple chiffon. "She wrote absolute trash, but she thought she was very important, putting on airs as if she expected us to curtsy and collapse over her. The whole thing was ridiculous, and after she left, I asked Clara whether she thought 'Madame' had a wind machine under her skirt to make all that chiffon billow.

"Well, Clara burst into the cutest little giggles. I think she was wondering the same thing but was too sweet to say it!"

It was ironic but fitting that the most fervent convert to Clara's "It" status was its creator. Originally Elinor had dismissed her as the means to a lucrative end, but once she observed Clara at work, her attitude altered dramatically. "Look!" Elinor would command, pointing out Clara to visitors on the *It* set. "She has 'It.' Oh, my! That girl will be one of the greatest some day. Notice how she sits there, totally unconscious of what she possesses." Unlike Gloria Swanson, whom Elinor had belittled in private, Clara commanded her respect and admiration. So complete was her confidence in Clara's abilities that, like Clarence Badger, Elinor simply encouraged Clara to do "the things that first came to mind" on camera. Off screen, she resolved to clean up Clara's act, ordering her to eliminate her gum chewing, "g" droppin', and good-natured profanity.

Clara had no patience for phoniness and pretension, so the more Elinor persisted, the more she resisted. Finally she began referring to her would-be benefactress not as "Madame," but "that shithead," and when the term reached Elinor's ears, her crusade to refine Clara came to an abrupt halt. Now Elinor turned her attention from her protégée to her public, embarking upon a cross-country lecture tour. Her topic: "It" and how to get it.

No one cared about the concept until Clara personified it. It was Clara whom audiences paid to see in *It,* and see *It* they did, in record-breaking numbers. Opening-week grosses doubled every other movie's in every city except New York, where *It*'s take was still a whopping fifty percent above all competition. *Variety* had no doubt about who caused the box-office bonanza: "This Bow girl certainly has that certain 'It' for which the picture is named, and she just runs away with the film. She can troupe in the front of a camera, and the manner in which she puts it all over the supporting cast in this production is a joy to behold . . . Clara Bow really does it all, and how."

*It* made Clara the ranking Jazz Baby of the Jazz Age. Literary authority F. Scott Fitzgerald cited her first in his flapper pantheon: "Clara Bow is the quintessence of what the term 'flapper' signifies as a definite description: pretty, impudent, superbly assured, as worldly-wise, briefly-clad and 'hard-berled' as possible. There were hundreds of them, her prototypes. Now, completing the circle, there are thousands more, patterning themselves after her." And just what did Clara signify? "It is rather futile to analyze flappers," answered Fitzgerald. "They are just girls, all sorts of girls, their one common trait being that they are young things with a splendid talent for living."

His words defined the most liberating decade in history. Women in the '20s did what their mothers had only dreamed of, and virtually every vocation included one at its forefront. Aviatrix Amelia Earhart crossed the Atlantic. Gertrude Ederle swam the English Channel. Miriam A. Ferguson was elected governor of Texas by an 80,000-vote majority. Edna St. Vincent Millay wrote poetry. Isadora Duncan choreographed dances. Anthropologist Margaret Mead studied sexual behavior in Samoa. Evangelist Aimee Semple McPherson preached her Foursquare Gospel to millions of devout believers. And Margaret Sanger established the first birth-control clinic in Brooklyn.

As renowned in their respective fields as all these achievers were, none made as indelible an imprint as Clara, whose success in *It* made her the foremost symbol of sex in a decade preoccupied with the subject. To a generation weaned on Mary Pickford, the change couldn't have been more radical or as welcome. Whereas "America's Sweetheart" (a phrase also coined by Ben Schulberg) had played presexual heroines, Clara's characters were not only conscious of their sexuality, but in full control of it. In American movies B.C.—Before Clara—depictions of flagrant female sexuality were of foreign and hence decadent origin. "The 'It' Girl" broke this mold. Born on native soil and descended from common stock, she was an ordinary girl with ordinary tastes and pleasures, of which sex was an especially fun one. As fresh and natural as her foreign predecessors were jaded and blasé, Clara brought sex into America's backyard, and since her countrymen could not utter those three letters comfortably, her two-letter label was a suitably coy substitute.

*It* changed Clara's life as much as her career. Now she was not just another famous name in an industry filled with them, she was the most famous name of all. No longer could she list her home address in the Los Angeles city directory as she had always done, for "the 'It' Girl" was expected to lead a life befitting her fame. Traditionally this meant a hilltop mansion staffed by a British butler, French lady's maid, Japanese gardener, and handsome chauffeur. Characteristically Clara broke tradition and bought a seven-room Spanish bungalow in the flats of Beverly Hills. Built a year earlier (stars were supposed to have residences erected expressly for them), her new home at 512 North Bedford Drive cost $15,000. Other stars thought the sum was embarrassingly low, but Clara did not see why she should live in a museum-sized mansion just because she had made a success. There was plenty of room in her bungalow for herself and her father.

Appalled by the thought of her eating Robert Bow's macaroni every night, Schulberg convinced Clara to hire a cook and maid. Her studio also worried about Clara negotiating Hollywood's hairpin curves, so against her wishes "a swell guy" named Herbert was hired as a chauffeur. Clara allowed Herbert to take her to and from Paramount but insisted on doing her own driving everywhere else. As a result Herbert did most of his chauffeuring for Clara's father, friends, and even her two servants.

Unpretentious and unaffected as she was, Clara could not live oblivious to her fame, nor did she want to. In five years she had made thirty-seven movies, and in her professional opinion, renown was simply a reward for hard work. Still, Clara could not help

viewing her stardom as too good to be true. The childhood fanta-
sies that had relieved the reality of her family's poverty, her father's
abuse, and her mother's seizures had been fulfilled beyond her
wildest dreams, and though she was thrilled, she was also frightened. What would happen when her fans discovered that this carefree, madcap flapper was actually a child of destitution, madness,
and despair? What would they say when they learned that the
supremely self-confident "It" Girl was, in reality, a slum girl devoid of self-esteem? The incongruity was so staggering, and the
dichotomy so complete that although Clara revelled in her new
reputation, she also felt like more of an emotional imposter than
ever. On *The Plastic Age* and *Mantrap* she had incorporated aspects
of her characters into her self, but *It* eradicated her identity forever. "Once Elinor Glyn called her 'the "It" Girl,' it changed Clara
completely," sighs Buddy Rogers. "She had always put on this act
because she was so shy and insecure. Now Clara *believed* she was
'the "It" Girl.' She tried to be vivacious, she tried to be fascinating,
she tried to be clever, and she just worked her body and mind and
soul to death."

Not quite; not yet. Clara's behavior was motivated by self-
denial, not self-destruction, and since "the 'It' Girl" was celebrated for her splendid talent for living, she began living up to her
celebrity. It wasn't difficult, especially when a stunning ex-
stuntman was cast as the leading man in her next movie, *Children of
Divorce*. He had appeared in one scene in *Wings* without Clara and
one in *It* with her, but since she had been publicly engaged to
Victor Fleming and privately promised to Gilbert Roland, nothing
happened until that November, when her affair with Gary Cooper
became the talk and envy of the town.

# 12

As a myth, he embodied the upright, down-home American hero. As a man, he remains an enigmatic, elusive figure.

Instead of distinguishing between the two, most biographies of Gary Cooper merge them, dutifully listing his professional and sexual laurels. Both were of legendary proportions: Cooper's stardom lasted thirty-five years, longer than any other leading man, and his off-screen conquests were both legion and catholic. "He was never a flamboyant swordsman," wrote Budd Schulberg, "but for all his quiet speech and diffident ways, Coop might have been the Babe Ruth of the Hollywood boudoir league. It was whispered down the studio corridors that he had the endowments of Hercules and the staying powers of Job."

"He had many girlfriends," admits Cooper's widow. "Looking as he did, you can see why." Since few of his silent films survive and those that do are rarely shown, modern audiences are unfamiliar with a time when, before his face was punctuated by the middle-aged crags that made it a cinematic Mount Rushmore, Gary Cooper was a man for whom the word "handsome" seemed an outrageous understatement. Six-foot-four, with a lanky torso ("lean clear through," gushed Elinor Glyn, though what she meant by the term is typically unclear), bowed legs, sandy blond hair, and blue eyes, he projected an irresistible combination of beauty and virility. "Women were so crazy about him, more than any other man I knew," sighed Paramount star Evelyn Brent, who cherished her affair with Cooper for the rest of her life. "I think what attracted people was he had a great shyness. He kept pulling back, and it intrigued people. He was a very quiet, quiet guy."

At the time, tales of the star who spoke softly but carried a big stick spread despite his gentlemanly silence. "I came to Hollywood," drawled Southern actress Tallulah Bankhead, "to fuck that *divine* Gary Cooper." (True to her word, Bankhead was soon seen literally chasing Cooper into his dressing room. Years later she was still bragging about their subsequent "one-night stand.") Yet to reduce Cooper from actor to satyr demeans a great talent and, according to all who knew him, a genuinely nice guy. Everybody liked Cooper, and the fact that his legend has been tarnished of late by printed but unproven allegations of closet homosexuality and ruthless ambition says less about him than us. In today's skeptical times, it is evidently unthinkable that such an easygoing and gentle man could prevail for four decades in an industry unknown for rewarding either attribute. That Gary Cooper did so makes him all the more fascinating.

When he entered Clara's life in late 1926, Gary Cooper had an interesting past and promising future. Born Frank Cooper in 1901, he was raised in Montana, where his father was a State Supreme Court judge, and educated in England, thus explaining his combination of western geniality and British reserve. At Grinnell College he drew cartoons for the school paper, then left Iowa for Hollywood, hoping that westerns would put his horsemanship to use. He worked as a stuntman until an agent changed his name to Gary (which he hated) and got him a small part in *The Winning of Barbara Worth.* Cooper was no actor, but he was a natural, possessing what Colleen Moore calls "that peculiar personality, that intangible quality that communicates on camera. Either you have it or you don't. Gary had it, and so did Clara."

Ben Schulberg saw *The Winning of Barbara Worth,* signed Cooper to a contract, and sent him to San Antonio for *Wings.* "Before *Wings,* no one knew Coop; he'd only done a bit part in one picture," recalls Buddy Rogers. "Dick Arlen and I took the train to Texas with him, and Coop didn't say one word the whole way except 'Yup' and 'Nope.' Dick nicknamed him 'Silent Sam.' " To Rogers and Arlen's astonishment, "Silent Sam" stole his sole scene in *Wings* from them. "He had that one damn scene with us," says Rogers, "and I don't know why it was so *strong.* All he did was take a bite of a Cadbury chocolate bar and put it down." In the film Cooper's magnetism renders Rogers and Arlen invisible, and upon his return to Paramount he was coveted more than any established leading man. Twelve-year-old Budd Schulberg remembers Cooper as catnip to women, "the secret dream and in many cases the literal love of the entire studio secretarial pool. All typing stopped, all eyes turned to devour what Father's main secretary described as 'the most beautiful hunk of man who's ever walked down this hall!' "

An actor with this effect belonged opposite an actress with a similar impact, so Cooper was yanked from westerns and war epics and, after a walk-on in *It,* was cast in *Children of Divorce.* Inspired by the shocking statistic that one in ten marriages was "doomed to disaster," Clara's follow-up to *It* was a tearjerker about Kitty Flanders, a flapper whose mercenary mother (Hedda Hopper) pressures her into marrying for money. During a night of drunken revelry, Kitty tricks Ted Larrabee (Cooper) into matrimony, and though Ted loves blond beauty Jean Waddington (Esther Ralston), both are children of divorce and thus refuse to resort to it. Fortunately Kitty rues her ways and commits suicide, leaving Ted and Jean free to marry.

Five writers worked on *Children of Divorce,* so there was no excuse for its flimsy story. The movie's most serious deficiency, however, was not its plot, but its hero. As a cowboy stranded in melodrama, Cooper was wildly miscast, and though his first scene was opposite Esther Ralston, it was Clara who coached him in rehearsals. "I always liketa help anyone who's new," she explained to a reporter, "so I was willin' t'go over and over the scene with him." The fact that this scene featured lovemaking was no doubt a further incentive, but not even Clara could allay Cooper's fear. On camera he panicked, "grunting and pointing" at Ralston because he was too timid to embrace her.

The next morning a garden party scene called for Cooper to jump a hedge on horseback, then hit his mark at a dead halt so Clara could hand him a cocktail. Unaccustomed to an English saddle and unnerved by the previous day's debacle, Cooper proceeded to turn sophisticated drama into slapstick comedy, spewing dirt and spilling champagne on Clara for twenty-three straight takes. Finally director Frank Lloyd demanded that Schulberg replace Cooper with a capable actor. Schulberg obliged with Douglas Gilmore, and Lloyd reshot the scene.

Clara's reaction to Cooper's dismissal is unrecorded, but the fact that Gilmore was fired and Cooper rehired the following day suggests that she campaigned on his behalf (on the other hand, Gilmore's performance may have been even more wretched than Cooper's, for he has since faded into oblivion). By now a trauma-tized Cooper was ready to quit movies altogether and seek work as a cartoonist. Aware of his attitude, Schulberg and writer Hope Loring urged Ralston to befriend Cooper and restore his confi-dence. She invited him to lunch "and chatted with him like a lifelong friend."

Suddenly Cooper interrupted her. "Esther, can I tell you a secret?" he asked shyly.

"Of course," replied Ralston.

Cooper hesitated again. "I think I'm in love," he finally said.

Ralston froze. "Oh, my goodness, I thought to myself, here I am happily married. I didn't mean to encourage this. I was only following orders."

When she said nothing, Cooper continued. "You want to know who?" he asked, smiling sheepishly. Still Ralston did not respond. "It's Clara," whispered Cooper, simultaneously relieving his confidante and puncturing her ego. "I'm in love with Clara Bow!"

The feeling was mutual. "While we was doin' [rehearsals], we fell in love," recalled Clara later. "If I wanted t'be the Clara Bow of the screen, I'd say—*and how!" Children of Divorce* began shooting on November 26, 1926; six days later, Victor Fleming returned from San Antonio to discover that his fiancée had replaced him with Cooper. In an announcement to the press, Clara termed her bro-ken engagement "temporary," apparently and presumptuously as-suming that Fleming would forgive and forget her infidelity in time. Another erstwhile fiancé swore he wouldn't: "That was the last of Gilbert Roland," admitted Clara. "He told me he'd given me three chances and he was finished."

"I will always love Clarita," declared Roland to Robert Bow, who was delighted by the break-up. "If she were only twenty-six,

God, how I would love her. But she is just a baby. She doesn't
understand men and she doesn't understand love."

Perhaps not, but Cooper kept Clara in practice. "Gary's such a
big boy, so strong, so manly, and so bashful," she gushed to a
reporter visiting the *Children of Divorce* set. "I always wanna rumple
his hair an' listen t'all his troubles." Esther Ralston got a more
graphic version. "Clara would regale me with stories of her love
affairs," says the actress. "She loved my shocked reaction to some
of the spicy details." On location one morning, Clara sidled up to
Ralston. "Esther, d'ya like Gary?" she asked innocently.

"I certainly do," Ralston answered. "He's one of the nicest
people I've ever worked with. Why do you ask?"

"Well, I like him, too," said Clara. "He's so sweet t'me. He
always lets me take my dog in the tub when he gives me a bath
every mornin'!' "

This tidbit was tame compared to what Clara purportedly told
Hedda Hopper, who inquired about her affair with Cooper. "All I
can say," shot back Clara, "is that he's hung like a horse and can go
all night."

Accurate or apocryphal? "I wouldn't put it past Clara," laughs
Esther Ralston. "She was an untamed little minx."

"Oh, yeah," concurs sultry beauty Lina Basquette, a self-described "bad girl" and good friend of Clara's. "She and Gary had a
pretty hot affair, and Clara talked about it a lot. She also used
pretty strong language to describe it, and in those days it was
absolutely taboo to utter anything like that in public. But Clara
would."

"Oh, she'd say that sort of thing to *anybody,*" agrees Tui Lorraine. "I had to listen to it night after night while she tried to go to
sleep: 'Oh, Gary is *sooo* gorgeous,' or, 'So-and-so is *wonderful,*'
making gestures of sizes and what-not . . . And *comparing* two
men. She did all that.

"Clara was a sensuous woman, there's no doubt about that.
She couldn't have been so madly in love with all these good-
looking men who *had* to be well-endowed, let's face it . . ."

Cooper also appealed to Clara for the same reason she appealed to everyone else: he exuded childlike, unpretentious charm.

His favorite exclamations were "Gosh" and "Gee," he seemed oblivious to his looks and blushed when reminded of them, and even though his affair with Clara did more for his career than any movie could, he loathed his label as her " 'It' Boy" and doggedly refused to discuss their romance. An on-the-set interview during *Children of Divorce* makes Cooper's reticence amusingly clear:

"How many scenes did you steal?"

"I don't steal scenes."

"Not even in *The Winning of Barbara Worth?*"

"That was just the direction. Anyway, you couldn't steal scenes from Clara Bow. Nobody could. She doesn't 'mug' the camera. Never that. She just naturally walks away with every scene she's in. She's marvelous. She has everything."

"When is the engagement going to be announced?"

"I don't want to stick to western roles."

"Yes, but what about you and Clara?"

"I don't dance."

"Are you two engaged?"

"I do like to ride. Give me a pack horse and a good mount and I'll be gone for a week."

"What about Clara?"

"She's a great actress."

Her acting could not save *Children of Divorce,* which had degenerated from a daring, topical drama to a hodgepodge of histrionics: Ralston was mechanical, Cooper unconvincing, and Clara uncharacteristically subdued in an unsympathetic role. Since it was preposterous to shelve the movie, Schulberg ordered an emergency resuscitation. Newly appointed assistant director Artie Jacobson coordinated Clara, Cooper, and Ralston's schedules (all had since started work on other films) so that after they had finished working all day, Josef von Sternberg could direct the "remake" of *Children of Divorce* all night. The nonstop schedule was so brutal that cameraman James Wong Howe fell asleep while shooting it.

One sequence von Sternberg reshot was Clara's death scene, and the result was so compelling that twenty years later, long after their romance and her career had ended, Victor Fleming believed that "To this minute, Clara Bow's death scene in *Children of Divorce* is the greatest ever done on the screen." Von Sternberg was equally effusive. "If Clara Bow ever makes the picture she can make," he declared at the time, *"then* you will see how great screen acting can be." The implication was obvious: Clara's talent warranted superior material, and Schulberg ought to furnish it for her.

There was less chance than ever of him doing so. After four consecutive hits in a single year—*Dancing Mothers, Mantrap, Kid Boots,* and her grand-slam smash, *It*—Clara was not just a star, but a commodity, and the more Paramount dropped her name to exhibitors as a synonym for certain profits, the more her career was at the mercy of monetary considerations. And although her four hits that year had been of high quality, it was becoming increasingly apparent that a *good* movie with Clara was an unnecessary bonus. As long as she was on screen, nothing else mattered. At least, not yet.

# 13

On January 24, 1927, the first Clara Bow formula film began. *Rough House Rosie*'s ingredients were basic: the silly, sexy escapades of candy factory worker Rosie O'Reilly, a girl with lots of "It" and little clothing. Blaming "a cross-eyed stork" for dropping her in a New York City slum instead of a Fifth Avenue penthouse, Rosie consults a Coney Island fortune-teller who foresees her fame as a dancer. Immediately Rosie dons a skimpy costume, creates an act ("Rough House Rosie and Her Smooth Little Roughnecks"), and becomes a cabaret star. Several mishaps and men later, she comes to her senses and reconciles with her boyfriend.

After the dismal *Children of Divorce,* which did respectable business due to Clara, *Variety* announced with relief that *Rough House Rosie* marked "Clara Bow's return to flippancy and [she's] much more at home than in sedate drawing rooms. Bow capers around the screen and will likely please her own particular audience." Since that particular audience was much of the one hundred million Americans attending movies each week, Clara's first formula film was her latest hit.

It also established three ground rules for future ones. *One:* Crowds came to see Clara make a spectacle of herself, not to see a spectacle starring Clara. Consequently costs were kept to a minimum, since the smaller the budget, the greater the profit. *Rough House Rosie* cost $225,000, one tenth of *Wings,* and recouped five times that amount. *Two:* If audiences did not care who was cast opposite Clara, why should Schulberg? Any up-and-coming or down-and-out actor (in *Rough House Rosie*'s case, alcoholic male model Reed Howes) would do. After *Children of Divorce,* even Gary Cooper was deemed too well known to work with her. *Three:* Clara and her screen characters must appear interchangeable. Like Betty Lou Spence in *It,* Rosie O'Reilly was a screen twin of the movie's star, and her ambition to become a Fifth Avenue "swell" was played strictly for laughs. Clara's off-screen exploits were also exploited. When Rosie blackens her boyfriend's eye in a lovers' quarrel, moviegoers were reminded that during *Children of Divorce,* Clara gave Cooper a shiner that halted shooting for several days.

What Rosie had and Clara lacked was perpetual energy. After a sleepless night, she often toiled from six A.M. until midnight, six days a week. "The public likes me in wild roles, [but] those're the ones that take the most pep," said Clara wearily, "and lemme tell ya, it ain't easy. My nerves is at their peak now." So was her career, so Schulberg maintained her grueling schedule despite her run-down condition. "Give me the maximum number of pictures we are to make with her in a given time," he ordered studio attorney Henry Herzbrun. Herzbrun's response showed that in the past five months, Clara had appeared in *Wings, It, Children of Divorce,* and *Rough House Rosie,* "and you can still use her in two more productions until August 16, 1927." Obviously her employers had no intention of giving Clara the rest she needed.

Her private life was equally overwhelming. Despite his placid nature, Gary Cooper possessed a jealous streak as strong as Gilbert Roland's, and for good reason: discussing marriage with Cooper had not stopped Clara from seeing Victor Fleming on the side. Cooper was furious, Fleming tolerant, and Clara torn helplessly between the two. "Gary was big and strong, but Vickie was older and understood me," she told an interviewer. "I needed someone t'soothe me. Vickie was like that. I mothered Gary, but Vickie mothered me." The virile director may have winced at these words, but he was still willing to accept Clara on her terms. Cooper wasn't, but Tui Lorraine believes he was better-suited to Clara anyway: "I adored Vickie, but he was a silent, aloof, 'man's man.' Gary was a boy, and Clara was a child herself."

While the pressure of choosing between Cooper and Fleming took an emotional toll on Clara, work on *Rough House Rosie* all day and retakes of *Children of Divorce* all night debilitated her physically. Not even injury was allowed to interrupt production, as she discovered during *Rough House Rosie*'s Coney Island sequence: "The big 'strong man' was hittin' the machine that sends an iron ball t'the top of the register. I was standin' next t'him, supposedta be admirin' his strength. He took one shot and landed the huge iron hammer kerplunk inta my cheek about a half inch from my eye. I was thrown ten feet, [but] after some doctorin' I went on with the scene, my face swollen and playin' with my good cheek t'the camera."

Finally Clara collapsed. Production on *Rough House Rosie* shut down for two weeks, a delay director Frank Strayer blamed on her vacillation between Cooper and Fleming. Headlines diagnosed her ailment as a nervous breakdown. Clara called this "ridiculous."

"There was no 'nervous breakdown,'" agrees Tui angrily. "They worked Clara so hard that she just dropped from exhaustion."

Clara's frail condition forced Schulberg to cancel her next movie and give her a three-month vacation. Meanwhile Paramount bombarded its biggest moneymaker with picayune bills for unreturned wardrobe items. A sample invoice includes a net brassiere valued at $1.25 and two black satin bloomers worth $5 apiece. When three bracelets worth a grand total of $14.15 could not be located, the studio demanded remuneration. Self-appointed "business manager" Robert Bow responded in his semiliterate scrawl:

> "Clara has not got this [sic] in her possession. Have serched [sic] her home. Must have been taken from her room or lost.
>
> Mr. Bow.
>
> Please stop these Bills.

"The 'It' Girl" was also charged twenty-five cents for every photograph of herself she requested.

Clara spent her convalescence furnishing her new home. Refusing to hire an interior decorator or devise a design scheme, she simply bought what she liked, and the result was an eclectic style (or lack thereof) that Louise Brooks would later label "Disneyland. Each room was different." A journalist invited to 512 Bedford Drive described it best: "It is just an ordinary stucco bungalow, but inside it is exactly like Clara. The beautiful and the bizarre, the exquisite and the commonplace, mingled in hopeless confusion.

"A gaudy doll in frowsy skirts and wig leans against a wonderful Ming lamp. A huge fuzzy teddy bear with a pink bow around his neck occupies a corner of the luxurious brocaded davenport. The center table is a fine thing of carved oak and the rugs are awful imitation Chinese. The lamps look as if they had come from the five-and-ten-cent store, but the shawl on the piano might be worn by a Spanish Infanta."

Clara's other prized possessions included a "Panatrope," the world's first electrically amplified and motored home phonograph; a photograph of the late Rudolph Valentino as *The Sheik* ("the greatest actor, bar none, who ever lived," she informed guests); and a made-to-order bed with a mirror in its canopy. "And facing you as you lay on it," chuckles Artie Jacobson, "was this great big gold Buddha with one red eye, one green eye. What a screwy dame she was! She was wild, and I loved her for it."

Clara's pride and joy was her "Chinese room," a nook devoid of light and done (or, in the general, condescending consensus, *over*done) in red-, gold-, and black-lacquered wallpaper; red and gold oriental draperies; thick Chinese carpets, cabinets, and lamps; a huge, specially made red-and-gold damask couch; a large, grotesque lacquer god perched on a carved pedestal; and, for occidental contrast, framed photographs of her favorite cowboy stars, Tom Mix and Gary Cooper. CLARA, wrote Mix, I HAVE NOTHING TO SAY. I ALREADY SAID IT. Cooper's inscription was less cryptic: TO CLARITA, WHOM I LOVE, WHOSE BEAUTY AND LIFE BY DAY ARE REAL AS THE SUN AT NOON, AND BY NIGHT HAVE ALL THE MYSTERIES AND ALLURE OF THE NORTHERN LIGHTS, WITH THE SOFTNESS OF THE SUMMER MOON. YOU ARE THAT. I LOVE YOU, GARYITO.

Like a scene from an Elinor Glyn romance, the Chinese room reeked of incense that rose in clouds from a brass burner. "Clara said it was a *loving* room, not a living room," laughs Tui. "I don't think Vickie approved too much." When Clara lured Cooper into her homemade den of iniquity, "Gary just gulped and said, 'Aw, gee.' "

Besides these trips to the Chinese room, Clara's favorite recreation was roller-skating up and down her driveway. The mob which rapidly amassed to watch her soon made this pastime impossible, so when Robert Bow ordered his daughter to fund his cleaning and dyeing store, Clara not only complied, but roller-skated there from Paramount with Cooper and Fleming's laundry slung over her shoulders. Her stunt publicized her father's business but did not prevent it from going belly-up due to his mismanagement.

Undeterred, Robert made Clara buy him a restaurant at 8801 Beverly Boulevard which he named "IT" after the house specialty, "the Official Clara Bow Sandwich." Clara brought pals but never let them pay, and her generosity, combined with Robert's ineptitude, closed "IT" within a year. Her father's failed restaurant cost Clara over $10,000.

By the spring of 1927 Clara's relationship with Cooper had reached an impasse, for Alice Cooper was dead set against a daughter-in-law like her. To keep abreast of her son's affair, Alice sent her husband to Paramount to glean information. "Judge Cooper was a dignified old man who knew his son was carousing with Clara night after night after night after night," recalls Teet Carle, a twenty-seven-year-old publicist who had just been assigned to her. "Gary was very shy about this stuff, so the Judge was trying to get somebody's opinion of the situation." Clara knew why. "His mother didn't like me," she said later, "and his mother ran his life."

Clara retaliated by flaunting her affair with Victor Fleming, now set to direct her next film, *Hula*. Following what she called "a silly fight" with Cooper over Fleming, their romance ended six months after it began.

Tui Lorraine believes that "if Gary had tried a bit harder, I think Clara would have married him. Really, she *should* have married him; it might have worked." After the breakup, Tui cornered Cooper on the Paramount lot. "Gary, why don't you marry Clara?" she asked bluntly. "You're made for each other."

Cooper turned crimson. "Too late," he said, mumbling about "a fellow she's flipped for." Not wanting to compromise Clara and Fleming, Tui dropped the subject.

For the rest of her life Clara "made light" of her affair with Cooper, mocking his maternal devotion and passivity. "Poor Gary," she would sigh when asked what caused their parting. "The biggest cock in Hollywood an' no ass t'push it with." Apparently her latter assertion was more figurative than literal, for despite Clara's claim that she never saw Cooper after their final quarrel, the couple enjoyed occasional, on-the-sly sex for another two years.

On June 9, 1927, Clara returned to work with Fleming on *Hula*. Paramount had reteamed them to capitalize on their romance and repeat their past success. But *Hula*, unlike *Mantrap*, had been devised to showcase Clara's skin, not her talent. The film's first scene set its tone: Hula Calhoun, an American heiress in the Hawaiian isles, skinnydips in a stream. Suddenly a bee stings her thigh. Naturally a close-up of the wound is necessary.

Hula loves no man until British engineer Anthony Haldane (Clive Brook) arrives. When she sees him for the first time, Clara does a triple-take identical to the one in *It:* her eyes bulge in innocent surprise, then survey Anthony with carnal rapture, and finally revert to their prior, permissible look. "You're a beautiful man, Anthony!" Hula informs him. She shows him her bee-stung thigh ("Clive wasn't nearly as excited over that as the audience," noted *Variety*), her predatory intentions plain. Because Hula has "It," her prey welcomes them.

But Anthony has a problem: his wife. "D'ya love her?" demands Hula. He assures her that they separated long ago. "Then what difference does it make? Kiss me, love me, begin again," urges Hula in a title banned by New York censors. Since Anthony is the soul of propriety ("Gad! I wish we *were* savages!" he tells Hula), he refuses to consummate their love without legalizing it first. So begins a tiff that comes to a titillating climax when Hula, enraged by Anthony's adherence to convention, gets drunk and goes native at a family luau. "I'll show 'em what my name means!" she vows as she ducks behind a bush, strips, and emerges in a grass skirt, strapless top, and lei for a bout of Hawaiian hipswaying. Hula's hula puts the locals to shame and drives men to a lusty frenzy.

While they fight for her favors, Anthony carries her off to his hut. "Oh, ya *do* love me, Saint Anthony?" she taunts in a flip religious reference that was also banned. Anthony admits that he does but begs Hula to be patient. Instead she dynamites Anthony's dam and forces his wife to file for divorce, and *Hula* ends with its heroine and her man legally united at last.

*Hula* followed the new formula for Clara's films: a low budget, a bland leading man, and a star supposedly playing herself. As such it was so derivative that even thirteen-year-old Budd Schulberg "cringed for *Hula,* a carbon copy of a carbon copy of a Clara Bow story." Budd also recalls his father planning to promote rival flapper (and former lover of Victor Fleming) Alice White as a "blonde Clara Bow" should the redhead's career decline.

*Hula*'s success precluded that possibility. Braving brutal reviews ("one of the feeblest excuses for a motion picture ever turned out of the Paramount studios," snapped the New York *Post*), the movie drew huge crowds who loyally ignored everything in *Hula* but Clara. "Paramount has the right idea with the Bow girl," remarked *Variety.* "This sap and flap picture will get to 'em, for Clara must be Clara. She's it doubly now, especially for the femmes."

That same month her phenomenal winning streak continued with the limited release of *Wings.* Specially equipped theaters showed the film's aerial battles in Magnascope, a process which expanded the screen to four times its normal size while a sound-effects track simulated the rat-tat-tat of machine guns, roar of propellers, and drone of motors in two tones to denote American and enemy planes. Though Magnascope seems crude in comparison to modern special effects, audiences in 1927 gasped aloud at the sight and sound of war waged before their eyes. *Hula* was formula Clara; *Wings* made movie history, and in an era when a month's run in a Broadway movie theater was considered excellent, *Wings* played a record-breaking *sixty-three* weeks before moving to another, larger theater down the street. Certainly its combat sequences were its main attraction, but Clara was the only cast member billed above the title, and her presence in a war epic attracted female viewers who would otherwise have avoided it.

Clara appealed as much to women as men, and in *Hula* it's easy to see why. Hula is less a sex object than a liberated heroine, flouting convention without guilt or punishment to get what she wants. Since all Hula or, for that matter, any of Clara's characters want is a good time and a man, it would be stretching the point to declare their sexual independence. Still, the aggressive role of these "It" girls in romantic courtship is a revolutionary upheaval of traditional feminine behavior. Given her gender's allegiance, it is no wonder that the title of Clara's next movie addressed them without mincing words: *Get Your Man.*

Prior to *Get Your Man,* two events, one professional and the other personal, affected Clara's livelihood and life. That August marked the first anniversary of her five-year Paramount contract, and already its terms were grossly unfair. "Miss Bow is now getting $1,500 a week from Paramount," editorialized the New York *Times,* "though being their best feminine box-office card. Her pictures have been grossing more than those of stars getting $5,000 and $6,000 weekly." Though neither Schulberg nor the studio could have foreseen how popular she would become in such a brief period, no offer was tendered to tear up Clara's current contract and replace it with one reflecting her true worth. Still believing her stupid and docile, Paramount ignored what was both a widespread and standard practice at other studios.

That month also marked the departure of Victor Fleming from Clara's life. On *Mantrap,* he had considered her a conquest; by *Hula,* "Vic was fascinated with her," says Billy Kaplan, the prop man on both movies. "It was a *very* serious thing." Clara remained in awe of her mentor-lover and deeply grateful for his guidance and support. "Vickie knew everythin'," she said later. "I admired him tremendously."

But admiration wasn't enough. At twenty-two, "the 'It' Girl" was neither ready nor willing to settle down with a man twice her age, even if he did provide the only stability she had ever known. "Vickie wanted to marry her," confirms Tui Lorraine, "but I don't think that he was social enough—or 'showy,' that's a better word for it." Later Clara would speak wistfully of Fleming, aware that she would never find another like him. "I believe the great love of her life was Victor Fleming," states publicist Teet Carle. "Clara used to talk about him, about what a wonderful man he was. 'Of all the men I've known,' she would say, '*there* was a man.' " For the rest of her life, Fleming and Clarence Badger remained her favorite directors.

Her parting from Fleming left Clara alone and confused. Since childhood, her conception of love had been founded on impossibly perfect movie romances; confronted with possible, imperfect ones, she clung to a dream hero and considered everyone else disappointing by comparison. "I really don't care 'bout men," she said that September, just weeks after her parting from Fleming. "I know four I like. Each one's got one thing that appeals t'me, but not one of 'em's got the combination." In love with a lover more ideal than real, Clara sought a fantasy composite of Artie Jacobson's steady dedication, Victor Fleming's soothing counsel, Gary Cooper's bashful prowess, and Gilbert Roland's macho passion. It was a romantic but hardly realistic hankering.

Her attitude toward marriage, however, was thoroughly pragmatic. "Marriage ain't woman's only job no more," Clara told columnist Dorothy Manners. "A girl who's worked hard and earned her place ain't gonna be satisfied as a wife.

"I know this," she concluded, "I wouldn't give up *my* work for marriage. I think a modern girl's capable of keepin' a job *and* a husband."

In an era when movie actresses yearned for domesticity in public while ruthlessly pursuing stardom in Hollywood, Clara's credo was heretical, and less outspoken actresses admired her for it. "She was her *own* man," says Dorothy Mackaill, who had known Clara since their WAMPAS Baby Star citation three years earlier. "She didn't care what people thought of her, and she was resented for it."

Casual affairs increased the resentment. Actors John Gilbert, Norman Kerry, and Warren Burke were diversions for Clara, who ended each liaison as capriciously as she began it. She never suffered, but her reputation did. *This girl's got more "Id" than "It,"* whispered gossips. *Clara Bow's a nympho.*

Given her notoriety, it was not surprising that in the fall of

1927, rumor linked Clara not to one lover, but the entire lineup of the U.S.C. football team. And given her notoriety, it was not surprising that such stories were accepted as true.

Were they?

# 14

In 1947, seventeen-year-old Kenneth Anger made *Fireworks,* a fif-teen-minute movie celebrating a sadomasochistic homosexual en-counter. The film's title derived from its climax, which showed a sailor's penis turning into an exploding Roman candle. Anger's hometown of Hollywood was hardly receptive to his work, so he moved to Paris, making underground movies and garnering lurid gossip about the industry which had disowned him. A book-length, "best of" compilation was published in France in 1959, wrapped in plain brown paper. Anger called it *Hollywood Babylon.*

Six years later, a pirated paperback edition of *Hollywood Baby-lon* appeared in America. It was banned within ten days. Finally, in 1975, the book received its official U.S. publication, altered and abridged but still filled with sensational, unsubstantiated allega-tions. "If a book such as this can be said to have charm, it lies in the fact that here is a book without one single redeeming merit," snapped the New York *Times.* But indignant reviews only ensured *Hollywood Babylon*'s success, for as its notoriety spread, so did its sales. So great was (and is) the demand for juicy Hollywood gossip that a sequel, *Hollywood Babylon II,* soon followed. It, too, sold well.

An especially scandalous chapter of *Hollywood Babylon* senior was "Clara's Beaux," a man-by-man inventory of just that. Accord-ing to Anger, Clara's beaux included actors, doctors, comics, and cowboys, all of whom were warm-ups to the main event: "Poor gregarious Clara took on Trojans by the bunch. She'd play party girl to the entire "Thundering Herd" (crack University of South-ern California football team) during beery, brawling, gang-bang-ing weekend parties, accommodating the fun-loving bruisers right down to the eleventh man: hulking tackle Marion Morrison (later known as John Wayne)."

Titillated readers accepted this assertion as proof of orgiastic twenties excess, and with *Hollywood Babylon* more accessible than

silent movies, Clara's professional accomplishments were suddenly eclipsed by her venereal ones. Now new generations discovered "the 'It' Girl" not on film, but in *Hollywood Babylon*'s caricature
of her as a nymphomaniacal flapper who took on the U.S.C. team.

The prelude to the legend occurred in November, 1926, when
Paramount sent Clara to San Francisco to promote *It.* Studio publicist and University of California-Berkeley alumnus Barney Hutchinson accompanied her, and to combine business with pleasure,
Hutchinson arranged for an appearance by Clara at the Cal-Stan-
ford game on November 20, 1926. At the end of the pregame
ceremonies, Clara's name was announced. She walked onto the
field, waved to the huge crowd, wandered over to a comfortable
spot on the grass, and sat down just as the band began to play.

Hutchinson hurried to her. "Get on your feet! Get on your
feet!" he hissed.

"What for?" asked Clara innocently.

Hutchinson couldn't believe it. "That's the national anthem
they're playing!"

Clara rose obediently. So limited was her experience outside a
movie studio, and so complete was her obliviousness to social
custom, that even the most familiar traditions were foreign to her.

But not even Clara could ignore the fever gripping Southern
California sports fans the following year. Former Yale coach Howard Jones had transformed the U.S.C. Trojans into a squad to rival
Cal-Berkeley's Bears and Stanford's Cardinals. The Trojans' 1927
statistics speak for themselves: eight wins, one loss, one tie and a
collective 281 points to their opponents' 51. Since Los Angeles did
not have a pro-ball team and sporting events were Hollywood's
favorite extracurricular activity, the movie colony supported
U.S.C.'s "Thundering Herd" with the same zeal that any town
would show its championship team. At home games on Saturday
afternoons, Trojan fans packed the university's Coliseum, cheering them on to victory and thrilling to the incredible gridiron feats
of star player and team captain Morley Drury.

To this day Morley Drury is known as "the Noblest Trojan of
Them All." He was a legend in his own time, too: during his
college football career, the six-foot, 185-pound Long Beach, Cali-

fornia, native became the first U.S.C. quarterback and "back back" to top 1,000 yards rushing in a single season, a record unbroken for thirty-eight years. Drury was inducted into the National Football Hall of Fame, the All-American team, and the Knute Rockne All-Opponent squad; Howard Jones called him the finest player he ever coached. Those who witnessed the outstanding finale to Drury's Trojan career saw sports history in the making: after running 180 yards and scoring three touchdowns against the Washington Huskies, Howard Jones took Drury out of the game five minutes early and ordered him to do two laps. As Drury jogged around the Coliseum for the last time, the crowd burst into a deafening, ten-minute-long chorus of cheers, applause, and whistles. Loudest among them were members of the Washington team, still on the field.

Hollywood was full of famous actors, but there was only one Morley Drury. Clara's curiosity was aroused.

She went straight to Teet Carle, a U.S.C. graduate who had handled the Trojans' publicity before joining Paramount to handle Clara's. "What's all this fuss 'bout a football game?" she demanded. Promising to let Clara see for herself, Carle bought tickets for the season's big game between U.S.C. and Cal-Berkeley.

It was Saturday, October 29, 1927. The sun was mild, the air crisp as 76,500 fans jammed the sold-out Coliseum. Carle and Hutchinson escorted Clara to her seat beside the tunnel leading to the Trojan lockerroom. As the team emerged and the crowd roared its welcome, Clara was treated to a close-up view of the powerful Trojan lineup: six-foot sophomore end Lowry McCaslin; barrel-chested fullback Harry Edelson; fleet-footed tackle "Racehorse Russ" Saunders; quarters Don Williams and Howard Elliott; the hulking Thomas twins, Max and Lloyd, from Jamestown, North Dakota; 190-pound tackle Jesse Hibbs, whose curly hair, baby blue eyes, and chiselled profile led Teet Carle to compare him to "a Greek god"; and finally the mighty Morley Drury himself. At Drury's entrance, the crowd's cheers became thunderous.

While Clara watched the Trojans take the field, Carle watched Clara: "She took one look at those big, beautiful guys in their crimson-and-gold uniforms and said, 'Where've these boys *been* all my life?' "

Carle gulped. "These are *students,* Clara," he reminded her nervously.

"How old d'ya think *I* am?" she shot back.

As usual, Drury was the day's hero. The Trojans trounced the Bears 13–0, due to what the Los Angeles *Times* called "Captain Morley Drury's marvelous exhibition. His day's toll will be remembered as long as they play football in the Coliseum. Driving through tackles in that irresistible way of his, the Trojan leader amassed the amazing total of 202 yards during his excursions here and there. Not only that, but he intercepted two forward passes, recovered California's only fumble when the Bears were hammering at the Trojan door, and ran his team in a faultless fashion. Drury was everywhere on defense and everything on offense . . . the fact remains that he turned in the greatest game of football we've ever lamped."

Clara was converted. She had seen Morley Drury in action; now she wanted to meet him in person. "How d'ya get in touch with these boys?" she demanded excitedly. Carle told her that U.S.C. had no dormitories, but most Trojans were members of the Sigma Chi fraternity.

"Ya mean Morley Drury is—?"

"Yes, Clara. Morley Drury is a member of Sigma Chi." Carle saw no point in prevaricating: if he didn't tell her, anyone could. Still, he sensed mischief in the making and "very quickly disassociated myself from the studio as far as U.S.C. and Clara were concerned."

After Carle had fulfilled his duty and chaperoned Clara home, she called Sigma Chi. A fraternity pledge answered the phone. "I wanna talk t'Morley Drury," said Clara.

"Who's this?" asked the pledge. She told him. He guffawed. She insisted. Familiar with fraternity pranks and expecting to be paddled for being fooled by this one, the pledge reluctantly delivered the message to Drury. "Morley, I don't know what to do, sir," he said sheepishly, "but some lady who says she's 'Clara Bow' wants to speak to you."

"Okay, kid," said Drury against his better judgment. "I'll take it." He knew he had fans in the movie business—in fact, director John Ford was visiting Sigma Chi at that very moment—but Clara Bow was different. He was *her* fan. He never missed her movies, and his buddies on the team knew it. This was obviously their doing.

Drury picked up the phone. Again Clara introduced herself. Again she was told to quit kidding.

Clara was losing patience. "I *ain't* kiddin'. I wanna meet ya. Where's this Sigma Chi thinga yours?" Drury gave her the address: 848 West Thirty-Sixth Street.

"Gimme fifteen minutes," said Clara. "I'll honk the horn."

Drury still considered the conversation a gag. Then Clara arrived with Tui Lorraine in tow.

"I was amazed," says Morley Drury. "We were *all* amazed."

Two hours earlier Clara had cheered the Trojans on to victory; now they stared at her in starstruck awe. "Bring a fella for Tui," commanded Clara to Drury, who invited fraternity brother Tom Dorsey. The foursome left Sigma Chi in Clara's car, driving aimlessly for several hours. Excitement had left Drury tongue-tied, so Clara chattered merrily, stopping the car only once at an illicit Hollywood bar where she and Tui had cocktails and the teetotaling athletes had Cokes. Afterward she returned Drury and Dorsey to Sigma Chi.

Inside the fraternity, fullback Harry Edelson was inconsolable. An injury on the field that afternoon had prevented him from accompanying Drury on his outing with Clara. When Drury came back, Edelson eagerly pumped him for information. "Relax," Drury assured him. "You didn't miss a thing."

"Nothing happened," reiterates Drury today. "We never got involved in a 'bedroom scene' or anything like that. We were too damn innocent."

But Clara never committed herself halfway, and the U.S.C. Trojans were no exception. Regular attendance at every home game was followed by regular entertainment at 512 Bedford Drive, where the U.S.C. players and their opponents that day would congregate on Saturday nights. Food was served (liquor wasn't) by

Clara's German cook, jazz was played on her Panatrope, and the Trojans danced with their hostess and her actress pals like Tui, Lina Basquette, and Joan Crawford. "We had a good time," says Lowry McCaslin, "but it wasn't *that* exciting." McCaslin always brought roommate Marion Morrison to Clara's parties, even though Morrison had been sidelined with a shoulder injury and did not play that season. (When Morrison could no longer afford to stay in school, film director and U.S.C. fan John Ford found a job for him as a grip at Fox. Morrison changed his name to John Wayne a year later.)

The quaint reality of these evenings hardly corresponds with the scurrilous rumors spread about them later. Even the wildest party, which ended in a four A.M. game of touch football on Clara's front lawn, was tame. She had asked All-American and Greek god look-alike Jesse Hibbs to teach her how to tackle; when he did, she practiced on him and broke his thumb. Following Clara's tackle and Hibbs's injury, a reporter wrote that Trojan coach Howard Jones had ordered his team to stay away from Clara Bow "individually and collectively."

The truth was more prosaic and, for U.S.C. fans, more fortunate. "Howard Jones had nothing to do with it," corrects Lowry McCaslin. "Jesse got hurt after the season ended. I know because I was there."

On another occasion, Clara's neighbors called the Beverly Hills police to complain about the noise. When more officers than necessary arrived for a routine matter, the Trojans panicked. They were breaking curfew, and trouble with the law meant suspension from the team. Clara explained their predicament to the policemen. "Okay, but hold the noise down," warned the officer-in-charge. Clara promised. The officer nodded, then paused. "We sure would like to meet Morley Drury," he added shyly.

Clara made the introduction and the officers left, but before the party could get going again, a drunken Robert Bow returned home. The idea of his daughter entertaining Trojans enraged Robert, and he evicted them "in record time," says Tui. Then Robert turned on Clara. "Why can't you act more like Lillian Gish?" he bellowed. It was a strange demand from a father who spent his nights (and his daughter's money) at Madame Frances's, a popular Hollywood brothel.

Though Clara's escapades with the U.S.C. team were not the lurid stuff of legend, they weren't entirely aboveboard, either. Her parties at Bedford Drive were no secret, but those held at another location were. "We just wanted to have some fun, kick up our heels a bit," explains Tui. Since Clara's paranoid father made fun difficult, she and Tui found a hideout from him. Now the two women would tell Robert Bow they were going to Joan Crawford's (a favorite alibi), then head to their getaway at the Garden of Allah, an eight-room, Spanish Colonial building at the foot of Laurel Canyon. Once the home of Alla Nazimova, Russian star of American films, the mansion was turned into a hotel on January 9, 1927. Gilbert Roland had escorted Clara to the opening festivities; later, long-term residents would include writers F. Scott Fitzgerald, John O'Hara, Dorothy Parker, André Malraux, and Alexander Woollcott, who described the Garden of Allah as "the sort of place you'd expect to find down the rabbit hole." Nazimova, who kept one apartment on permanent reserve for herself, had built her pool in the shape of the Black Sea as a reminder of her native land.

That fall in 1927, the Garden of Allah became the final stop of the Young Hollywood set. Lina Basquette and Joan Crawford were regulars. Buddy Rogers brought Janie Peters, a next-door neighbor who would soon change her name to Carole Lombard. When Earl Burnett's famous Biltmore Hotel Orchestra played "Goodnight, Ladies" one last time at two A.M., its musicians segued to the Garden of Allah and jammed on Clara's favorite jazz tunes all night long. Meanwhile she and Tui drove to Sigma Chi to pick up the Trojans, who sneaked out through a special window.

It was a risk Morley Drury couldn't resist. "I loved to dance," he admits. "It was the only thing I liked better than football."

The revelry in Clara's room was not as appealing to other Garden of Allah residents. When songwriter Nacio Herb Brown pounded on the wall demanding quiet, his anger puzzled Clara. "Imagine wanting to lead a quiet life or *sleep!*" laughs Tui. "She couldn't understand it."

The parties usually ended with a sunrise swim in the hotel

pool. Since the vice squad was a highly publicized and feared judicial presence in Hollywood, skinnydipping was unthinkable, and besides, Clara felt a form-fitting, belted bathing suit showed off her figure just fine. So did her smitten guests, and Tui Lorraine remembers "muscles being flexed all over the place like yo-yos" as Trojans in swim togs posed for Clara.

One night the group decided to swim while it was still dark and narrowly escaped serious injury. Before anyone did any diving, one Trojan stuck his foot into the water and discovered there wasn't any. The empty pool was being cleaned.

"Jeez!" shrieked Clara. "The goddamn thing's dry!"

Suddenly she froze at the sound of a familiar voice. Having learned of Clara's whereabouts, Robert Bow had come to the Garden of Allah to investigate. The sight of his daughter in a swimsuit surrounded by football jocks sent Robert into a fury, and as he dragged her off, Clara apologized to the Trojans for the premature end to the party. Tui followed the Bows, shouting to make herself heard above Robert's tirade. "If you don't shut up," she threatened, "I'm going back to the North Pole!"

"Fine with me!" screamed Robert. This surprised Tui. Robert had recently made sexual advances toward her, so she naively assumed he was in love. He wasn't—yet.

Her father put an end to Clara's parties at the Garden of Allah. Though she remained a devoted Trojan fan and continued to host an annual dinner for the team at her home, Robert Bow made sure the friendship stopped there. His enforced separation deprived Clara of the male camaraderie she had enjoyed since childhood. Whether she was acting feminine while dancing with Morley Drury or being a tomboy and tackling Jesse Hibbs, the Trojans accepted her, and since they were as well known in Hollywood as she was, her celebrity never affected their companionship. *Hollywood Babylon* portrays 1927's U.S.C. gridiron heroes as beer-swilling, gangbanging louts; the facts, however, reveal a group of well-behaved boys who were, in Morley Drury's own words, "too damn innocent" to be anything else. It is an ironic truth that despite subsequent, decadent stories, the Trojans kept Clara *out* of trouble, not in it. For the first time in her life, she had money, fame, and fun, and had finally found a group of friends with whom she felt comfortable. When Robert forbid her to see them, Clara was left alone and lonely once again.

She was not welcome anywhere else.

# 15

"She dislikes gossip and is unquestionably one of the most gossiped-about women in Hollywood," wrote *Photoplay* of Clara. What the magazine did not mention was the town's tacit policy of excluding her from all social functions. Even twelve-year-old Budd Schulberg realized that "there was one subject on which the staid old Hollywood establishment would agree: Clara Bow, no matter how great her popularity, was a low-life and a disgrace to the community."

Her sin: In an industry trying to forget its outcast past and adopt affectations to suit its exalted present, Clara had remained herself, and as such was a constant reminder of her and, by implication, everyone else's lowly background. "Her Brooklyn accent and dreadful manners would reproach [them] with their common origin, making her presence an insulting reminder of their uneasy position in 'high society,'" wrote Louise Brooks. When Brooks married director Edward Sutherland, she won instant access to the Pickfair-San Simeon set. Having idolized Clara since *Dancing Mothers,* Brooks planned to invite her to a dinner party, but when she mentioned it to her husband, "Eddie recoiled in horror. 'Oh, no, we can't have *her,'* he said. 'We don't know what she'd *do.* She's from *Brooklyn,* you know.'" So were several pillars of the Hollywood community, but they had renounced their humble beginnings. Clara had not, and her lack of pretension sealed her social fate. It is no coincidence that shortly after she and Tui traveled to Yosemite National Park to visit Joan Crawford on location for *Rose Marie,* Crawford shunned Clara once she found future husband Douglas Fairbanks, Jr., and the social pinnacle of Pickfair within reach.

Clara's forthright sexuality alienated her from potential female sponsors within the Hollywood elite. "Clara wasn't well liked amongst other women in the film colony," says fellow outsider

Lina Basquette. "Her social presence was taboo, and it was rather silly, because God knows Mary Pickford and Marion Davies had plenty to hide. It's just that they hid it, and Clara didn't." Unlike Pickford and Davies, Clara disregarded Hollywood's unwritten code of correct sexual conduct: a woman could do whatever with whomever, as long as she kept her door and mouth shut. Unique and sophisticated as it seemed, Hollywood actually possessed the same sexual double standard as any small American town: a man who pursued women was a "stud"; a woman who pursued men, a "slut." Since a large majority of Hollywood actresses would have fallen into the latter category had they stayed in their hometowns, the emphasis on appearances was imperative, for all that separated Pickford and Davies from Clara was their self-made social position. "The women in the film colony liked to put on the pure, virginal act," says Lina Basquette, "whereas Clara just called a spade a spade. She didn't care what anybody thought. She just went ahead and did what she wanted to do." This brazen attitude outraged Hollywood socialites, who condemned Clara not for what she did not know, but because she did not care. Ignorance was forgivable. Rebellion was not.

As the rebel without a cause, Clara was often her own worst enemy. Though amusing, her social blunders were both blatant and avoidable: when director Frank Tuttle invited her to dine with his family at the elegant Beverly Hills Hotel, Clara arrived in a belted bathing suit. "It was a shocker," one of Tuttle's daughters remembers. It was also a violation of both the hotel's dress code and Hollywood's rule of formal dress for evening engagements, yet Clara couldn't fathom the fuss. Why should something *she* wore make someone *else* uncomfortable? And why did Mrs. Tuttle get so mad just because she used their towels as makeup rags?

Clara even scandalized the scandalous, as Judge Ben Lindsey learned. The mild-mannered, middle-aged Lindsey had caused a furor with *The Companionate Marriage*, a book which advocated premarital sex as a crucial determinant of a couple's compatibility. If fewer women approached the altar as virgins, wrote Lindsey, fewer divorces would come before his bench in Denver. His theory lost Lindsey his judgeship, and when Colorado conservatives hounded him out of the state, he found refuge with empathetic Hollywood liberals like Ben and Ad Schulberg, who made the judge their house guest while a local bench was bought for him. The Schulbergs intended to present Lindsey to their equally enlightened friends, but he had other plans. As Budd Schulberg recalls, "the apostle of unmarried sex in America wanted to interview one of its most celebrated practitioners."

Judge Lindsey asked to meet Clara Bow.

With great reluctance, the Schulbergs invited her to their home. She arrived late and tipsy; ever genteel, they overlooked both details and introduced her to Lindsey. "Hiya, Judge!" whooped Clara. "Ben tells me ya believe people oughta have their fun without havin' t'get married. Ya naughty boy!" Giggling, she pulled Lindsey to her and planted a big, wet kiss upon his lips. Mrs. Lindsey looked askance at her hostess. Ad Schulberg's expression indicated that she had expected as much.

Lindsey had planned to query "the 'It' Girl" about her views on sex and marriage. Clara had little interest in discussing either, demanding instead that the judge dance with her. Lindsey obliged, stumbling clumsily across the Schulberg living room as he tried to follow Clara's nimble feet. Meanwhile, and to everyone's mounting panic, Clara had begun a gambit of her own: "beginning with the judge's top jacket button, she said, 'Rich man . . . poor man . . . beggar man . . . thief . . . ,' her busy little fingers unbuttoning with each designation. By the time the childhood game had brought her to 'Indian chief,' Clara Bow was undoing the top button of Judge Lindsey's fly." Clara was practicing what Judge Ben Lindsey preached; panic-stricken, he fled from her arms to his wife. The Lindseys left the Schulbergs' in a self-righteous huff.

Afterward Ben Schulberg reprimanded Clara, who sulked like a naughty child. "Well gee whiz," she pouted, "if he believes in all that modern stuff like ya say he does, how come he's such an old stick-in-the-mud?"

Her point was lost upon her self-presumed social betters.

Shunned by socialites and forbidden to fraternize with Trojans, Clara found a friend and ally in Adela Rogers St. Johns. A novelist, journalist, and screenwriter (she wrote a draft of *Children of Divorce*) whose father, renowned criminal lawyer Earl Rogers, once defended Clarence Darrow on a charge of jury tampering, Adela was a tough, smart, and independent woman who believed her sex superior: "This country got into trouble," she once declared, "when women came down to equality with men." Though eleven years older and more worldly than Clara, the two women had plenty in common: both preferred the company of virile men (Adela married her latest lover, Stanford halfback Richard Hyland, that year, then divorced him when he called her "half-witted"), and both were role models for other women. Adela had risen from a seven-dollar-a-week cub reporter for the Hearst syndicate to its "World's Greatest Girl Reporter," covering major news events and interviewing movie stars with such revelatory results that she was called the "Mother Confessor of Hollywood." Aware that such pieces must paradoxically debunk yet perpetuate their subject's stardom, Adela could turn an ordinary life into extraordinary reading.

In the fall of 1927 Adela was assigned by *Photoplay* to profile Clara. She arrived at Paramount and was taken by a studio publicist to Clara's dressing room, located in the "number one" spot on the lot (star prestige was measured by dressing room location; Clara's was on the corner closest to the executive offices). Clara was not there, which Adela later considered "an omen. [She] is never, at least in my experience, where she is expected to be. Trying to locate her at any given time is a week's work, partly because she changes her mind with every new impulse and partly because she is always surrounded by thoroughly incompetent people whom she either happens to like or is sorry for." Finally Clara was found with Tui Lorraine in a projection room watching the day's rushes, and Adela was introduced to "a very young girl, with amazing red hair obviously but beautifully and effectively dyed, and the most restless, brilliant, and arresting black eyes I had ever encountered."

Clara apologized for the mix-up and invited Adela to dinner at her home. Tui reminded Clara that it was the cook's night off and all that was left in the house was gin—"and no lady ever drinks *gin.*" Clara tried calling her house to confirm this, but her phone number had been changed because too many people knew the old one and she could not remember the new one. She dialed several numbers which sounded right. All were wrong. Apologizing again, Clara invited Adela to dinner at the Ambassador Hotel the following night. Having extended the invitation, she immediately retracted it: "Sorry, I forgot. I gotta date with a *gorgeous* man. 'Least, I *think* he's gorgeous. He'll prob'ly turn out t'be a dud." Clara told Adela to drop by her house beforehand and wrote down her address. It was two blocks wrong.

The following evening Clara forgot to tell her maid a guest was coming, so Adela was denied admittance until Robert Bow appeared, allowed the journalist to enter, then disappeared without a word. Adela was left alone in the bizarrely decorated living room, "unable to read because I couldn't find any books."

Finally Clara and Tui arrived. Clara looked exhausted. "She rehearsed a scene forty times with some sap leading man," explained Tui. "She runs errands for almost everybody over there."

"Ya gotta be regular," sighed Clara. "Even more when you're up. I remember when I was scratchin' for a job. Pola Negri useta ride by me in her limousine like I was part of the roadbed. But I ain't gonna high-hat anybody. First, 'cuz I know how it feels. Second, 'cuz this is a funny game—you're here t'day and gone t'morrow. How 'bout a drink?" The three women had one highball each, which was all Clara allowed herself during shooting. Then Tui left. Clara was ready for her interview.

Adela was apprehensive. Her subject "was slumped in the corner of the davenport. It seemed to me that she would give me nothing. She looked tired and almost stupid, in spite of the feverish glitter in her eyes."

"Then, as we started to talk, she came alive."

The interview lasted until dawn. As Adela listened with rapt astonishment, Clara spoke of her incredible past in vivid, unsparing detail. The tenements, the hunger, a life without hope or love. Frederick Gordon, and Johnny's deaths before her eyes. Her father's absences, her mother's "spells." The butcher knife. Sarah Bow's death, for which Clara still blamed herself. The Fame and Fortune Contest, coming to Hollywood, and then, five years later, becoming the biggest box-office draw in movie history. Men: Gilbert Roland, Gary Cooper, Victor Fleming. And despite her success and suitors, loneliness. Always loneliness.

Adela sat transfixed throughout. "I do not know why she talked as she did," she wrote later. "Once started, she could not stop. It was as though a dam had broken and the words poured out without volition; as though she had not for years talked to anyone who might sympathize and understand."

Adela called her all-night conversation with Clara "the peak of my experiences. Before me rolled a mind entirely untrained, grappling in its own way with the problems of a sophisticated and civilized world. There is hammered into her soul a fear of life, and that is why she desires to live fast and furiously, why she must seek forgetfulness in mad gaiety."

Beginning that night, Adela befriended the real Clara beneath her "It" Girl veneer, and the truth behind the myth fascinated and frightened her. "There seems to be no pattern, no purpose to her life," she wrote at the time. "She swings from one emotion to another, but she gains nothing, stores up nothing against the future. She lives entirely in the present, not even for today, but just for the moment. And you go on loving her, feeling sorry for her, and praying that she won't get into any real trouble." Clara had acquired experience but not profited by it, and Adela feared that when she finally and inevitably did learn her lesson, it would be a devastating one. Given the disasters that would soon occur, her worries were justified.

Adela thought Clara's story too raw to retell in standard Mother Confessor style. Instead she convinced *Photoplay* to run it as a first-person narrative; the effect, Adela believed, would be most gripping coming directly from Clara, just as Adela had heard it herself. In an unprecedented decision, the magazine's editorial board agreed, and "My Life Story, by Clara Bow as told to Adela Rogers St. Johns" appeared in three consecutive issues. Though Clara's Brooklyn dialect and colorful vocabulary were cleaned up, the tale's grisly details were left alone. To her further credit, Adela did not concoct a happy Hollywood ending. From the first lines of its first installment, "My Life Story" portrayed its subject unlike any prior magazine piece: "I think wildly gay people are usually hiding from something in themselves," wrote Adela for Clara. "The best life has taught them is to snatch at every moment of fun and excitement, because they feel sure that fate is going to hit them over the head with a club at the first opportunity." This was Clara's essential credo, and though she had neither the acumen nor ability to verbalize it, Adela did. The resulting life story, composed of Clara's facts and Adela's interpretation of them, remains gripping.

Ironically "My Life Story" ensured Clara's social exile within the Hollywood community. Even those who reacted with sympathy recoiled at her candor, for in an era when poverty and mental illness were causes for embarrassment and shame, "the 'It' Girl" was associating herself with both. And in an industry which treated truth as a burden, not a virtue, Clara's unflinching honesty was considered yet another display of bad manners. While everyone else buried their pasts, she exhumed hers. While everyone else conformed, she rebelled. Now Hollywood rendered its hypocritical verdict: "My Life Story" was touching, but was it truly *necessary*? What point was there in dredging up old, sordid memories?

Adela ignored such disapproval and appointed herself as Clara's protector. She arranged for her brother, Bogart Rogers, to take control of Clara's finances from Robert Bow, who had managed to squander much of Clara's $1,500-a-week salary on, among other investments, his cleaners and restaurant. She accompanied her to U.S.C. games, where Clara appeared in a bright red sportsuit, bright red slippers with high gold heels and buckles, bare legs, and a bright red beret perched jauntily over one ear.

Adela tried to reason with her new friend. All that red, she said, was positively *barbaric*. And a lady always wears *stockings* in public. And why come to a football game in *high heels*?

"Why not?" asked Clara innocently. "I like 'em. They make me feel good."

It was, suggested Adela, a question of *taste*.

Clara wasn't insulted, but she wasn't convinced, either. "My taste suits me," she replied. "And I gotta live with myself more than anybody else does."

Nonplussed by such reasoning, Adela said nothing.

Clara also became a frequent guest at Adela's ranch in Whittier, where she was re-presented to Hollywood society. Adela hoped her protégée would charm the assembled company and be granted a social reprieve, but Clara invariably turned opportunity into calamity. A typical blunder occurred at a gathering that included Colleen Moore, *It* scenarist Hope Loring, and guest-of-honor William Randolph Hearst. During dinner, Adela and Loring encouraged Clara to enroll in college courses, a daunting prospect for someone with a ninety-hour work week and seventh-grade education. Clara listened politely, "agreed with us, admired our platitudes—and went right on being Clara Bow." In this instance, being Clara Bow meant telling a dirty joke with graphic gestures and a punchline which, recalls Colleen Moore, had its narrator squatting to make her point. "I was as shocked as everybody else," Moore admits, "but I had to laugh inside, she did such a first-rate job." If others felt likewise, none were willing to say so in the presence of the prudish guest of honor. Clara's performance was received in silence.

Meanwhile the vigilant governess of Adela's two children, twelve-year-old Billy and ten-year-old Elaine, refused to allow her charges to sleep under the same roof as Clara. So vehement was the governess, and so intimidated was the normally formidable Adela, that the St. Johns children were usually taken against their will to their grandmother's for the weekend. Both adored Clara: "She was so warm and affectionate, with soft skin; hugging her was like hugging a kitten," recalls Elaine. "Of course, my governess disapproved of her so heartily that I rarely got to see her."

Clara knew it. "I'm crazy t'see your kids," she would tell Adela as soon as she arrived. "That little Billy is such a darb, he reminds me of Johnny." Adela knew about Johnny, so her lame excuse that her son was spending the weekend with his grandmother made her sick with guilt, especially when she witnessed Clara's wounded reaction: "her eyes met mine and I winced. They began to smolder, her face hardened. 'Oh well,' Clara said. 'What'd I expect?'"

Although Clara preferred the company of the St. Johns children to Adela's adult guests, to Elaine's disappointment she was invariably "dragged down and made to watch the tennis matches.

She never played, just watched." While Clara watched the tennis matches, wives watched Clara. Adela remembers one doubles game where she was partnered with the wife of a handsome actor. During the match the actor and Clara sat on a canvas swing beside the court, four feet apart from one another, in full view of everyone. Yet when the match ended, the wife stormed over to her husband and smashed her racquet over his head. The couple departed prematurely "amid tears and recriminations."

Clara couldn't understand it. "Why do they always think I want their husbands?" she would ask Adela wearily. "Most of 'em are no bargains that I can see." Aware of Clara's strict code about married men, Adela nonetheless found herself furious when her own husband, football hero Richard Hyland, scrambled eggs with Clara late one night. In the eyes of other women or the presence of other men, Clara was guilty until proven innocent, and although Adela remained a loyal friend and ally, invitations to Whittier soon dwindled, then disappeared. "You'll fail as I did," Hope Loring had warned when Adela made Clara her Galatea. Adela later admitted as much: "I did fail as she had, as Elinor Glyn had. But I think now it was because we were offering oyster forks to a wounded creature who needed the true Bread of Life."

Now Clara had neither. The most popular girl in America was a Hollywood pariah whose presence was not even missed at the premieres of her movies (Clara would wait a month, then go incognito to a neighborhood theater). "Mosta my friends're ones I knew before I paid income tax," she told a fan magazine, "and their names don't mean nothin' t'nobody." To Hollywood society, this was precisely the point: Clara was without social prestige, and no degree of fame or adulation would secure it for her. Uninvited to private parties and unnerved by mobs which formed whenever she appeared in public, "the 'It' Girl" passed sleepless nights playing poker, Parcheesi, darts, or craps with her cook, maid, and chauffeur.

One premiere she missed would acquire historic significance. In December, 1927, as the Trojan season ended, Los Angeles audiences cheered a movie whose actions were accompanied by synchronized *speaking*. Despite frenzied public response to the on-screen songs of Al Jolson, *The Jazz Singer* was considered a novelty, not a threat to silent filmmaking.

There was no reason to believe otherwise, nor to suspect that in the wake of *The Jazz Singer,* a time bomb had been set, and that even for a career as phenomenal as Clara's, its clock was steadily ticking.

# 16

*Get Your Man* reteamed Clara with Buddy Rogers, her leading man in *Wings*. As usual, its plot was pure formula: "It" Girl goes to Paris, spots a Frenchman who catches her fancy, and crashes her car into a tree outside his château to gain admittance. Once ensconced, she wins his love and his noble family's blessing.

Under pressure from his progressive wife, Schulberg assigned *Get Your Man* to twenty-nine-year-old Dorothy Arzner. Before shooting, Buddy Rogers was asked whether he would allow a woman to direct him. Rogers replied that he would let anyone direct him; in fact, he was flattered anyone *wanted* to.

Clara didn't feel as honored. "She bitched to me about having a woman director," reveals Tui Lorraine. "After all, girlfriends like me she could lose, but a gorgeous man was 'divine,' and Dorothy Arzner was going to make one less man around."

Before *Get Your Man* began, the director set a ground rule for the star: "I told her, 'Now, I don't want a lot of men around here, and I don't want any nonsense going on.' So Clara, who was really a very sweet and charming child, would sit in her dressing room with the door wide open and say, 'See? No one in here!' "

Arzner was astounded by Clara's innate artistry. "She was just automatically a natural. A marvelous actress, full of animation and projection of her thoughts and emotions." What impressed the director most was how Clara, with no formal training, could possess such infallible instincts. "The whole thing was emotional with Clara; she understood the emotional content of every scene. Whichever way she did it was so *right,* so *alive.* It was like a dancing flame on the screen.

"They all called Clara 'the "It" Girl,' the outstanding 'flaming youth.' Well, she was all that, but I think she was also the one flaming youth that *thought.* "

Arzner never forgot the final scene of the movie, which was

shot at four A.M. Exhausted and distracted, she gave one last direction to Clara and Rogers through her megaphone: "Now you come together, meet in the middle, and we fade out."

As the crew burst into laughter and began repeating the line, Clara rushed over to Arzner and threw her arms around her. "She don't know what she said!" yelled the star in defense of her mortified director. Then Clara comforted Arzner, assuring her that "the boys'll tryta twist everythin' into a double meanin' on ya, see. Anythin' for a laugh." Her dignity restored, Arzner got the shot and brought in *Get Your Man* for $200,000, fifteen percent less than the budgets of both *Rough House Rosie* and *Hula.*

One month before *Get Your Man*'s production, Paramount gave Ben Schulberg a $100,000 bonus and promotion for relinquishing all rights to Clara's contract. Schulberg had served as associate producer on all her Paramount films; now, as newly appointed general manager of the entire studio, he no longer needed the contractee whose popularity had brought him to Paramount in the first place. Ironically *Red Hair,* the last of Clara's films personally supervised by Schulberg, was also the most lavish. Hoping for a hit of *It* proportions, Paramount allocated $340,000 to *Red Hair,* purchasing *The Vicissitudes of Evangeline,* a long and deservedly forgotten Elinor Glyn novel, for $50,000 and asking the authoress to refashion it for Clara. By now Clara's fame had surpassed her "It" creator's, so when Madame Glyn demanded a prologue depicting "Clara Bow and myself talking on the set among electricians, etc.," her suggestion was ignored and she was replaced by Agnes Brand Leahy. So complete was the identification between star and screen character that each of Leahy's drafts referred to *Red Hair*'s heroine as "Clara," while the film itself was known at Paramount as "Spring Bow," the studio's new, seasonal breakdown of her releases (beginning in 1928, Paramount promised exhibitors one Clara Bow movie each winter, spring, summer, and fall, thereby guaranteeing them at least one certain hit per season). *It* director Clarence Badger was hired, and a theme song called "Red Hair" was commissioned. Clara's hair was bleached, then hennaed to render it redder than ever.

Special care of Clara's hair and the large budget for "Spring

Bow" were due to a shrewd gimmick by Ben Schulberg: audiences at *Red Hair* would see exactly that. The film's opening reel was shot in two-strip Technicolor, a primitive process involving white-hot lights, heavy makeup, and exorbitant film costs. In Clara's case, the effect was worth the expense: moviegoers were mesmerized by the sight of "the 'It' Girl" silhouetted against a green background, her fiery tresses offset by a tight white-belted bathing suit.

Otherwise, *Red Hair* had little to recommend it. Leahy's story made the plots of Clara's prior films seem Byzantine by comparison: redheaded, gold-digging manicurist Bubbles McCoy bewitches three elderly lechers, who shower her with expensive presents. When Bubbles finds true love with a man her own age, she throws a wild party, strips, and leaps into a pool to prove her devotion to him. What wasn't nonsensical was derivative, and what was derivative was intentional: Clara played a manicurist (her *Mantrap* profession) called McCoy (her *Kid Boots* surname) who gets her man in a watery clinch (her *It* technique).

Two weeks into production on *Red Hair,* another Bow made headlines. Twenty-two-year-old first-cousin William Bow had recently arrived in Hollywood from Brooklyn, and although Clara had seen him only a half dozen times in her life, she welcomed "Billy" Bow into her home, invited him to her Garden of Allah parties, and promised to find him a job at Paramount. He returned the kindness by selling liquor in Robert's restaurant to two customers who promptly identified themselves as government agents. Once arrested, Billy pleaded guilty and was sentenced to two months in the county jail, where he gallantly denied any connection to Clara until a judge threatened him with another fifty days. Billy retorted that his movie-star cousin would fix everything, including the judge.

Clara confronted reporters with typical candor. "Sure, Billy's my cousin," she said. "He's in jail, and I ain't gonna get him out. I'm tired of puttin' out for my relatives.

"I don't see why this hasta go in the newspapers," she added, confused and upset by the adverse publicity Billy's imprisonment had brought her. "I didn't have nothin' t'do with it. I been workin' on this picture night and day." For the first time, Clara was receiving front-page coverage she did not covet.

By the end of the press conference, Clara was already relenting. "Oh well, I may help Billy out," she sighed. "I'm softhearted. He oughta have some money. I gave him some for Christmas." Billy's fines amounted to several thousand dollars. Clara quietly paid them, forgave her cousin, forgot the incident, and found him a job as a grip at Paramount.

An inadvertent problem caused by Clara during *Red Hair* set a subsequent precedent for all movies featuring female stars. A sequence in the film called for Bubbles McCoy to jump off a boat (yet another *It* riff) and swim ashore, so the film's cast, crew, and two hundred extras traveled to Catalina Island to shoot aboard a rented ferry. That morning, Clara apologetically informed Clarence Badger that she was menstruating. Since it was still considered unsafe to submerge a bleeding woman in cold water, Badger had no choice but to suspend shooting until Clara had recovered.

When word of the delay reached Paramount, Ben Schulberg was furious. Two hundred extras would have to be paid for another day's work and another night's housing on location with the cast and crew, while the rental fee for the ferry would double. Schulberg blamed assistant director Fred Flick and fired him.

Fellow assistant director Artie Jacobson found out about Flick's dismissal, circulated a petition among his peers protesting it, and delivered the document to the front office. Nothing happened. Desperate, Jacobson informed Clara, who immediately stormed into Schulberg's office and demanded that Flick be rehired. "Freddie ain't no mind-reader, ya know," she told him. "If ya gotta fire somebody, fire *me.*"

"She raised such hell that they put Freddie back on salary," remembers Jacobson. "And from that point on, every assistant director had to know the menstrual cycle of every star. We carried little books." To his surprise and concern, Clara's revealed that she menstruated twice a month.

That spring, Clara in Technicolor turned *Red Hair* into her biggest hit since *It.* "Bow plus Glyn equals underwear," reported *Variety,* "and that goes in this release, and plenty."

At the time America was still a culturally stratified country, with city dwellers and country folk possessing stereotypically polar tastes. Clara bridged the gap more than any other star, filling both rural and metropolitan movie palaces in which, for an admission price of sixty-five cents, liveried attendants led patrons through cathedral-like lobbies, up plush carpeted staircases beneath crystal chandeliers, and finally to their seats of velvet, all while a thirty-piece orchestra serenaded them from the pit below. Those glorious, garish examples which survive have since been converted into office buildings or legitimate theaters, for no current star's movies could fill them seven times a day.

Clara's did. A key-city survey taken upon *Red Hair*'s release conveys exhibitors' awe at her unprecedented popularity. "This Bow girl is the greatest box-office natural of the female gender the entire Coast has," reported a 2,200-seat Los Angeles theater, "and the way the populace flocked to the Loew house signified that fact. Clara Bow drags 'em in of all ages, and they sure went for this one." In San Francisco a 2,700-seat theater "exceeded even the fondest expectations and ended the week with a near box-office record. Clara Bow drew 'em in. Long waiting lines were almost constant to see *Red Hair.*" In a 4,000-seat Kansas City cinema, "Clara Bow is the best bet on the screen. When the 'It' girl goes up in lights over a local house, the employees know they are in for a workout. *Red Hair* was no exception." Business in a 4,500-seat Chicago theater was "well above normal." In New York, Clara's stiffest competition was herself: eight months after its release, *Wings* was still playing to full houses.

Aware that Paramount's biggest box-office draw was also, in proportion to her popularity, Hollywood's lowest-paid star, Schulberg informed Clara that beginning with *Red Hair,* the studio would give her a $10,000 bonus for each film. All payments would be placed in her studio-controlled trust fund, where they would accrue until 1931 unless her employers found cause to withhold them.

In other words, the bonuses would belong to Clara in name only. She had no legal access to them for four more years.

Clara fumed. She was underpaid, overworked, and ashamed of the undress-for-success formula of her films. A decade earlier, Gloria Swanson had made the shift from slapstick comedy to serious drama with historic results. Clara wanted desperately to do the same, and the support of several people fueled her ambition. Tui Lorraine believed her best friend's harrowing background made tragedy more appropriate than comedy, while Elinor Glyn declared that "the 'It' Girl" actually belonged in "particularly tragic parts, for which she had a far greater aptitude than for the comedy scenes which I had to make her act in my films." At Paramount, production supervisor Paul Bern was urging Clara to fight for roles which would reveal her dramatic talent. Lightweight comedies, warned Bern, would not captivate the public forever; what would happen when her "It" hype diminished? If Clara did not make the transition soon, Schulberg would continue exploiting her until it was too late.

Aware of how important her next movie could be to her career, Clara confronted Schulberg and pleaded for a serious role. To her astonishment, he announced that Paramount had just purchased *Ladies of the Mob,* a true story by a "lifer" in Folsom Prison published in H. L. Mencken's *American Mercury* magazine. Schulberg boasted that Paramount's adaptation of *Ladies of the Mob* would provide Clara with the greatest challenge of her career. Production, he promised, would begin as soon as her next comedy had finished. When Clara offered to go off-salary until *Ladies of the Mob* was ready, Schulberg reminded her that a refusal to work put her in violation of her contract. Only physical infirmity could prevent her from making another comedy.

Clara made sure it did. For the past few months, she had suffered from sporadic abdominal pains diagnosed as appendicitis, and an appendectomy had been recommended at her convenience. During the U.S.C. football season, she had been too busy; awaiting *Ladies of the Mob* and unwilling to work on anything else, the operation seemed an ideal solution. It was the same stunt she had pulled four years earlier, when late-night sinus surgery rescued her from *Painted People* and Colleen Moore.

But Clara was sicker than she thought. Her irregular menstrual cycle and abdominal pains led a specialist named Toland to advise not only the removal of her appendix, but her ovaries as well. The medically correct term for this operation was "castration." Afterward Clara would never bear children.

The thought of herself, America's foremost symbol of female sexuality, as a barren woman without reproductive organs was inconceivable to Clara. Recently she had decided to leave movies, marry, and raise a family when the right man came along, and though he had not appeared yet, she had no intention of jeopardizing this dream. Clara consulted other doctors frantically, and several felt an appendectomy sufficient. Bolstered by their difference of opinion, she begged Toland to remove her appendix and leave her ovaries alone. He made no promises.

The operation was scheduled as a simple appendectomy, with only Clara and her doctor knowing otherwise. "Dr. Toland is very anxious there be no publicity, and so am I," she wrote in an uncharacteristically formal and confidential letter to Schulberg. "I imagine you feel the same way about it, so it might be a good idea to tell the publicity department to say nothing whatsoever if they can help it." After Billy Bow's arrest, Clara had realized that any event involving her received national attention. Filled with shame and fear of her impending surgery, she hoped to avoid it now, but privacy was impossible. Even though Schulberg honored her request and Teet Carle remained silent, her hospitalization was front-page news. Even the New York *Times* covered what was, to its knowledge, a routine operation.

Toland performed the appendectomy at St. Vincent's Hospital on February 13, 1928. He did not remove Clara's ovaries, but warned that her symptoms would most likely recur until someone did.

Clara had begged her father and Tui to visit her in the hospital all day every day. Robert Bow soon grew bored and left, citing urgent business matters. Tui comforted Clara by telling her she looked "pale and interesting." Actually, she seemed worn and weak. So listless was Clara that she even ignored the hive of doctors swarming outside her room.

To Tui's surprise, one exceptionally handsome intern flirted with *her*. "I wasn't used to being such an obvious object of attention when Clara was around," she claims, "but this joker kept giving me the 'glad-eye' right in front of her." Tall, rugged, and athletically built, the intern resembled a younger version of Victor Fleming right down to his deep voice, though its tone was mellowed by a rich Southern accent. As glib as he was good-looking, the intern introduced himself as William Earl Pearson, a twenty-six-year-old Texan who had come to Los Angeles for his urology residency. At the end of their conversation, Earl Pearson asked Tui to dinner. She declined. The next day he asked again. Once more she turned him down. The invitations continued during each of Tui's daily visits.

Meanwhile Clara showed signs of rapid improvement, wearing a new negligee in which she truly did look pale and interesting. Her swift recovery led to an early discharge, and Tui arrived to escort her friend home. Entering Clara's hospital room unannounced, she was greeted by the sight of the ailing patient and dashing intern locked in a passionate embrace.

Pearson blushed and beat a hasty retreat. Clara giggled. Tui glared, and on the way back to Bedford Drive, she teased Clara about the intern.

"I think he's *gorgeous*," gushed Clara.

"He made a pass at me first, and *I* gave him the brush," Tui reminded her.

"You ain't interested in Earl, are ya, Tui?" Tui told Clara contemptuously that she was welcome to him. "Good," sighed Clara, " 'cause I think I've flipped for him."

"Just your type," snapped Tui. "Short on brains and long on other organs." Again Clara giggled.

Accustomed to her friend's fleeting infatuations, Tui figured Earl Pearson's bedside manner would soon fade from Clara's memory. She was wrong. Later that night, Clara put a record on her Panatrope, turned up the volume full blast, and sneaked a phone call to St. Vincent's. Robert Bow did not overhear her, but

Tui did. "Okay, sweetie, but come as soon as you're off-duty," cooed Clara into the receiver. "I'll be waitin'." Kissing noises followed her invitation.

Earl Pearson became Clara's first serious relationship since Victor Fleming the previous summer. Almost as ardent as Gilbert Roland, almost as tall as Gary Cooper, and almost as tough as Fleming, Pearson appeared to be both a composite of and an improvement upon them. He came from a wealthy family and was well educated. He had no interest in the movie business, focusing instead on the urology practice he planned to establish once his internship ended. Stable, smart, and an evident Southern gentleman, Clara's new lover seemed ideal even if Robert Bow did refer to him as "that sonofabitch." But Pearson, like Fleming, could not be bullied. He was devoted to Clara.

He was also married. Clara knew it but could not help herself. "He told me he had just been married," she explained later, "but that he and his wife was always squabblin' and fightin' and didn't understand each other.

"I never had no date with a married man in my life," she continued, "an' I wouldn't've had no dates with this one if he'd had any kids. But he didn't." Though Pearson had indeed left his wife in Texas, Clara was nonetheless breaking her cardinal rule. By becoming involved with another woman's husband, she was looking for trouble.

By the spring of 1928, Clara's celebrity was beyond measure. *Red Hair* and an appendectomy treated as news of national import had increased her fan mail to over eight thousand letters per week, more than double any other Paramount star (her closest competitor, Buddy Rogers, received three thousand). Considered second to box-office grosses as a gauge of star power, fan mail was monitored carefully by Paramount, which established a Fan Mail Department responsible for tallying, then answering every letter to every star. In Clara's case, this proved a Herculean task. That May the Postmaster of Los Angeles announced that 33,727 fan letters for her had passed through his office, many addressed simply to "The 'It' Girl, Hollywood, U.S.A." It was the most mail any star at any studio had ever received in one month's time.

Clara could hardly read all these letters, but those she did affected her deeply. Seven years earlier she had written to *Motion Picture*'s Answer Man about her favorite stars. Now the favorite star herself, she tried to make the dreams of her own fans come true. Teet Carle remembers one Saturday morning when Clara, who was not scheduled to shoot that day, dropped by the studio on her way to Long Beach where, she said, she intended to sell popcorn. "Maybe youse guys wanna come and get a picture of me," she added as an afterthought.

Bewildered, Carle asked Clara what she was talking about. She showed him a fan letter from a boy whose parents sold candied popcorn from a booth on the Long Beach pier. Both parents were ill, and the boy had written Clara because "if you came down, I know I could sell enough popcorn to pay their doctor's bills."

It was Clara's first free moment since she had received the letter. She was on her way.

Carle couldn't believe it. "She would have gone there all alone and been *mobbed.* People would have torn her clothes off! That was what made Clara so wonderful, yet such a problem; she never realized she was a *star*. I used to say to her, 'Clara, stars don't *do* what you're doing!' "

Carle and two studio photographers accompanied Clara to Long Beach. Sure enough, when word of her presence spread on the pier, "they stormed her," says Carle. "And I'll never forget the expression on that boy's face when Clara told him she'd come to sell popcorn."

Other encounters with fans ranged from comic to chilling. One night a blond behemoth in overalls pounded on the door of 512 Bedford Drive demanding entrance. Clara called the Beverly Hills police. "Of course I know whose house it is," roared her uninvited visitor to patrolmen who arrived minutes later. "It belongs to Miss Bow. And I came all the way from Iowa to propose marriage to her, only she won't open the door.

"Where I come from," he continued, "when anybody comes to the door and knocks, why, we invite them inside. Now how's about getting me in to talk to Miss Bow?" Clara's suitor clutched his wedding gift, the title to his farm back in Iowa, in one oversized paw. Eventually he was persuaded to return to it without her.

Once Tui Lorraine borrowed Clara's roadster and was followed for several miles by three men. After a high-speed chase (Tui usually drove her own Daytona Beach racing car), Tui lost control of her vehicle and jumped a curb. Her pursuers pulled up beside her, saw that she was not Clara, and sped off. When Tui was trailed again the next night, Paramount hired private detectives to protect Clara. The episode made headlines.

On another occasion, a special delivery letter arrived at Clara's home from a "Mr. Rand" of the U.S. Secret Service. "An inmate of the Illinois State Hospital for the Insane who was raving about murdering you has escaped," he warned. "He says that you have the soul of a flying horse and that you are going to give birth to Jesus Christ and on top of that he is going to marry you." Rand promised Clara that he would come to California to serve as her bodyguard.

Terrified, Clara turned the letter over to Schulberg, who contacted the federal government. He was informed that the Secret Service employed no agent named Rand.

Again detectives were hired to protect Clara. The incident was never made public.

After a month of recuperation from her appendectomy and a tactless letter from Ben Schulberg ("I am sorry that you did not go through with your original plan to have the major operation you were told would be necessary, instead of the superficial, minor operation that you did undergo"), Clara was eager to begin "Summer Bow," her first dramatic star vehicle. Certainly *Ladies of the Mob* was dramatic; from its grisly prologue depicting a man's electrocution to its fade-out on the criminal hero (Richard Arlen) and heroine (Clara) resolving to serve the prison terms they deserve, the film was a radical contrast to Clara's formula comedies.

No prints of the film survive, but reviews and personal memories indicate that Clara's first drama was as insipid as her comedies, though once again she transcended her material. Tui Lorraine, who never bothered to attend her best friend's movies, made an exception for *Ladies of the Mob* and witnessed a performance by Clara which made her potential clear. "I could see it, all right; *anyone* could. It was quite obvious that Clara had the talent to become a serious actress."

What was obvious to Tui was overlooked by critics. Instead of commending "the 'It' Girl" for acting without "It," *Variety* conceded only that "fans who come to see Clara do her usual flip flapper will be disappointed, but the unusual seriousness will probably constitute an interesting contrast."

No criticism could stop *Ladies of the Mob* from opening strong, but soon the backlash began. "We don't want to see you suffer," ran a typical fan letter. "You stand for happiness to us. Keep on laughing and dancing." Soon theater attendance reflected such feelings. "Poorest vehicle Clara Bow has been seen in here," said Seattle; in Detroit, "Bow drew but didn't please." "*Ladies of the Mob* seemed [a] poor vehicle for Clara Bow," complained Minneapolis exhibitors. "Bow, always surefire here, didn't flap enough to suit her followers." The verdict on *Ladies of the Mob* was in: Clara could handle drama, but audiences did not want her in it. And though the movie turned a respectable profit, "respectable" was a disappointing result compared to her formula comedies.

One could conjecture that if Paramount had followed *Ladies of the Mob* with equally serious vehicles, perhaps Clara's fans would have grown accustomed to the change and a new image might have been molded for her as the studio's star dramatic actress. Certainly Clara was willing. "She wanted terribly to go on to other dramatic parts," confirms Tui Lorraine, "but Schulberg wouldn't have it, because the money kept rolling in from the silly tripe she was doing." The comment is an indication of the economic factors that controlled Clara's career: she was not just a star, but the most lucrative asset of a powerful corporation which sold its annual program on the basis of her four films. Taking artistic chances, which to his credit Schulberg had done with *Ladies of the Mob*, meant a monetary risk, and Paramount had no intention of letting Clara's dramatic ambitions interfere with corporate profits. "Clara was making money doing the hula," explains studio photographer John Engstead. "Why not keep on making millions with her doing just the same thing?"

Confinement to formula comedies robbed Clara of the only fulfilling area in her life: her work. As her respect for her movies dwindled, so did her energy and enthusiasm. Once she had toiled for twenty hours a day without complaint; now she balked after twelve. In interviews she refused to discuss "It," saying she was sick and tired of the subject. She spoke of leaving films after her Paramount contract expired for marriage and motherhood. "The world expects Clara Bow t'be divorced a short time after marriage, but I take marriage serious," she declared. "I wanna think about it before doing it, and when I do marry, I wanna make a success of it." Clara added that she had no man in mind yet.

Naturally she did. Earl Pearson said his wife would soon file for divorce.

Between his Southern charm and his status as Clara's ranking boyfriend, Pearson had become a well-known figure in Hollywood and Malibu, where Clara had rented a three-bedroom beach cottage for thirty dollars a month. Still *déclassé* compared to neighboring Santa Monica, Malibu became a summer retreat of stars like Dorothy Mackaill, Clara's fellow 1924 WAMPAS Baby Star, and former lover John Gilbert. Adela Rogers St. Johns used her beach home there as a hideaway for herself and an Italian boxer named Enzio Fiermonte. Ad Schulberg brought her son Budd but instructed him to stay away from "the ignorant, the wastrels, the low-lifes" like Clara, whose all-night gin and jazz parties (anchovy paste squeezed onto saltine crackers was also served) could be heard all the way downshore to the Schulbergs'. Budd disobeyed his mother and brought Clara tomcods he caught in Malibu Creek. She welcomed him warmly, fussing over the tiny fish and showing them off to her friends.

Besides Earl Pearson, two other men had their own keys to her Malibu cottage: Artie Jacobson and Jack Oakie. An ex-vaudevillian, Oakie met Clara on "Fall Bow," an inane trifle called *The Fleet's In* that cast Clara as a "taxi dancer" who performs "the Clara Bow Stomp" with sailors for a dime a song. As a stage veteran reliant on verbal patter, Oakie fretted about how he would express emotion on film. Director Malcolm St. Clair led him to Clara's set. "Watch this," he ordered.

As a trio of musicians began playing a popular song requested by Clara, Oakie watched her tear up a picture of leading man James Hall, then throw the pieces into a wastebasket. Oakie was spellbound. "Nobody on the screen ever tore up a picture with so much feeling."

Then came the kicker. "Now!" shouted St. Clair over the music. Instantly Clara sank to her knees, digging pieces of the torn picture from the wastebasket and reassembling them frantically on the floor in front of her. In two gestures, she had expressed her anger for Hall and the love hidden behind it. No words or titles were necessary.

"Cut!" said St. Clair, then turned to Oakie. "See?"

Oakie did. "The redhead," he realized, "was one of the greatest emotional actresses ever." She could turn even the simplest action into a moving one.

Flattered by his admiration and delighted with his infectious good humor, Clara became Oakie's ally and pal. She urged St.

Clair to build up his supporting role, and when she discovered that Oakie was not under contract to Paramount, she went straight to Schulberg. "Get that boy," commanded Clara. "Don't let him get away." It was wise advice: within three years, Oakie was the studio's star comedian.

While Earl Pearson worked hospital shifts, Oakie, Jacobson, and Tui kept Clara company in Malibu. Another regular guest was Elijah "Buddy" Fogelson, a Texan whom Clara had met in San Antonio while filming *Wings* two years earlier. Fogelson had no interest in the movie business either, boasting instead that one day he would strike oil in his homestate. He had a beautiful voice and often composed silly songs about Clara and Tui on his ukelele.

One afternoon Clara interrupted the sunbathing, swimming, poker playing, and imbibing with a breathless announcement. "C'mon, everybody!" she said. "We got tickets t'go see *Dracula!*" The play had come to Los Angeles and caused a sensation due to its hypnotic star, a Hungarian named Bela Lugosi who spoke no English and performed his role phonetically. Clara found this fascinating. She herded everyone into her car and told Herbert to drive them to the Biltmore Theater. Beneath her fur coat she wore only a bathing suit.

Clara sat transfixed throughout *Dracula,* and when the final curtain fell, she made a beeline for Lugosi's dressing room. "How d'ya know your lines?" she immediately asked him. Lugosi, who still spoke no English, gesticulated that he learned from cues by other actors. Without further ado, Clara invited him home.

Though Tui Lorraine lived in Hollywood's Warner Kelton Hotel, most of her time was spent at Bedford Drive or in Malibu with Clara. When Tui did return to her hotel room, the phone would soon ring. "I'm lonely," Clara would pout. "I can't sleep. C'mon over." Tui always did.

Clara wasn't the only one who wanted her near. Tui was twenty-one and, except for one drunken encounter she could not remember, a virgin. To Robert Bow, this made her all the more enticing. "You better watch it, Tui," teased Clara one evening after her best friend had refused to give her father a goodnight kiss. "I think Daddy's in love with you. How's about you bein' my mother?"

"Not on your goddamn life," snapped Tui. "You're older than I am, and besides, I don't believe in marriage."

Clara grinned. "We'll see."

Tui wanted to discuss another matter. At her maid and cook's request, Clara had been signing blank checks for household expenses. Tui knew that after a five A.M. cup of coffee, Clara rarely returned home until late evening, by which time she had already eaten lunch and dinner. Yet Tui had noticed dozens of canceled checks for large amounts lying around the house. For someone who barely ate at home, she remarked dryly, Clara was spending a small fortune on food.

The next time the two German servants went shopping, Tui made sure to check the amount of the grocery bill against the check used to cover it. It was half of what Clara was charged. Upon direct questioning, Herbert admitted that the maid and cook had urged him to pad the gasoline bills. Although he refused, he had said nothing to Clara because he was sure that with her trusting nature she would not believe him.

Tui went to Clara with the evidence. Her temper ignited by the betrayal, Clara fired the two women. They blamed Tui and vowed revenge.

A week later, the phone rang in Tui's hotel room. She assumed it was Clara; instead it was the desk clerk calling from downstairs to warn her that two policemen were on their way up. Entering Tui's room, they identified themselves as U.S. Immigration Department officers. Tui, a New Zealand citizen and British subject, had entered the country with neither a passport nor visa. As an illegal alien, she faced immediate deportation.

The officers advised Tui to call a lawyer. Panic-stricken, she called Clara. Robert Bow answered the phone and reassured Tui that he would handle the matter. Relieved and grateful, Tui thanked him and hung up. The officers asked her whom she had called.

"Robert Bow, my fiancé," she replied haughtily. No one was more surprised by the announcement than Tui herself.

Tui was taken to the County Jail, where she spent a nightmar-
ish weekend while the $1,000 bail posted by Robert (with Clara's
money) was delayed due to a report that Tui was also a carrier of
venereal disease. Immigration Department officials disclosed that
this information, as well as the tip about Tui's alien status, came
from two unidentified German women.

Tui's release from jail did not solve her problem. Facing imminent deportation, only one solution seemed obvious: marriage.
"Clara needed a mother and I needed a father," she explains,
omitting the fact that if she intended to remain in America, she also
needed a husband. Prior to her arrest, Tui had dismissed Robert
Bow as an irascible old pest; facing exile from a country and industry she loved, she married him in San Bernardino on September
22, 1928. On the marriage certificate, Robert listed his occupation
as "retired businessman" and his age as forty-five. He was actually
fifty-three.

Though Tui considered her marriage a convenience, Robert
regarded it as a love match and consummated his third wedding
with an ardor which left his young bride "disenchanted with what
marriage was all about. If there is such a thing as a male nympho-
maniac," she declares today, "Bob was one. A woman can put up
with just so much and then she wants a *rest*, if you know what I
mean."

News of Tui's marriage to Robert Bow baffled those who knew
her and amused everyone else. "It came as a complete surprise to
members of the film colony," reported the press, assuming that the
farcical facts spoke for themselves.

In this instance, they didn't. What most at Paramount knew,
and what the newspapers didn't dare print, was that although
Robert Bow "was pretty crazy about Tui, Tui was pretty crazy
about *Clara.*"

Tui Lorraine Bow, it was whispered in the jargon of the time,
"was on the lavender side." Tui went "that way."

Clara did not realize it; nor did she even know that female
homosexuality existed. When she had asked Tui "t'be real buddies, just like the two guys in *Wings,*" Clara had envisioned the
camaraderie shared by Buddy Rogers and Richard Arlen in her

movie. Tui happily obliged, and if it all seemed like an ideally close
friendship, to Clara it truly was. When Bela Lugosi visited her
Malibu cottage one weekend and all three bedrooms were already
occupied, Tui volunteered to sleep with Clara, who agreed without
hesitation. She could hardly suspect what she did not understand.

Tui had married Robert Bow when Clara, deeply infatuated
with Earl Pearson, began drifting away. Since her best friend
wanted a husband, Tui felt it pointless to reveal her true feelings,
let alone act upon them. When actor Nils Asther teased Tui about
her "lovely friendship with Clara" with a "knowing, wicked grin,"
Tui blushed and told the truth. "Clara adores men only," she
sighed. "Heterosexual to the core, you know."

Mr. and Mrs. Robert Bow lived in Tui's hotel room but spent
their time at Clara's. "We became sort of a family group, the three
of us," says Tui. If so it was a strange dynamic, with the husband
"shockingly jealous" of his daughter, the wife secretly pining for
her stepdaughter, and a naive Clara delighted that her father and
best friend had fallen in love. Ironically (and, if the situation were
not so bizarre, comically), Robert resented Tui for preferring
Clara's company to his own but hated it even more when his
daughter took her stepmother on double dates with other men.
When they sneaked off to San Pedro for a romantic shipboard
dinner with two naval officers during the shooting of *The Fleet's In*,
Robert flew into a rage. Had he known his wife's nature, his reaction would no doubt have been different.

Not surprisingly, Robert's marriage to Tui Lorraine barely
outlasted his brief union to Ella Mowery four years earlier. Within
months Tui had learned that her husband was luring "a number of
little dears" to Clara's beach cottage on nights when no one else
was there. Late one evening, Tui and her own female consorts
piled into her racing car and drove to Malibu armed with powerful
flashlights. Silently they crept along the shoreline until they
reached Clara's cottage, where the sound of squeaking bedsprings
and "grunts, groans, snorts, and squeals of delight" greeted them.
Tui hoisted the bedroom window, aimed her flashlight, and hit her
target, "two of the barest asses any of us are likely to see." Emitting
a bloodcurdling shriek that sent her husband tumbling out of bed

in alarm, Tui played the wronged wife and demanded a divorce. She was granted one on the less scandalous grounds of "mental cruelty."

Tui disregarded her lawyer's advice and in lieu of alimony asked only for eighteen months' rent, a total of $648. But cutting her ties with Robert Bow meant doing the same with his loyal daughter, and for Tui this proved unbearable. Finally she forced a showdown, bracing herself with gin and arriving unannounced in Malibu to confront Clara. "I don't see why we can't still be buddies and see each other," she pleaded.

Clara glared back. "We're through," she told Tui. "And don't think you're gonna get any more money from Daddy. He ain't got any."

This was too much for Tui. Hurt and drunk, she stormed off, drove back to Bedford Drive, and collected her belongings. On her way out, she passed the Chinese room and saw an enormous photograph of her stepdaughter winking invitingly at her. Tui defaced it.

She never saw Clara again.

# 18

*Three Weekends* was Clara's weakest formula film yet. Even its title, a diminution of Elinor Glyn's *Three Weeks,* was derivative, yet so surefire was the "Bow plus Glyn equals underwear" equation that in return for the use of her name, Paramount paid Elinor $25,000 and gave her story credit. As additional insurance, *It* and *Red Hair* veteran Clarence Badger directed it.

Though Clara approached her role in *Three Weekends* with characteristic gusto and professionalism, she could not save a plot as skimpy as her wardrobe. Influential film critic Richard Watts, Jr., denounced the insipid formula for her films, charging that "because Miss Bow has had the misfortune to be labeled the 'It' Girl, she must be a sort of Northwest Mounted Policeman of sex, who gets her man even if she has to bludgeon him. The result is a series of films in which a particularly engaging star gets coy and elfin all over the landscape, battering down the resistance of some man who, for an unaccountable reason, is cold to her loveliness. The formula is particularly annoying when applied to one of the most pleasing stars of the cinema." Watts's point was not lost upon his wide readership, which grew increasingly aware of how alike Clara's films had become.

Though Watts did not know it, the question of what to do with Clara once her formula failed was already being pondered by Paramount executives, one of whom wrote an anxious memo to *Three Weekends* production supervisor Ben Zeidman. "The final scene is so utterly in the style of a two-reeler as to be unworthy of consideration in a Clara Bow picture," reproached the executive. "My main criticism, however, is of the story as a type of Clara Bow picture on this year's program. Where is that superior, more sincere, more generally dramatic flavor which we are to understand will characterize the Bow productions this year? In the words of Mr. Lasky,

Bow has about reached the limit of development along the old line."

As the memo makes clear, Paramount president Jesse Lasky had finally realized that Clara needed better material. Nevertheless Ben Schulberg, Lasky's subordinate within the studio hierarchy, defied orders and approved *Three Weekends* for production. When it generated the same sizable profits as all of Clara's comedies, Lasky, who reported to Adolph Zukor and Paramount stockholders in New York, was put in a no-win position. The movie business was a function of commerce, not art; how could he reprimand Schulberg for sticking to formula when "Winter Bow" was one of the studio's biggest hits that season?

A calamity in Clara's private life precluded Lasky's concern about her material. While *Three Weekends* was shooting, Elizabeth Pearson arrived in Los Angeles hoping to reconcile with her husband. He picked her up at the train station in Clara's new Cadillac limousine. She wondered how an intern could afford such a luxurious automobile. Pearson assured her that it belonged to "a friend."

His wife decided to find out who that friend was.

It wasn't difficult. For eight months Clara had kept her relationship with Earl Pearson relatively quiet, but encouraged by his promises of divorce, Clara soon began referring to Pearson in interviews. One was particularly explicit. "I have found the one man who brings complete happiness into living," she was quoted as saying. "I am sorry, but I cannot tell you his name. He is not in the motion picture profession. I would gladly tell you if it weren't that I must protect him.

"He is married. He has not been living with his wife. There are no children.

"I love him. As to my getting married, if it were possible now, I'd do it."

After reading this and listening to local gossip, Elizabeth Pearson confronted her husband. He confessed his love for Clara, assuming his wife's knowledge of the affair would expedite a divorce. It did, but not as Earl Pearson planned. Instead of returning docilely to Dallas, Elizabeth Pearson informed her husband that

she would file for a local divorce, cite Clara Bow as "co-respon-
dent" in her complaint and bring suit for "alienation of affections"
against her. She would seek $150,000 in damages.

Clara couldn't believe it. "The wife was gonna sue me for
alienation!" she said later with lingering astonishment. "Blam!
Like that! One hundred and fifty thousand smackers! Why, I'd
never even *seen* that much coin before."

At the time it was no minor matter. "The 'It' Girl" was
naughty but no homewrecker, and a divorce suit portraying her as
one could destroy her career. Clara was expected to tow the same
virtuous line as her screen characters, not overstep it. As she had
seen for herself, even a so-called sexual libertarian like Judge Ben
Lindsey reacted like a reactionary to her teasing; if her fans were
less hypocritical than Lindsey, that did not mean they were less
judgmental.

One vengeful wife could ruin Clara and she knew it. "I don't
want no publicity," she wailed when informed of the imminent
lawsuit. Paramount didn't either: with the career of its most important asset at stake, the studio had no intention of allowing Clara to
be portrayed as an alienator of affections in court and in headlines.
Since Lasky was in New York and Schulberg in Chicago on business, studio attorney Henry Herzbrun took charge of the affair. On
October 13, 1928 he drafted a letter in Clara's name retaining
prominent Los Angeles lawyer W. I. Gilbert to represent her in
"any action or proceeding which may be commenced against me
by one Elizabeth Pearson," then sent a telegram to Clara in
Malibu, where she and Pearson were hiding from the private detectives his wife had hired. Herzbrun's instructions were curt and to
the point: GIVE BILL [sic] RAILROAD TICKET TO HIS HOME AND SUCH
EXPENSE MONEY AS HE ACTUALLY NEEDS. Clara did. Earl Pearson
returned to Texas without his wife.

That same day, Teet Carle prepared a statement for the press
in case the story should break. Signed by Clara, the dignified,
blanket denial amused those who knew her better than to believe
it. "I was a patient in St. Vincent's Hospital in February of this
year," began Carle for Clara. "Among those who attended me was

an intern. When I was discharged, because of his knowledge of my case the Doctor continued to attend me during my convalescence.

"I did not know that Dr. Pearson was a married man until some time after our acquaintance began. With me the Doctor is merely a member of the passing throng made up of the life that comes to those in screen work. The hospitality extended to him was exactly the same as that shared by many another during this period.

"I am not purposely hunting for newly wedded husbands. I can't use all of my spare time to shoo them away. It is regrettable, of course, if true, that the Doctor has lost any affection which he may have had for his wife, but I deny that I had anything to do with it. The public should know that the present suit is the result of failure to extract any part of my salary. Clara doesn't scare."

The statement's final declaration was also its final falsehood. With Lasky and Schulberg's approval, Herzbrun was already in the process of dissolving Clara's studio-controlled trust fund, which contained $26,000 deposited by Paramount a year earlier. Her contract had stipulated that she would receive the entire sum in 1931 unless she became "involved in a public scandal," and though the Pearson affair was not public, it was sufficiently scandalous for Paramount to exercise its contractual privilege and retain its $26,000. The money Clara had considered hers in name only was no longer even that.

Paramount also held an additional $30,000, the total of three $10,000 bonus payments from *Red Hair, Ladies of the Mob,* and *The Fleet's In,* with the same stipulation: any scandal, no money. The provision enabled Henry Herzbrun to offer Elizabeth Pearson the entire $30,000 if she kept Clara out of her divorce suit and altered its grounds from "alienation of affections" to "failure to provide." His offer was made on October 17, 1928.

Later that day, Elizabeth Atwood Pearson filed for divorce from Dr. William Earl Pearson. The charge: failure to provide. To Paramount's immense relief, not a word of the truth reached reporters, nor was Teet Carle's press release ever publicly issued.

Back in Texas, Earl Pearson's family made plans to exile him to Germany, and though she did not reply to them, Clara subsequently bragged about receiving "the longest cablegrams ever sent over the ocean." DARLING, wired Pearson, CAN YOU FEATURE MY LONELINESS, MILES FROM MY LOVER? HONEY, LOVER, I AM SO LONELY FOR YOU. WHY DO WE HAVE TO BE SEPARATED EVERY TIME? LET ME HEAR FROM YOU. I NEED YOU. EARL. He did not mention that his wife was also in Germany trying to reconcile with him. Despite her presence, Pearson's lovesick cablegrams to Clara continued.

She was more upset about the $56,000 their affair had cost her. A hastily scribbled entreaty to Schulberg reveals the confusion in Clara's life and finances following the Pearson fiasco:

> Dear Ben,
>
> Didn't have time to wait for you because after rehearsal I had to go to the beauty parlor to have my hair dyed a dark red so that it wouldn't photograph too light. I just wanted to ask you with tears in my eyes if there wasn't some way we could fix up that income tax on the $25,000 I lost in the law suit. If you can't help me in the matter, I'll have to pay the government an extra $5,000 next year and it will spoil my whole New Year because I can't afford it really. Please think it over and see if there isn't some way out of it for me.
>
> Maybe the organization could charge it to something or other because after all the money was never mine anyhow!
>
> Be a pal and use your influence, Ben.
>
> Clara
>
> P.S. Pardon pencil please.

By now Clara was earning $2,800 a week, a pittance compared to Pola Negri's $6,000 a week or Colleen Moore's $125,000 per picture. Still, $5,000 amounted to less than two weeks of her salary. That she could not afford it was shocking.

By late 1928, *The Jazz Singer*'s success could no longer be attributed to a passing vogue or stroke of luck. The competition between movies and radio had changed sound on film from a novelty to a necessity, and every major studio rushed to supply the sudden demand for "talkies" that guaranteed large grosses by virtue of their gimmick alone. One of the first to jump aboard the talkie bandwagon was Elinor Glyn, who appeared as herself in a two-reeler devoted to her favorite topic: *What Is IT?*

Paramount acknowledged the craze by sending special effects engineer Roy Pomeroy to study sound technology with experts from Western Electric. Armed with his new knowledge, Pomeroy returned to Paramount in the summer of 1928 and transformed his office into a "soundstage." As the only studio employee skilled in sound recording, Pomeroy wielded more clout than even Ben Schulberg. His salary shot up from $250 to $2,500 a week, he barred everyone from his studio-within-a-studio, and he informed his superiors that the sooner they realized no talking picture could be cast without his approval, the better off Paramount talkies would be. Helpless, executives had no choice but to obey.

One month after Clara's out-of-court settlement with Elizabeth Pearson, Paramount released *Interference,* its first all-talking picture. When *Three Weekends* appeared a few weeks later, talkies were already so prevalent that it was assumed "Winter Bow" was "silent because the boys evidently figure Clara is strong enough to stand without a sound crutch." She was, but not for long. If Clara wanted to stay in movies, she would have to speak in them like everyone else.

It was a potentially catastrophic prospect. At Paramount, rumors flew that an inflection, pitch, tone, or accent which did not please Roy Pomeroy could jeopardize even the most secure stardom. Pomeroy, they said, could not only record a voice, but doctor it to an actor's disadvantage. "See that man there?" actor Richard Dix asked Esther Ralston, pointing to Pomeroy. "Well, you'd better be nice to him. He can make a baritone out of you and a soprano out of me." Paramount's announcement that its 1929 program would be all-talking, followed by the mass migration from New York to Hollywood of actors with trained voices and stage experience, was considered conclusive proof by silent film stars that their own voices would not record adequately.

Although Pomeroy did not possess the skill or knowledge to alter voices on purpose, the fears of silent stars were furthered when Clive Brook, a Paramount actor with prior stage experience, recounted his ordeal in the sound engineer's studio. After Brook finished recording his voice test, Pomeroy played it back for him. Brook listened, aghast: "I heard a deep, strange voice come booming out of the loudspeakers. It was not, I told myself, Clive Brook. It alternately faded into nothingness and then rang out in a thunderous crescendo. 'Was that my voice?' I asked. Pomeroy smiled at me. 'Yes, but you couldn't recognize it, could you?' " Actors regarded Brook's experience as proof of Pomeroy's "doctoring" and awaited their own tests with mounting panic. A jittery pact was struck by Buddy Rogers, Richard Arlen, Gary Cooper, and Jack Oakie, the studio's top male stars. With clasped hands, the foursome vowed that if one did not "pass" his voice test, the others would allocate ten percent of their salaries to him.

Voice tests were administered in Pomeroy's studio without shooting a foot of film. For once, Clara was given star treatment: *her* voice test would also be recorded by a camera, with Dorothy Arzner directing a scene from *The Wild Party,* the forthcoming, all-talking "Spring Bow." No other Paramount actor was accorded such a privilege.

No other actor needed it as much, either. Although Clara's filmed voice test consisted of one brief scene, followed by her facing the camera to introduce herself and her voice, she was petrified. She had heard all the horror stories about Pomeroy, she was already ashamed of her stammer, and she was certain that speaking in a movie would result in nationwide humiliation.

On December 13, 1928, only days before her test, Clara was given a 102-page shooting script of *The Wild Party.* Riffling through it, she could not fathom how she was supposed to memorize so many lines (clinging to her silent film vocabulary, she called them "titles") when just saying her name seemed daunting enough.

Though her test progressed smoothly during its shooting and recording, the results confirmed Clara's fears, and when the projectionist ran the film and Pomeroy played back the synchronized wax discs, she literally screamed in anguish. The sound of herself on screen was everything she had expected and worse, and although Dorothy Arzner reassured her, Clara was inconsolable. "How can I be in pictures with a voice like that?" she wailed. Then she burst into tears.

# IV

## Talkies

"Talkies are spoiling the oldest art in the world—the art of pantomime. They are ruining the great beauty of silence. They are defeating the meaning of the screen."

– Charlie Chaplin (1929)

"We didn't need words. We had *faces* then."

– Gloria Swanson as Norma Desmond,
*Sunset Boulevard* (1950)

# 19

Silent films were never silent. During shooting, studio stages resounded with the cacophony of carpenter's hammers, cranking cameras, hissing klieg lights, "mood" music, and directors exhorting actors through each scene. Doors leading to and from the stages squeaked open and slammed shut. Executives conferred, extras chatted, and even actors carried on conversations. A typical example occurred during *Kid Boots,* when Clara, supposedly quarreling with Eddie Cantor on camera, was actually giving him words of encouragement.

Silent films were never shown in silence, either. The best theaters featured hundred-piece orchestras playing original scores composed for specific films, and even small towns employed organists to vamp an accompaniment based on the emotional content of each scene. That today's audiences are often made to watch so-called "silent" films in silence is both an injustice to their makers and viewers. No one thought of them as silent until talkies took their place.

Talkies caused a chaotic and bewildering flux within the film industry. *Fortune* magazine called the technological transition "beyond comparison the fastest and most amazing in the whole history of industrial revolutions," while those who lived through it call the change "overnight." In truth, it wasn't much longer: in 1928, the majority of American movies were silent; by 1930, all were sound. (The sole holdout, Charlie Chaplin, released *City Lights,* his final silent masterpiece, in 1931, a decision considered career suicide at the time.) In their frenzied rush to spend tens of millions of dollars converting facilities, replacing equipment, and signing theatrical talent, the movie industry never paused to mourn the demise of a medium which, over the past three decades, had been transformed from a crude turn-of-the-century novelty to the most modern, influential, and often exquisitely subtle of art forms.

What succeeded it seemed a travesty. Since the ideal speaking
voice to a sound engineer was a level one, actors were ordered to
speak in a monotone. Heavy, cumbersome cameras which took
eight men to lift (versus the portable ones for silent films) were
encased in soundproof booths which remained stationary during a
shot, rendering impossible angles which had been commonplace a
few months earlier. Because of this, the visual fluidity which characterized silent filmmaking was replaced by static talkies which
were nothing more than photographed stage plays. In love with
the sound of their own dialogue, these movies made certain every
action and emotion was not only seen, but *heard.* Few are bearable
today.

No one suffered more than the stars of these primitive efforts.
Accustomed to performing amidst incessant, noisy activity, actors
in talkies now worked, ironically enough, in total silence. As soon
as the sound engineer (who now outranked the director) said,
"Action," a funereal hush fell over the soundstage. Meanwhile
actors crept gingerly into camera range, avoiding normal steps that
could record as stomps on sensitive recording equipment known
to pick up everything from outside street traffic to the rumbling of
an empty stomach. Only when an actor hit a designated "mark"
could dialogue be delivered, with each word enunciated slowly,
clearly, and not at all realistically in the direction of an immobile
microphone looming above. Off camera, the director would watch
with contentment, then cringe as the sound engineer bellowed
"Cut!" from within his recording booth. "No good for sound," the
engineer would announce. It was the most dreaded phrase heard
on a soundstage. It was also the most common.

By this time makeup was streaming down an actor's face,
melted by brutally hot lights which were used because they did not
hiss like kliegs did. Since air conditioning also made too much
noise, soundstages were sweltering.

Talkies not only changed the way movies were made, but the
way they were watched. Gazing at a silent screen upon which
mouths moved but did not speak, audiences had idealized not only
how stars sounded, but what they said. Talkies turned these fanta-
sies into a single, concrete reality, and fans whose minds had

"listened" to their favorite silent film stars were bound to feel disappointed. What voice could possibly fulfill one hundred million different expectations? No matter how appealing a star's voice was, its actual sound could not compare to its imagined one.

A generation later, the musical classic *Singin' in the Rain* exploited this frantic period for comic purposes. At the time it was no laughing matter. "Mike fright," a term which originated when radio performers froze before going "on air," was now an occupational hazard in Hollywood as well. By late 1928, seven colleges of "voice culture" had established themselves in Beverly Hills, where they did a thriving business by promising panicked actors they could (and this was said with dead seriousness) teach them how to talk. The shrewdest stars hired New York "thea-tah" actresses as private coaches: Gloria Swanson worked with Laura Hope Crews, while Colleen Moore, whose future hung in the balance of a voice test in which she was told to recite "Little Bo Peep," hired Constance Collier. Others were impervious. "Eeet is all foolishness," proclaimed Pola Negri. "Eeet is a fad, a curiosity. I do not think of eeet at all. Bah!" Negri's reaction to the news that Paramount would not renew her contract remains unrecorded.

Clara was left to fend for herself. Relaxed, her voice was low, throaty, and sensual, with a coarse Brooklyn accent somewhat within her control. Nervous vocal tics, however, were not, for the stammer that had plagued Clara since grammar school still returned when she became overwrought. Then her regular speech would accelerate to such a frenzied pace that she would finally "hang up" on a word, stammering its first syllable until her mind caught up with her mouth. The faster she spoke, the higher-pitched her voice sounded, until by the time of the hang up, she reminded Buddy Rogers of "an excited little girl." Typically and uncharitably, Sam Jaffe thought her voice "whiny."

"We were at fault," Jaffe concedes. "We should have taken six months to train her." Easily said six decades later, but as 1929 began, America was clamoring to hear its screen favorites speak, and Clara's first talkie was, with the possible exception of Greta Garbo, the most eagerly anticipated vocal debut of all.

MGM waited two years before allowing Garbo to appear in a

talkie. Paramount gave Clara two weeks. After her filmed voice test in mid-December of 1928, and despite her devastated reaction to it, *The Wild Party* went into production on January 2, 1929. That she began her first talkie lacking sufficient preparation or self-assurance was unimportant to Paramount. "Spring Bow" would talk whether Clara was ready or not.

Louise Brooks finally met her idol during this traumatic period. A decorative but not particularly popular featured player, Brooks reported to Roy Pomeroy's studio one day and discovered Clara curled up in the corner of an oversized couch, "wearing her usual sweater and skirt, in absolute ignorance of her own physical beauty. She never gave a damn about her soft fluffy baby hair, pure skin, beautiful mouth and perfect teeth."

Brooks sat down and introduced herself. To her surprise and delight, Clara "just began to talk. She knew all about me." Brooks could not know that Clara had been too awed by her elegance and style ("so damn beautiful," she would whisper to Tui Lorraine whenever they passed Brooks on the Paramount lot) to make any overtures at friendship. But when Brooks made the first move, Clara responded with warmth and candor.

Listening to her chatter nervously, Brooks realized how "stunned and helpless" Clara felt in the face of widespread gossip which mocked her voice and accent and considered her failure in talkies a foregone conclusion. "They make me feel so terrible," confided Clara to Brooks, "that I-I-I-I can't *talk.*" Just discussing the subject made her stammer. Several days earlier, she continued, Schulberg had sent Ruth Chatterton, a stage actress just signed to a long-term studio contract, to Bedford Drive. "I beat it out the back door," Clara confessed, then repeated herself miserably. "They make me feel so t-t-t-t-*terrible* . . ."

Listening to Clara's musical contralto, Brooks could not believe what she was hearing. "She was Hollywood's top female box-office star! She got 30,000 fan letters a month! But she already knew that she was finished."

As her confidence plummeted, her popularity reached its peak. The day after *The Wild Party* went into production, a national survey of 2,700 theater owners and managers named Clara the favorite star of moviegoers, with Colleen Moore a distant runner-up. Two days later *Wings* went into general release after seventeen months of sold-out shows in major cities. The film's phenomenal success and thrilling aerial effects earned it the Best Picture award from a new organization called the Academy of Motion Picture Arts and Sciences. At the first annual AMPAS awards ceremony in the Blossom Room of Hollywood's Roosevelt Hotel, Clara accepted an Academy statuette (not yet nicknamed "Oscar") for *Wings* from master of ceremonies Douglas Fairbanks, who also presented her with an honorary scroll for her contribution to it.

All of these accolades and the feverish anticipation of her first talkie boosted Clara's fan mail in January, 1929 to 45,000 letters, more than double any star's in movie history. But instead of instilling hope, her incredible celebrity only intensified the pressure of working under conditions which rumor claimed she could not handle.

Paramount was still grappling with those same conditions. Roy Pomeroy's reign of terror had ended when a studio policeman barred Victor Fleming from entering Pomeroy's studio to watch him work. This time the sound engineer picked the wrong director to bully, for Fleming went straight to Schulberg's office. "What the hell is this, Ben?" he demanded. "This sonofabitch can't direct every picture. Are you going to have one director for sound? It's here to stay; we're *all* going to have to find out about it." Realizing that Fleming was right, Schulberg sent several engineers to study at Western Electric. When they returned, Roy Pomeroy was expendable. He left Paramount shortly thereafter.

All of this was small comfort to Clara. With or without Pomeroy, the strange new procedure still applied, and as hard as she tried, she could not seem to adjust. "We had quite a time in the beginning," recalled director Dorothy Arzner of her trials with Clara on *The Wild Party*, "because to be aware of the pantomime which she was accustomed to, then have *words* to remember, was very difficult for her." If Clara emoted as she had in silents while speaking, the effect would be comic in its extremity. Talkies required a restraint she had never developed and rendered useless the abandonment she had. Darting about the set was an impossibility in scenes requiring actors to stand still and spout pages of dialogue. In two weeks' time, Clara was expected to transform herself from a visually to a verbally communicative actress. To an innate talent without theatrical training or studio support, it was all overwhelming. Clara felt "constant fear" throughout *The Wild Party*'s production.

Arzner and assistant director Artie Jacobson did all they could to help her. The stationary microphone hanging above the soundstage was attached to a fishpole so Clara could move more freely instead of halting below it whenever she spoke. Likewise, a deal was made between Clara and the crew: once a scene had been "blocked," she would not deviate from it during the "take." This enabled the cameraman to light her properly in rehearsal and the sound engineer to know in advance where she would stand when she spoke. While Clara waited nervously in her dressing room, Jacobson would then conceal the mike in a prop near her mark so she would not be so conscious of it. A pillow or vase were common hiding places.

Of course, this trick could only work in medium or close-up shots. Master shots meant the mike must loom above the set in full view of Clara, who was developing a dangerous habit: while playing a scene with another actor, her gaze would travel upward toward the off-camera mike. Unaware of what she was doing until it was too late, Clara would shoot Arzner a panicked glance when she heard the director call "Cut!" over the sound engineer's objection. Again and again Arzner would take Clara aside, explaining the problem gently. Clara would apologize, shedding tears of embarrassment and frustration.

*The Wild Party* was regulation Bow formula: "It" girl goes to college and gets her man, who in this case is also her anthropology professor (Fredric March). In her first scene of the film, Stella Ames (Clara) enters her dorm room dragging a heavy trunk, hits her mark, halts, turns, faces the camera, and talks: "Just a working girl," she sighs, gesturing to her trunk. Her phony, painstaking articulation is obvious.

Everyone in *The Wild Party* talks in tranquilized fashion, pronouncing each word as if learning English aloud. Several other sound-related snags occur: when Stella and her pals scandalize a costume party by wearing skimpy bathing suits beneath their raccoon coats, their syncopated dance steps record like a stampede. Later a conversation between Clara and another actress conducted across a room leaves the latter, presumably farthest from the mike, whispering while Clara, positioned closer to it, seems to be shouting.

Her voice itself is more successful. Though its Brooklyn honk comes and goes (Stella prefers a wild "pahtee" to an anthropology "cleeass") in a role where it should not surface at all, her most serious vocal deficiency, the low-to-high progression of pitch, works to her advantage. Deep and throbbing in her dramatic scenes and shrill and childlike in her comedic ones, Clara's unusually broad range is the most appealing aspect of her speech. Still, it is her silent work which remains most effective, and Arzner wisely shot many long, loving close-ups of Clara reacting to off-camera events as if to demonstrate that she does not need dialogue to express emotion. Her ability is all the more impressive when one learns that these close-ups were shot not with other cast members feeding her lines from behind the camera, but with Clara staring straight into narrow strips of nonreflecting black cloth known as "niggers." That she could communicate without words under such conditions was amazing. It was also outmoded.

Legend contends that Clara's first talkie was a disaster. Actually it could not have been anything but a hit unless her voice had been comical, and contrary to Clara's belief, it wasn't. "Laughing, crying or condemning, that Bow voice won't command as much attention as the Bow this and that, yet it's a voice," *Variety* assured exhibitors. "Enough of a voice to insure a general belief that Clara can speak, as well as look—not as well, but enough." "Miss Bow Talks!" headlined the New York *Times,* and though its review dismissed *The Wild Party* as "intended for dwarfed intellects," it noted that "Miss Bow's voice is better than the narrative. It is not overmelodious in delivery, but it suits her personality."

Qualified critical praise was beside the point; the most popular movie star in America had made her first talkie, and everyone wanted to see it. Even the *Times* critic was awed by the "tremendous crowd" which filled the theater.

It was the same everywhere else. Buffalo reported "skyrocketing" business. House records were set in Providence and Philadelphia. Grosses were "hot" in Chicago. *The Wild Party* was "packing 'em in" in Washington. San Francisco had "one of its big weeks of the year." Business in Portland "started off with a bang." "Will accept Bow in anything here," marveled Los Angeles in reference to the high grosses Clara generated despite *The Wild Party*'s poor reviews.

Outside these major cities, her sound debut was shown in silence. Theater owners refused to convert their facilities for what was still considered a fad.

To publicize *The Wild Party,* Paramount planned a "personal appearance" tour, a publicity gimmick which brought actors to theaters for in-person promotions of their latest films. The prospect terrified Clara, whose problems on *The Wild Party* made her more self-conscious of her voice than ever. Talking into a mike was tortuous; speaking in public seven times a day was unthinkable. Paramount had no confidence in her, either, so when Clara begged to be released from this contractual responsibility, a compromise was reached. Instead of a multicity tour, she would fly cross-country by propeller plane for a one-day "p.a." at Brooklyn's 4,000-seat Paramount theater.

It was a decision based on business, not sentiment. By 1929, Brooklyn was New York City's most populous borough and hence a major market for the movie industry. This was the decisive factor, though there were others. In Brooklyn, Clara's accent would sound normal. In Brooklyn, two million people thought of her as a local girl made good. And in Brooklyn, where she had not been since her stardom, the prospect of a highly publicized homecoming excited everyone but sixty-seven-year-old Clara Bow, who slammed her door in the faces of reporters inquiring about the namesake niece she had thrown out of her house eight years earlier.

As an unknown, unloved slum dweller, Clara had waited eight

hours for matinee idol Wallace Reid's personal appearance at a local theater. Now she was the most popular star in movies, and thousands of fans braved the bitter winter cold to welcome her home. Policemen outside the Paramount theater tried to stop the mob from overflowing onto DeKalb Avenue and jamming traffic. "Hours for seats!" warned ushers. No one budged. With patriotic if hyperbolic pride, a local paper likened the scene to Lindbergh's return to America.

Clara's brief appearance before each show was greeted with a deafening ovation. Dressed in a black taffeta gown, with a cape dyed to match her hair, diamond earrings, and the gold evening slippers she wore to both football games and formal events, she stepped nervously toward an on-stage microphone amidst frenzied applause. "If ya wanna go inta movies and ya work hard, ya can get where I've gotten in six years," she told her audience. A dreamy sigh swept through the theater. "I hope youse all prouda me," she added. The crowd cheered its answer. Then she left the stage and the movie began.

Her reception touched Clara deeply. "I really wanted t'cry out there," she told reporters backstage. "Y'know what I mean? So many of 'em wanna see me personally, but there ain't time. I suppose they think I'm high-hattin' 'em." One journalist asked how she felt about talkies. Clara hesitated and then sighed. "I ain't so crazy 'bout the movie business like I once was," she admitted.

Outside the theater, fifty urchins who could not afford tickets besieged her. Clara gave them each a personal autograph. "Why didn't you answer my letter?" demanded one of her uncles. Clara explained that she had received 45,000 letters that month. Then she apologized guiltily for not opening them all.

When she returned to Hollywood, her latest lover was waiting. Twenty-eight-year-old ex-prizefighter turned stuntman Jimmy Dundee was a rugged Irishman whose superhuman coordination enabled him to roll under cars and leap off cliffs without injury. Studio gossip linking Clara to Fredric March must have amused Dundee, who not only worked on *The Wild Party*, but lived with Clara throughout its production. She didn't love him, but she did enjoy Dundee's amiable personality. When he considered a return to the ring, she turned her backyard into a training camp, complete with boxing and gymnastic equipment.

By now Clara had also found a new best friend. Born in Kentucky in 1904, Daisy DeBoe was a slim and stylish bleached blonde with liquid blue eyes, a leonine face, and a no-nonsense manner. As a teenager, she had migrated to Los Angeles and chosen hairdressing over high school. A client suggested she change her name to DeVoe and recommended her to Paramount, who hired Daisy as an on-location hairdresser in 1924. Two years later she was in San Antonio working on Victor Fleming's *The Rough Riders* when Clara arrived for *Wings,* but the two women did not meet until a month later, when Daisy was sent to San Pedro, California for *It.*

Clara immediately took a liking to this tough and independent hairdresser with a work ethic as strong as her own. Like Clara, Daisy had supported herself since age sixteen. Like Clara, she regarded her role in the movie industry as a job, not a birthright. And like Clara, she had no intention of devoting her entire life to it. At the time it did not seem significant that the emotionally indomitable Daisy was a polar opposite of the emotionally fragile Clara; antithetical as their temperaments were, the two shared the same realistic attitude toward a profession based on illusion. It was a logical basis for friendship, and after Tui Lorraine (who hated Daisy) married Robert Bow, Clara demanded her favorite hairdresser for all her movies. Soon she and Daisy were inseparable.

It was hardly a surprising development. A hairdresser tended to a female star from six A.M. until midnight. She was the first person the star saw each morning and the last to bid her farewell at night. With the exception of the script girl, whose responsibility to the director kept her occupied all day long, a hairdresser was often the only female crew member, as well as the only one expected to serve the star exclusively. And in an industry which rated actresses by appearance, a skillful hairdresser was indispensable to a female star. This was especially true for Clara, whose hair was her most famous attribute. Daisy not only knew that the most celebrated redhead in America was actually auburn, but how to rectify it. The "secret recipe" she concocted for Clara was little more than a basic bleach-plus-henna procedure, but when Daisy applied it, the results were as spectacular in life as they appeared on film. Meeting Clara for the first time, Adela Rogers St. Johns had been struck by how "obviously but brilliantly and effectively" colored her incendiary orange-red hair was. This was Daisy's work, and in the days before artificial dyes, it was no small achievement. Even twenty years later, brunette actress Rita Hayworth was subjected to an elaborate dyeing process whose results, though photographically perfect, made her red hair look pink in reality.

Daily shampoos, rinsing, drying, and styling followed by eighteen hours on a soundstage, provided ample time for Clara to confide in Daisy. She was bitter about the $56,000 price tag of Elizabeth Pearson's divorce suit. She hated talkies and vowed to retire as soon as her contract expired. She resented her cousin Billy Bow, her business manager Bogart Rogers, and her new Hungarian cook and maid for abusing her generosity. Even Robert Bow, whom Clara had supported without complaint since age sixteen, was becoming intolerable. The last distraction she needed on the set was a father propositioning extra-girls and mooching cigars from executives.

Finally Daisy had heard enough. "You don't have to live like this," she told Clara. "If you don't like it, why the hell don't you *do* something about it?"

Clara shook her head sorrowfully. "I can't. I just can't." She had asked Robert to find a job. "I'm your father," he had retorted. "You *owe* me." Clara believed him.

"Get yourself someone with a strong will," advised Daisy. "Someone to run your affairs and be there for you when you need it." Clara sighed and said she would try.

Shortly thereafter, Daisy was summoned to Ben Schulberg's office. "Bow needs somebody to go in and clean out that mare's nest she lives in," he said bluntly. "Interested?"

Daisy was. "She needed somebody with a strong will to give her a 'thumbs-down' on anything she shouldn't do," she explains. "Well, that was me all over." In return she requested a raise from her seventy-dollar-a-week salary. Schulberg said that since Daisy was no longer a Paramount employee, her wages would be paid by Clara.

With that Daisy was promoted from studio hairdresser to personal secretary. Clara was not present.

As Daisy turned to leave, Schulberg's voice stopped her. "By the way," he added casually, "I might need you to do some reporting for me from your new job."

"You mean *spying?*" snapped Daisy.

"Just tell me what goes on inside there," Schulberg persisted. "For the studio's sake."

"No dice," said Daisy. "I don't work for the studio anymore, remember?"

Schulberg made no reply, but Daisy "knew I was on the list. I had talked back to 'the mighty B. P. Schulberg'—the louse."

Both she and Clara would regret it.

# 20

Daisy discovered that Clara had not exaggerated her wretched state of affairs. Here was a $5,000-a-week star leading a $100-a-week life, and an unseemly one at that. Even Clara's closetful of slacks, sweaters, and tam-o'-shanters looked shabby.

Her home was a shambles. Its floors were filthy, unwashed by a maid who wore high heels to work. Its beams were so termite-infested that they shifted whenever anyone walked beneath them. Finally one fell from the living-room ceiling and almost killed Clara.

Assuming an inspection of the house had been made when Clara bought it, Daisy checked business manager Bogart Rogers's records. To her astonishment, they revealed that not only was 512 Bedford Drive still mortgaged, but Clara was so far behind in her payments that she faced foreclosure on a property she could have owned outright with just three weeks' salary.

Daisy was outraged. "There's no reason you should lose your house with the money you're making!" she lectured Clara. "No reason except Bogart Rogers isn't paying the bills." Excluding the $56,000 paid to Paramount and Elizabeth Pearson, Daisy calculated that Clara had earned roughly $200,000 in two years. She spent nothing on herself, owned no valuable jewelry or clothing, and traveled only to New York at her studio's expense. Yet when Daisy was hired, Clara's bank account balance was $16,000. Who had squandered her savings?

It was, of course, a rhetorical question. "They were all bleeding her dry," says Daisy. "Her father, her cousin, her business manager, and her two servants." Daisy struck back by firing Bogart Rogers, evicting Billy Bow, and cutting off Robert's access to Clara's account. Informed of this, he demanded to see his daughter.

Daisy didn't mince words. "I don't like you any more than you like me," she warned him, "so stay away from here, or we're gonna tangle."

"How dare you?" sputtered Robert.

"You bother her and I'll punch your lights out," snarled Daisy. "Now scram."

Robert did, taking an apartment of his own and returning to his former residence only when Daisy was not there. Ever dutiful, Clara continued to support him.

Her father was not the only one who resented Daisy's influence. "Daisy DeVoe was a pain in the ass as far as I was concerned," says Teet Carle. As Clara's publicist, Carle was accustomed to dealing with "the most cooperative star in the world. *Anybody* could get to Clara." Daisy put an end to such easy access. "She figured Clara needed a strong-armed dame to take charge," Carle recalls, "so she appointed herself to decide whether Clara would do this or that. She kept people away from Clara, and Clara didn't know anything about it."

What she did know was that her home was finally a haven. Gone were its freeloading relatives, corrupt employees, and unpaid mortgage. Its rooms were exterminated and its beams replaced. Her maid wore flat shoes to scrub floors. Her wardrobe included fashionable gowns which befit a star.

Not every change was welcomed. Clara refused to banish her bootlegger, though Daisy did so anyway. She balked at an enforced diet, even though she had gained weight since *The Wild Party*. She felt guilty about ending her open-house parties and sorry for the strangers Daisy turned away at the door. Then she felt guilty for feeling guilty.

Blaming her nervousness and chronic insomnia on the pressure of talkie production, Clara vowed to quit movies once her contract expired. "If you're planning to retire, you'd better save your money," Daisy told her.

Clara sighed miserably and said she didn't know how. "I know what a hundred dollars is," she reflected. "That usedta be a dream t'me, t' have a hundred dollars. I still get a bigger kick outta a hundred smackers than my whole salary."

Daisy decided that if Clara could not save her money, then she would save it for her. With this objective in mind she contacted California Trust Company official Benjamin Odell, who convinced Clara to establish a trust fund of her own. She was wary, but Odell promised that Paramount would have no control over Trust PR-875, which was opened in May of 1929 with her $16,000 bank balance. It was hardly enough to retire on, but if Clara deposited half her salary each week (and Daisy planned to make sure she did) until her contract expired, her trust would eventually exceed $250,000. Then Clara could leave films forever and never work again.

Besides the trust fund, Benjamin Odell opened a "Clara Bow Special" checking account that gave Clara and Daisy dual signing privileges. In theory, Clara could write a check for any sum she chose; in practice, Daisy kept her on an allowance. She also paid her $75-a-week salary from this "Special" account.

Saving money seemed more important than ever, for Clara's career no longer depended on her quantity of "It," but on the quality of her material. Fortunately Ernst Lubitsch, the director who had cast her in *Kiss Me Again* four years earlier, had been made production supervisor of her latest movie. When Lubitsch read the script for 1929's "Summer Bow," a pallid "It" Girl-goes-to-the-circus story called *Pink Tights,* he ordered it recast, rewritten, and reassigned to protégé Lothar Mendes, whom Lubitsch felt understood Clara's untapped potential.

He was right. Also set under the big top, *Dangerous Curves* boasted a serviceable plot, snappy dialogue, and a role for Clara modeled on herself, not her image. Beneath her wisecracking bravado, bareback rider Patricia Delaney seems wracked by sorrow, and although she's a grown and very beautiful woman, Pat is nonetheless portrayed as a lonely little girl whom the other characters call "Kid." It was a radical departure from Clara's usual roles, and though "It" is not in evidence in *Dangerous Curves,* a more subdued and haunting quality is.

Sixty years later, the progress from *The Wild Party* to *Dangerous Curves* appears so vast that it is difficult to believe the two movies were shot within a month of each other. Clara's first talkie remains a primitive production with lethargic pacing and stilted dialogue, while her second is visually inventive, briskly paced, and loaded with appropriate, atmospheric lingo. "Those two bimbos ain't so dusty," observes one small-town sheik of Pat and a fellow bareback rider. "Get back in line, ya overgrown, half-baked, sawed-off igno-ramus," snaps Pat in a single breath when a rival rider hogs the spotlight.

Lines like these would sound strange *without* a streetwise ac-cent, and *Dangerous Curves* allows Clara's to work to her advantage. By contrast, the vocal impediment of cast member Kay Francis ("wavishing Kay Fwancis," a critic once called her) wreaks comic havoc on her love scenes. Clara suffers no such hindrance. When Pat Delaney serves "cawfee" to the "meeahn" she adores, Clara is pronouncing her words as her character would. Freed from the pressure of perfect diction, her performance is charming, moving, and unmannered.

There were still serious problems. The mike overhead loomed like an enemy, and in take after take Clara would involuntarily stare at it in terror. She had always prided herself on her professional-ism, so when her mike fright delayed *Dangerous Curves'* production, her confidence was undermined to the point where, during the shooting of one especially talky scene, Clara could endure no more. Frustrated and ashamed of her mistakes, she swore violently at the mike, then burst into tears and sank to the ground, sobbing and whimpering. Lothar Mendes summoned Lubitsch, who rushed to the set, calmed Clara, and ordered witnesses to keep silent. Though word of the incident never reached the press, details spread throughout the studio and fueled rumors that Clara could not cope with sound technology.

Ironically, reviews of *Dangerous Curves* hailed her bright future in talkies. "New chapter in the Clara Bow career promises well," reported *Variety*. "Fans had begun to tire of this star in the flaming sex appeal role, but renewed interest greets this experiment of casting her in a sympathetic role of sentimental force." Once again, Ernst Lubitsch had come to Clara's rescue, this time by giving her the chance to show how well-suited her voice and accent were to a truer-to-life character than "the 'It' Girl" of her formula films.

Having encouraged Lubitsch to change Clara's image, Paramount now proceeded to thwart his effort. That year the studio released sixty-one movies, more than one a week. *Dangerous Curves* disappeared in the glut. Good reviews and great grosses (Clara's second talkie played to sellout crowds) did not matter; before favorable word-of-mouth could travel, Paramount had yanked *Dangerous Curves* from distribution.

Though accustomed to professional exploitation, Clara had always avoided its infringement upon her private affairs. All her lovers had been honorable. All her lovers valued privacy.

Not Harry Richman.

"Don Juan himself never had more girls," declares Harry Richman in his memoirs, modestly titled *A Hell of a Life.* "Without bragging, I can say I had every single one I went after. Every well-known whore in the country was my friend." Apparently Richman got what he paid for, though the distinction between girls and whores seems to have escaped him.

So does humility. A preferred Richman pastime was to visit a neighborhood diner, order coffee and doughnuts, and watch his overworked waitress's expression when he paid his ten-cent tab with a thousand-dollar bill. Dismissing Al Jolson as a jealous rival, Richman crowned himself "King of Broadway" after a real royal, the King of England, arranged for a private command performance. "May God bless and keep you," said Richman to the Queen with characteristic, cock-o'-the-walk bluster. "I wish I could afford to!"

He was born Harry Reichman in Cincinnati, Ohio, in 1895, the son of immigrant Jews. At age ten he played piano in local saloons, at fifteen he left home to tour in vaudeville, and at twenty he served as accompanist to Mae West ("Jesus, what a woman! What a woman!"). By 1920, Harry Reichman had gone solo as Harry Richman, refining his song-and-swagger act to a trademark tux, high silk hat, and cane. With his powerful build, perpetual suntan, brilliantined hair, blue eyes, and lusty baritone, Richman possessed an undeniably commanding stage presence. The fact that he lisped made no difference; his brassy, somewhat vulgar style typified the twenties entertainer. He introduced "I Can't Give You Anything but Love" and "When the Red, Red Robin Comes Bob, Bob, Bobbin' Along," among others. "On the Sunny Side of the Street" was composed especially for him. Irving Berlin loved his version of "Blue Skies" so much that he wrote "Puttin' on the Ritz" for Richman. It became his theme song.

In 1924 Richman opened the Club Richman at 157 West Fifty-sixth Street, just around the corner from Carnegie Hall. With its namesake as host and star, the Club Richman achieved instant renown. Its six-dollar cover charge was not prohibitive, yet entry was restricted almost entirely to the royal, rich, celebrated, and criminal. Representing the latter category, Al Capone arrived from Chicago in a custom-made, bullet-proof Rolls-Royce with thirty-two bodyguards in tow. The gangster enjoyed Richman's performance so much that he guaranteed his safety for life.

But becoming the toast of Manhattan did not content Harry Richman. He wanted national recognition, and since the fame he sought came only to movie stars, he decided to become one, accepting a $75,000 offer for one film (quadruple what Clara was paid for hers) from producer Joseph M. Schenck. Richman wanted his movie debut to do for him what *The Jazz Singer* had for Jolson, so a barely fictitious story of songplugger-turned-star "Harry Raymond" was devised. Lest audiences fail to make the connection, the movie would be called *Puttin' on the Ritz*, and Richman would perform his theme song in it.

His arrival in Hollywood, where he was just another Broadway star trying to break into talkies, was a painful reminder of how unknown Richman was outside Manhattan. Schenck recommended a publicity stunt. "Nothing sells pictures like a big romance between the stars," he explained. Richman immediately asked who the biggest female star in America was. Schenck seemed amazed at his ignorance. "Clara Bow, of course."

"I had to hold on to myself to keep from fainting," Richman remembers with typical reserve. "Clara Bow. Every time I'd seen her on the screen, I'd thought, 'Oh, boy, if I could just spend a night with that . . .' It never occurred to me that she might be mine."

Now that it had, the two men wasted no time. Schenck called Schulberg, who gave him Clara's unlisted phone number. Then he called Clara. Aware that she received few invitations, he disregarded decorum and invited her to dinner that night. A few hours later, the doorbell rang. Richman beat the butler to it.

He was not disappointed. "There stood Clara Bow, one of the most luscious, sexiest women I ever saw in my life. Off screen she was even more beautiful. 'Ripe' was the only word for that figure of hers." Richman introduced himself formally. His guest was not impressed. "The name's Clara," she told him, "not 'Miss Bow.' An' you can be sure we're gonna get along." Taken aback by her forthright, unpretentious manner, Richman dropped his guard and entertained her with bawdy stories and songs. She rewarded him with a goodnight kiss. He forgot about publicity and fell in love.

So runs Richman's version, though those who witnessed the subsequent, relentlessly publicized romance refute it. "A ham who exploited her," sneered Louise Brooks of Richman. "A scum-bum," agrees Daisy DeVoe. "He used Clara for her fame." The most damning revelations come from Richman himself. "Every place we [went], every eye was focused upon us," he crows in *A Hell of a Life*. "She was the biggest star in the country. And I was out with her."

To his delight, Clara's celebrity was contagious. "Because I was seen with her everywhere, people began to recognize me. " 'Richman!' " they would shout at premieres. The newspapers would print photographs of us on the front pages; if one of us went out without the other, the reporters would make an issue of it. I began to feel like a star myself. Someone was always wanting me to attend something, or to introduce someone, or to show up for some occasion because they knew I would bring Clara." That he lists these perks with such pleasure indicates his view of the relationship.

Had she felt more secure when she met Richman, Clara would have pegged him for a publicity-monger and shunned him as such. But at the time she craved attention as much as he did. Secrecy and a narrowly averted scandal with Earl Pearson, followed by the professional trauma of talkies, made a public romance appealing to her. The massive coverage her unofficial engagement to Richman received in mid-1929 reassured Clara that, despite studio gossip, she was still the most famous star in movies. She needed the confidence and did not resent Richman for inadvertently providing it. Likewise, she did not begrudge him the $5,000 he earned for one week's work at a local theater even though it was *her* appearance at curtain calls which drew crowds. Richman alone meant little. Richman with Clara broke the theater's house record. Her morale needed the boost.

If her indiscreet lover is to be believed, the relationship's firmest basis was physical. "One of the greatest things about Clara was that she had an appetite for lovemaking that was at least the equal of mine," marvels Richman. "Every time I was ready, she was; and believe me, there was hardly an hour when I was not ready. The instant I saw her I was ready, and twenty minutes later I would be ready again." Each night, the couple rushed back to Bedford Drive from their respective studios and ate a hurried dinner. Then Richman spent the night "with that rich, delicious body in my arms." A bearskin rug he purchased "for the obvious purpose" was a favorite trysting place, and often a huge Great Dane he gave Clara would curl up beside them. She gave Richman a photograph of herself and her new pet. MY DEAREST, wrote Clara in her childish scrawl, THE BEAUTIFUL THING ON THE RIGHT IS OUR FIRSTBORN SON AND I CALLED HIM DUKE. AREN'T YOU PROUD? She signed it TOOTS, Richman's nickname for her.

Richman bought Clara a baby grand piano so he could serenade her in private, then publicly dedicated his latest hit, "You Can't Stop Me from Falling in Love with You," to her. "The very moment I laid eyes on you / I knew that I had met my Waterloo," its first verse began. Clara thanked him with another autographed photo: TO MY NAPOLEON, FROM HIS WATERLOO—AND HOW!

A third inscription required no explanation: TO MY GORGEOUS LOVER HARRY, gushed Clara. I'LL TRADE ALL MY "IT" FOR YOUR "THAT." YOUR LITTLE TOOTS.

The public devoured such items, and the press reported them faithfully. Never before had a movie star conducted so brazen an affair, and although Clara did not realize it, a double standard was set: the more notorious her relationship with Richman appeared, the more necessary a legal union between them became. After Roland, Fleming, Cooper, and now Richman, even Clara's most devoted fans felt "engagement" a lame euphemism for her liaisons. "Clara's engagements are about as frequent and enduring as the average girl's headaches," fumed one newspaper editorial. Her reputation was tarnished further when Richman departed for New York and she followed, and instead of observing proprieties and at least registering at a hotel, she stayed at his Beechhurst, Long Island, mansion. The fact that Daisy accompanied her fooled no one. Clara was living with her lover.

Back on his home turf, Richman paraded Clara around like a prized trophy. He wanted her to play hostess at the Club Richman, but like the heroine in *It*, she insisted they "do it up right" at Coney Island. What Clara wanted, Richman granted, so along with Daisy and boxer Max Rosenbloom (known as "Slapsy Maxie" for his sloppy fighting style), the couple rode the Ferris wheel and ate at Nathan's, the hot dog stand where Clara had sliced buns a decade earlier. Since Coney Island in midsummer attracted a million people a day, her presence caused pandemonium.

A photograph taken that night shows them pressed against a protective wooden barricade as fans swarm behind them. Richman preens, a proprietary arm around Clara. As always, she dominates the image, but not for the usual, photogenic reason. Here her face is puffy, her eyes are glazed, and her red hair runs amok in uncontrolled curls. One hand cups her chin; a half-smoked cigarette dangles from the other. She looks fat, tired, and far too worn for a twenty-three-year-old. Richman was ten years older than Clara. In this photograph they seem the same age.

That summer of 1929, Clara felt older and more at odds with her image than ever. The latest portrait she had given to Richman showed her in a somber pose, and its inscription was more wishful than true: TO MY SWEET DARLING HARRY, she wrote, JUST YOUR GROWN-UP CLARA AND I KNOW YOU UNDERSTAND THIS ME AS FEW OTHERS HAVE EVER DONE. THIS IS *ME*—THE *REAL* ME—BELIEVE IT OR

NOT. It was the closest Clara could come to acknowledging this private, tormented side of herself. Richman paid no attention.

Even worse was an incident he was not aware of. One day during their trip to New York, Clara and Daisy decided to shop for a fall wardrobe at several department stores. Inside their taxi, Clara suddenly asked Daisy if she would mind taking a side trip to Brooklyn. Daisy said she would not mind at all.

Clara gave the driver an address, and eventually the taxi halted before an imposing building. "Leave the meter runnin'," ordered Clara. Evidently she did not intend to stay long.

Daisy studied the unmarked building, which obviously was not residential. "Where are we?" she asked.

Clara hesitated. "Nuthouse," she said finally. Then she linked arms with Daisy and approached it.

Inside, an elderly woman without a uniform greeted them. Clara identified herself. The woman left her and Daisy standing in the hallway. They did not enter further; nor did they remove their coats.

Minutes later, two thin and frail women were brought into the hallway. Clara greeted them gently. They looked at each other in bafflement. It was clear that they had no idea who their visitor was.

After some awkward chatter by Clara, the two women were taken away. Neither had uttered a single word.

Back in the taxi, Clara was unnaturally quiet. "Guess that was a waste of time," she murmured finally. "They didn't even know me."

"*Who* didn't?" asked Daisy. She still had no idea who they had just visited.

Again Clara hesitated. "My mama's sisters. My aunts." She sighed. "I been payin' for 'em to stay in that place and they don't even know me no more."

"Oh, I'm sure they do," lied Daisy.

"No," said Clara, "no, they don't. But I tried." She stared out the rear window as the asylum receded in the distance. "I tried, and I ain't never goin' back."

Daisy wasn't so sure. At the time, insanity was considered as hereditary a trait as height or weight and hence was hidden in shame and fear. Clara rarely discussed her mother with Daisy, but when she did, all she would say was how "crazy" Sarah Bow had been. Now Daisy had seen Sarah's two insane sisters.

*My God,* she thought as she watched Clara stare out the window. *She's going to wind up in there with 'em.*

# 21

*"The Saturday Night Kid* had been kicking around Paramount for a couple of years as a perfect title for Clara Bow," remembers Joseph L. Mankiewicz. "By 1929, it had been sold to exhibitors as a coming attraction for her." Ben Schulberg ordered Mankiewicz, a neophyte writer without credentials or credits, to concoct a vehicle for Clara based on the presold title. Mankiewicz devised six different stories. Schulberg rejected them all. That he had assigned a novice to "Fall Bow" in the first place indicates his cavalier attitude toward Clara's career.

Instead of rectifying the error by replacing Mankiewicz with an experienced writer, Schulberg simply lifted the plot of *Love 'Em and Leave 'Em,* a 1926 Paramount silent. *Variety* was stunned: "Selecting a moderately good program silent release to be remade with dialogue is a hazardous venture," it warned. Undaunted, Schulberg added personal insult to professional injury by assigning Edward Sutherland to direct *The Saturday Night Kid.* Two years earlier Sutherland had ignored the pleas of wife Louise Brooks and refused to invite Clara to their parties.

It was not an auspicious start, and it soon grew worse. Clara read *The Saturday Night Kid* script, liked it, and then learned that the part she had assumed was hers, a sexy shopgirl who steals her sister's money and man, actually belonged to second-lead Jean Arthur. Evidently Schulberg was willing to cast her in uninteresting roles, but not unsympathetic ones, with the result that "Arthur was so good that we had to cut and cut and cut to keep her from stealing the picture," said Sutherland. "Not that she was better than Bow, but the *part* was better." A typical "star turn" would have called for Clara to terrorize her competitor. Instead she encouraged Arthur to make the most of her role.

Devastated by Roy Pomeroy's recent pronouncement that her foghorn voice would prove fatal to her talkie career, Arthur was forever grateful for Clara's support. "I loved her," she declares in the voice that would soon be considered her best attribute. "She was so generous, no snootiness or anything. She was wonderful to me."

Next to the petite Arthur, the 132-pound Clara looked heavier than ever, and her weight problem seemed even more apparent when a curvaceous ash-blonde appeared one day on *The Saturday Night Kid* set. "The closer she came, the more interesting she became," explains assistant director Artie Jacobson, "because she was wearing this black-crocheted dress with *not a stitch* on under it. From where I sat, you couldn't tell whether she had put it on or *painted* it on." It was visibly apparent that the voluptuous stranger was a natural blonde.

While the crew ogled the visitor, Clara summoned Jacobson to her dressing room. "Who the hell is *that?*" she asked him.

Jacobson checked a casting office memo a messenger had just handed him. "Don't know," he told her. "Says here her name's Jean Harlow."

"Well, what's she doin' here?" demanded Clara. Jacobson assumed that Harlow, like Clara's cousin Billy Bow, had been given a minor role in the movie.

"Oh yeah?" snapped Clara. "Well, you tell 'em t'take her off this goddamn set and never bring her back. I don't want her in the picture."

"Why not?" wondered Jacobson disingenuously. "She's a no-body."

"Are you kiddin'? If she dresses like that for an interview, how's she gonna dress in a *scene?* Who's gonna see *me* nexta *her?*"

Jacobson called the casting office and told them to take Jean Harlow off *The Saturday Night Kid.* To his astonishment, the request was refused. Harlow had a "friend" in the front office with even more clout than Clara, and although Jacobson never discovered who her patron was, few besides Ben Schulberg could overrule the studio's most important actress.

Within days it didn't matter, for Clara's jealousy of Harlow turned to sponsorship. "She was simply fascinated by her," says costume designer Edith Head. When Head designed a bias-cut dress which Clara was too fat to wear, she not only approved it for Harlow, but asked Teet Carle to have pictures taken of them together. "See if ya can help her out," Clara urged Carle. "She's a good kid." Carle reminded her that stars never posed with bit players. Clara laughed. "She's gonna go places," she assured him. "You'll see." Reluctantly Carle arranged a photo session.

A picture of Clara with anyone was guaranteed to run in thousands of newspapers. It was Harlow's biggest break yet.

Clara's reversion to type in *The Saturday Night Kid* was a dangerous setback from *Dangerous Curves*. She needed another role like Pat Delaney to expand her range; Paramount devised "Fall Bow" from a catchy title already promised to exhibitors. Ironically, a formula film that allowed Clara little opportunity to act was accepted as confirmation that she could speak. "The shopgirl lingo rolls off her tongue perfectly," reported *Variety* of *The Saturday Night Kid*, "with plenty of 'ain'ts' and that inevitable bedtime undress peep." Most critics paid more attention to Clara's girth than her performance. Their verdict: The "It" Girl had more "It" than ever, especially around her midsection.

Not surprisingly, Clara hated both *The Saturday Night Kid* and Edward Sutherland. "A horrible picture," she wrote of the movie. "A lousy no-good bastard," she said of its director.

She felt likewise about her fiancé. At first Harry Richman's shameless publicity-seeking had been a welcome diversion from the press-shy lovers of her past, but his King of Broadway–sized ego was unbearable. One morning in Malibu, Richman boasted incessantly to Clara, Artie Jacobson, and Jacobson's girlfriend Gloria of an omelette created by him for the Club Richman to cure hangovers, then cooked it for Clara with obnoxious fanfare. She shot him an exasperated glance, tasted the omelette, and put her fork back on her plate. "This is from the Club Richman?" she asked in wide-eyed wonderment. Richman nodded, beaming proudly. Clara's eyes narrowed. "Well, send it back!" she snarled, scooping up the omelette and hurling it into Richman's face.

"She reverted right back to her macaroni days," laughs Jacobson in reference to the food fights he refereed at the house on

Hollywood Boulevard. "But Richman was so crazy about Clara that he didn't even get mad."

Instead he bought her a $2,000 bracelet. He also took her to Agua Caliente, a chic casino just over the Mexican border. Clara loved to gamble, as an ad-libbed moment in *The Saturday Night Kid* makes clear. In the movie, her tenement landlord challenges her to craps. Instantly she sinks to her knees, palms the dice, and caresses them excitedly. "Rabbit dice, multiply!" she exhorts. "Do it for the starvin' Armenians!" Rolling well, she rocks up and down in childish delight. "Oh mama, I'm hot!" she squeals. "Fever, fever down in Georgia!" Whether on film or in Caliente, Clara's zeal to gamble is apparent, and soon she and Richman were regulars at the casino. When work kept him in Hollywood one weekend, he urged her to go without him. She did, met a handsome Mexican croupier, and disappeared for three days. Richman finally traced the two to Malibu and drove there, parking down the road and sneaking up to her cottage. He could hear Clara and her guest inside. "Heartsick, as low as I've ever been at any point in my life," he returned home and drank himself to sleep. The next day he bought Clara a platinum-covered clock and an antique table on which to display it.

It was too late. Clara began begging off their nightly bouts on the bearskin rug, saying she should rest before her early call in the morning. Richman had never known her to either need or want sleep, so the next time she gave this excuse, he nodded, departed, parked his car down the street, and waited. Sure enough, Clara emerged fifteen minutes later, wearing a red beret to match her red roadster. Instead of pursuing her, Richman "went with a whore, because going with a paid lay was getting back at Clara."

The following night Richman trailed Clara to her destination: Gary Cooper's house. She was inside so long that he finally abandoned his stakeout.

On the third night, Richman confronted Clara. She denied everything. He told her he had followed her. "Cheap sonofabitch, followin' me," she said disgustedly.

"Why did you cheat on me, Toots?" whined Richman. "I thought we loved each other."

"So what?" shrugged Clara. "Nobody's gonna own me."

Richman had backed himself into a corner. "She told me that she was going to behave exactly as she pleased, and I could take my choice. It was on her terms or nothing." His response: a $5,000 engagement ring, the first Clara had received from a fiancé. When she accepted it, he called a press conference to record its presentation. The couple's "official" (and, in the opinion of many, long overdue) engagement made headlines, and headlines made Harry Richman jubilant. "Now I knew Clara was going to be mine," he exulted.

She was more concerned with her career. Following the latest fad for Broadway-style revues, each studio was featuring its entire roster in a plotless movie filled with skits and songs. At first Paramount resisted the trend, but enormous public response led Schulberg to line up the most spectacular array of talent yet. Every star at the studio would appear in *Paramount on Parade,* and every major director would work on it. Naturally Clara would have a sequence of her own. For some inexplicable reason, Schulberg decided she would sing in it.

Clara couldn't believe it. To talk on screen had been traumatic enough; to *sing* seemed inconceivable. How could she possibly compete with internationally acclaimed *chanteur* Maurice Chevalier or "boop-boop-a-doop" Broadway sensation Helen Kane? She had neither training nor experience; Chevalier, Kane, and other musical performers in *Paramount on Parade* had years of both. If Schulberg wanted her to sing, why hadn't he ever arranged for her to take lessons? Why didn't he do so now? Whether from deliberate sabotage or rank incompetence, Clara faced yet another fearsome professional ordeal.

*Paramount on Parade* was the first film scheduled for production on the studio's brand-new "soundstage," a huge facility in which four talkies could shoot simultaneously. None had the chance, for days after the stage had been built, alarmed cries of *"Fire!"* swept through the studio. The chaos roused Clara from her dressing room, and as she stood on its steps watching the blaze, Ernst Lubitsch rushed past her. "I hope t'Christ it's the soundstage," he heard Clara mutter.

It was. Before it had been used even once, the new soundstage had burned to the ground, leaving Paramount in a potentially disastrous position: its films were talkies and its stages were not soundproof. Since the studio released a new movie a week to its six hundred theaters, it could not sustain the slightest delay in production. Without a soundstage, production was put in a stranglehold.

It was a desperate situation, and Ben Schulberg made a swift decision: while the soundstage was rebuilt by day, talkies would shoot at night. Production on the old stages now began at six P.M. instead of six A.M., and makeshift soundproofing was achieved when studio seamstresses sewed huge canvas blankets together and technicians hung them along the walls and ceiling. Combined with the white-hot lights, the insulation from these blankets made the stages more sweltering than ever, but there was no alternative. No talkies meant no work.

The soundstage fire postponed the shooting of Clara's song, so Paramount sent her to San Francisco to promote *The Saturday Night Kid,* which opened on Friday, October 25, 1929, the day after "Black Thursday" devastated Wall Street. Now considered a catastrophe of instantaneous impact, the crash actually affected few outside New York's financial district for another year, and since there was no precedent for the Depression that followed, there was no expectation of it. And because Clara's money was held in trust, not invested in stocks, she paid no attention to the crash.

Indeed, her condition that fall seemed more fragile than the economy's. Talkies had shattered her professional security. Harry Richman had exploited her in an emotionally unfulfilling relationship. Chronic insomnia had robbed her of rest. Without Daisy, Clara would have broken down completely; as it was, she almost did anyway. After interviewing 1929's most popular movie star, *Photoplay* reporter Lois Shirley wrote a pitiless but honest piece portraying Clara as the pathetic wreck she was. Instead of profiling her subject in purplish fanzine prose, Shirley reprinted Clara's frantic rambling verbatim. "I always wanna cry," she said, running her fingers through her hair. "I could cry any minute. Had no childhood. Worked like a dog all my life. Get up in the mornin'—go t'work. Work, work, work. Go home at night. Can't sleep. Think too much. Think about everythin'. Mind goes on and on and on. Think 'bout my life, 'bout the new picture, 'bout my lines.

"Really, my nerves is shot," added Clara as if it weren't obvious. "My contract has two years t'go. Maybe after that I might have enough dough t'go away and stay away."

Shirley noticed several bottles of sedatives beside the bed. Clara claimed none of them helped, then admitted how much ostracism and ridicule in Hollywood hurt her. "Everybody yells at me t'be dignified, but what're dignified people? Snobs!

"I'm a curiosity in Hollywood," concluded Clara. "I'm a big freak because I'm myself."

Her listener was stunned. "The most famous woman in pictures," she realized, "is a pitiful, tired child who has called to life and heard only her own echo."

The "pitiful child" was suffering from serious medical problems. In November, 1929, Dr. Wesley Hommel urged Clara to undergo the same operation she had originally opposed and still dreaded. She would lose at least one ovary. If both were removed, she would never bear children.

Desperate for secrecy, Clara informed only one man of her impending castration. GRIEF STRICKEN BY MESSAGE, Earl Pearson cabled in reply from an ocean liner bound from Europe. REST, SWEET DARLING. HAVE NURSE KEEP ME INFORMED.

To protect her privacy, Dr. Hommel told Paramount that Clara had suffered an emotional collapse that would necessitate a month's hospitalization. Since her contract entitled her to eight weeks' paid sick leave anyway, Paramount had no choice but to cancel "Winter Bow" and plan how to use her breakdown to its benefit. "Believe we should take every advantage afforded us in our contractural relations with her, allowing us to add the time she is confined in the hospital to her contract, so that we do not lose all of the money we pay her while she is ill," ran a dispassionate executive memo. Clara's condition did not merit comment.

While she awaited surgery, the studio fed the press a lame account of postappendectomy "adhesions" which required excision. Meanwhile Dr. Hommel sent his patient to Sylvan Lodge Hospital, a secluded four-room duplex for private patients and their personal physicians. Clara was so frightened that she rented an adjoining room for Daisy, but was still too ashamed to tell her best friend the truth. Instead she said she was having a hysterectomy.

A breakdown, adhesions, or a hysterectomy? Gossips weighed all three falsehoods, then dismissed them in favor of a fourth. Daisy heard about it when she mentioned to a studio hairdresser that Clara was in Sylvan Lodge and the woman smirked knowingly. Sylvan Lodge, she told Daisy, was a favorite spot for stars to terminate unwanted pregnancies. Apparently everyone except Daisy knew that Clara had battled with Harry Richman, broken their engagement, and aborted his child.

Daisy doubted it. Clara's menstrual troubles made the possibility of pregnancy unlikely; what's more, a woman spent two to three days, not four weeks, recuperating from such a procedure. Since pregnancies stalled careers, Hollywood actresses routinely received abortions from licensed physicians, whose well-appointed offices and flourishing practices were a far cry from the back-alley butchers encountered elsewhere. Finally, in an only-in-Hollywood irony, the husband of gossip columnist Louella Parsons was both the unofficial house doctor at Madame Frances's bordello and the movie industry's most popular "clap doctor."

A different irony existed in Clara's case, one which explains but does not excuse why the alleged father of her purported, aborted child did not discourage rumors he knew were not only inaccurate, but impossible. For Harry Richman had a secret of his own: he was sterile. The King of Broadway shot blanks, and since his royal ego would not allow him to admit it, he chose to tarnish Clara's reputation instead.

On November 20, 1929, Dr. Hommel operated on Clara. Only one ovary was removed. She could still bear children (though not by Richman) and nurture her dream of retirement, marriage, and motherhood once her contract expired.

After a year of professional upheaval, emotional distress, and physical trauma, 1929 ended with Clara overcoming all three. First, she was discharged from Sylvan Lodge in mid-December fully recovered and thirty-two pounds lighter. Then an exhibitors' poll named her the top box-office draw for the second year in a row, a citation which confirmed her success in talkies. It was a boost her flagging confidence needed.

Clara spent the days between her discharge and Christmas preparing for her favorite holiday of the year. Already her Yuletide generosity was legendary: from producers to prop boys, everybody on the Paramount lot got a Christmas gift from Clara. Solid-silver flasks, leatherette cigarette cases, and bejewelled trinkets were specially ordered for each recipient, then engraved with a personal inscription. Clara expected nothing in return. "That was the way she liked to spend her money," says Teet Carle. "On everyone but herself." Since Clara's taste tended toward the garish, Daisy chose each item for her.

From New York, Harry Richman was reminding reporters that Clara had promised to marry him at some future but still unspecified date. She would not comment on either her fiancé or new lover Guinn Williams, an ex-rodeo rider nicknamed "Big Boy" for his muscular build. Involved with yet independent of both men, Clara ushered in the New Year by traveling to New York for a month's vacation.

Richman made sure her arrival lacked any semblance of privacy. Alerted in advance, the throng inside Manhattan's Grand Central Station on January 22, 1930, was so huge that one hundred redcaps linked arms to prevent it from spilling onto the tracks. At nine A.M., the Twentieth-Century Limited pulled into its track. Wearing his nattiest raccoon coat and black slouch hat, Richman ran alongside it, peering into each window eagerly. Photographers followed, and so did the crowd, knocking over redcaps and cordons alike as they converged upon a car surrounded by Pullman porters. A woman stepped from it. The crowd cheered wildly, then groaned in disappointment at the sight of Daisy DeVoe. They were still groaning when another woman emerged in a fur coat, a cloche hat, and flame-red spit curls framing her face. This was Clara Bow.

As the crowd roared, Clara hugged her rag doll, surprised and unnerved by the tumultuous reception. Instantly Richman rushed to her, encircling her waist with one arm and fending off everyone else with the other. "Why, what's all this?" he demanded indignantly, feigning surprise at the presence of reporters with whom he'd been chatting for the past hour. "What is this all about?" As he spoke, Richman posed for the cameras. Clara clung to him timidly. A photographer asked her to kiss Richman. She blushed but complied. A reporter questioned her about the couple's marriage plans. She shrugged vaguely, explaining in a hoarse whisper that she had a cold and could barely talk. Another reporter asked Daisy what the two women did during their trip.

"Oh, nothing much except play pinochle all day long," she replied.

For the next three weeks, Richman flaunted Clara all over town. She was the center of attention at the Club Richman and the Cotton Club, where she watched Cab Calloway perform and hobnobbed with Broadway comic Fannie Brice, heavyweight champion of the world Jack Dempsey, cartoonist Peter Arno, socialites Jock and Liz Whitney, and gangster Dutch Schultz. She and Richman attended twelve Broadway plays, including *Strike Up the Band,* a George Gershwin musical, and *Strictly Dishonorable,* a Preston Sturges comedy. Such lighthearted, lightweight fare was Richman's favorite. It is both characteristic and revealing that Clara preferred *The Last Mile,* a bleak prison drama starring Spencer Tracy.

At the annual New York Automobile Show, Richman's public displays of affection reached their ostentatious peak. Clara casually admired a custom-made, aquamarine Isotta-Franschini with eighteen-carat-gold fixtures. Cost: $18,000. Richman wrote a check on the spot. She drove straight to Sheepshead Bay, her old Brooklyn neighborhood and the one where cousin Billy Bow's family still lived. Apparently Clara was too embarrassed by Richman to bring him along.

He would have reveled in the community's reaction. As word of her presence spread through Sheepshead Bay, adults and children alike climbed trees outside William Bow's home to catch a glimpse of Clara. Soon the crowds were so large that a police convoy was formed to escort her back to Manhattan. En route, she insisted on stopping at the station to personally thank the officers for their aid.

Ultimately Harry Richman's public campaign to win Clara backfired. Scrutiny of the couple, whose marriage plans were the subject of daily tabloid speculation, grew so intense that she finally called a press conference in her hotel suite. There Clara issued a rather bizarre statement: she would not marry Richman, she told reporters, because she was expecting a nervous breakdown and had to return to Hollywood to experience it "in the proper surroundings."

Actually, what awaited her in Hollywood was her latest professional challenge, and to everyone's surprise, Clara turned it into a triumph. "True to the Navy," her song in *Paramount on Parade,* was not memorable, and neither was her singing, which wavered between a sexy contralto on low notes and a shrill soprano on high ones. "I sorta half-sing, half-talk, with hips-'n'-eye stuff," Clara told an interviewer candidly. "I don't like it, but the studio thinks my voice is great." So did audiences, who cheered louder for "True to the Navy" than any of the twenty other numbers in *Paramount on Parade* except Maurice Chevalier's. Schulberg was so delighted by the response that he ordered the song expanded into a story. To make sure moviegoers associated "Spring Bow" with her song in *Paramount on Parade,* the film was given the same title: *True to the Navy.*

For a woman facing castration and collapse just three months earlier, it was a remarkable recovery, and although Clara did not know it, the best was yet to come. She was about to meet the man of her dreams.

# 22

George Beldam was born in Chicago in 1903. His father was a horse trader around the city stockyards, an area whose inhuman conditions were exposed by muckraker Upton Sinclair in his 1906 novel *The Jungle*. By that time George Beldam's father had developed a bronchial condition aggravated by the stench of freshly slaughtered livestock. Doctors recommended a warmer, cleaner climate, so he, his wife, and their two sons migrated to a small town in Southern California called Hollywood.

To a boy from the big city, it was a thrilling change. Cowboys straight out of the Zane Grey westerns he devoured were now neighbors and friends, and young George Beldam idolized them all. Molded by the myth of the Wild West hero, he spent his spare time exploring trails in the Hollywood Hills atop a mare his father had given him. During these expeditions, George Beldam would survey the vast, undeveloped San Fernando Valley and nurture his sole ambition: to have a home on the range of his own.

At Hollywood High School the aspiring rancher was a star athlete who caddied for Wallace Reid on weekends. But George Beldam was more interested in horses than movies, so he organized a charity rodeo at Hollywood High with fellow student Joel McCrea and invited local cowboys to participate. When his own mare kicked up dust and irritated his father's bronchial condition, he sold his horse, buggy, harness, saddle, blanket, and bridle to McCrea for eighty dollars. "Even then it was a terrific bargain," says McCrea today. "But that's the kind of guy George was."

All who knew him agreed: George Beldam was a model youth. Easygoing, friendly, and unfailingly polite, he was a cross between homespun cowboy and perfect gentleman. "A darling boy," sighs one girl who grew up with him. "The epitome of decency and honor," declares another. "George was like a grown-up Boy

Scout." In this case, it was said without the slightest condescension.

George Beldam read of the mythic westerner's moral code and applied it to himself. Mothers urged sons to follow his example; fathers urged daughters to attract his attention. The latter often replied that they were already trying: standing over six feet tall, with broad shoulders, dark blond hair, blue eyes, and a disarming grin, George Beldam had movie-star looks to match his Boy Scout manner. Still he expressed no interest in a movie career, preferring a steady job and steady income. The preference turned into a necessity when his father died and left George Beldam the sole provider for his mother and younger brother. At twenty-one he began driving a truck for the Blue Diamond Building Materials Company. Ranching would have to wait.

What followed seemed straight out of a fan magazine: during a delivery to the Fox studios, George Beldam was "discovered" and offered a contract. He confessed that he couldn't act. Fox responded that if George Beldam could ride, he could work as a stuntman in westerns just as Gary Cooper had. The notion of falling off horses for a living struck George Beldam as ludicrous, but he accepted the offer.

After four years of stunt work for Fox, George Beldam was cast in John Ford's *Salute*. Another stuntman, ex–U.S.C. Trojan Marion Morrison, was also in the film, and the two became close friends. Coincidentally, Morrison changed his name to John Wayne just as George Beldam's name was changed for him, a result of Fox's search for a screen cowboy to succeed Tom Mix and Buck Jones. To embody the heroic, euphonic "Rex Bell," the studio screen-tested several young and handsome cowboys, George Beldam and Joel McCrea among them. To his astonishment, George Beldam was chosen. Henceforth he would be known as Rex Bell.

The prospective star's reaction was characteristically sensible. "I'm not going to hang on forever like most of these boys do," he told reporters. "In a year or so, if things aren't beginning to line up for me, I'm going to quit and go into some sort of business outside the movie game. After all, this isn't the only life in the world, and it can make you plenty miserable if you let it." Rex Bell regarded movies as a means to his end, which was not stardom, but ranching.

When Rex met Clara, she was engaged to Harry Richman and involved with Guinn "Big Boy" Williams. Neither could stop her from taking yet a third lover, though what began as a casual affair soon became a serious relationship. "She's the first girl I was ever really in love with," Rex admitted. Clara reciprocated by dropping Big Boy Williams and putting Rex on the phone whenever Richman called from New York.

Robert Bow's hatred of Rex was typical, and as such Clara ignored it. More disturbing was the enmity between her lover and best friend, each of whom competed with the other for Clara's trust. Caught in the middle, she tried to ignore their mutual animosity and concentrate on "Spring Bow."

*True to the Navy* opens with a soda shop waitress (Clara) serving her sailor beau (Rex) a sundae. Between her 32-pound weight loss and his form-fitting sailor's suit, the two make a stunning couple, though their one scene together cannot enliven the ensuing film. "Slow in tempo, sappy in story, bearing the stamp of perfunctory production, and no help to the star," charged *Variety*. "Bow has seldom been so unimportant in a picture. Studio didn't strain themselves looking after her interests." It was an inexcusable blunder: after receiving excellent dramatic and musical reviews for *Dangerous Curves* and *Paramount on Parade,* Clara was abandoned in her most hackneyed formula film ever. Apparently Ben Schulberg still believed her name alone would entice audiences into theaters.

Therein lay the problem. Paradoxically, Paramount considered no other star as important as Clara, yet it treated no other star as carelessly. Deemed too reliable a draw to "waste" in first-rate material, she watched with understandable frustration as another Brooklyn-born, redheaded actress named Nancy Carroll won the plum roles which rightfully belonged to her. Already loathed as "the biggest bitch on the lot" (a title inherited from talkie casualty Pola Negri), Carroll was cute, but no Clara, and that was both the problem and the point—Carroll needed good material and Clara did not. Thus Carroll starred in film versions of hit Broadway shows, while Clara languished in formula films based on presold titles. Her voice had never been better, but her films had never been worse.

As her career slumped, so did her reputation. Both were addressed in *Variety*'s review of *Love Among the Millionaires,* which ended with the ominous observation that "it will call for a lot of faith from Clara Bow admirers to accept her in this sweet wishy-washy part after the bum publicity she's been getting." By the time these words about 1930's "Summer Bow" were published, such "bum publicity" had escalated from minor incident to major scandal. It began when Al Jolson wisecracked on a nationwide radio program that Clara slept "cater-cornered," an expression whose implication was apparent. Jolson was calling Clara promiscuous, and when he did, listeners laughed knowingly.

The second slur occurred in April, 1930, when a Grinnell College newspaper's gossip column reported that Clara had given birth to triplets and implied that the student columnist had fathered them. It was a sophomoric prank which did not deserve Paramount's attention, yet studio attorney Henry Herzbrun threatened Grinnell's president, the paper's editor, and the columnist with legal action unless an immediate retraction was made. "Miss Bow has not seen the [offending paragraphs] and we do not propose to call them to her attention," huffed Herzbrun, reminding them that the previous year, Paramount had adjusted Grinnell alumnus Gary Cooper's schedule so that he could return to its campus for a reunion. Surprised and distraught that a major movie studio would bully a small midwestern college, all three parties apologized profusely, admitting that it was a tasteless joke and assuring Herzbrun that no one at Grinnell questioned Clara's virtue. The point was that everyone at Paramount did, and the studio's overreaction to a bit of bad college humor is indicative of her reputation not in Iowa, but in Hollywood.

Meanwhile a St. Louis journalist named Harry Brundidge had traveled to Hollywood to profile several stars, one of the first non-Hollywood correspondents to do so. "Paramount opened its doors to him," remembers Teet Carle. "We wined and dined the guy." Since Clara was Brundidge's favorite star, Carle arranged for an extensive interview in which "Clara was most gracious. She did everything she could to help him."

Brundidge returned to St. Louis to write his articles, which were compiled in book form and distributed nationally. When Carle read it, he was horrified: Clara was portrayed as herself, chattering candidly about past fiancés with characteristic impropriety. "Gilbert Roland was the first," she began. "He's got another mama now, but I still got tender thoughts about him. Not that I want him again. Not me—I wouldn't have him on a bet.

"Then I met Victor Fleming, the director," continued Clara. "There's a man for ya. He gave me a lotta good advice, but he was too darn old for Clara—and besides, I had Gary Cooper comin' up.

"Gary was a swell boy, but jealous. I didn't wanna get married. I went everywhere and did everythin'." Before she could begin discussing Harry Richman, an overwhelmed Brundidge steered the conversation onto a general course: how did Clara hold on to her men? "If ya wanna keep one after ya catch him," she advised, "be nice t'him one day and give him plenty of hell the next." Then "the 'It' Girl" revealed her golden rule: "Never lie to a man unless ya absolutely know ya can get away with it."

After the interview, Brundidge was passing the newly rebuilt Paramount soundstage when he heard a familiar, raucous peal of laughter. Turning, he spotted Clara amidst a crowd of male extras engaged in a lively game of "Spittin' at a Crack," a popular slum pastime won by the player whose saliva hit its sidewalk target. Brundidge ended his profile of Clara by noting that she did not miss a shot.

A book which characterized Clara as coarse and loose was the last sort of publicity she needed, but at least being the defenseless butt of Jolson, Grinnell, and Brundidge's barbs brought a measure of sympathy. When she caused trouble, the results were calamitous, and this time no one could be blamed but Clara. As a shocked nation soon discovered, she was her own worst enemy.

Anatomy of a scandal:

*Sunday night, June 15, 1930.* Accompanied by Daisy, Clara arrives in Dallas, Texas, and registers at the Baker Hotel as "Daisy Hamilton." The horn-rimmed glasses she wears in disguise do not work. Within hours the local press learns of her presence.

*Monday, June 16.* The manager of a local Paramount theater pleads with Clara to make a personal appearance prior to showings of *True to the Navy.* She refuses, confessing that her fans frighten her. "When they stare at me, I get the creeps," she says. "If they would only treat me like a regular human bein', it would be all right." Finally and reluctantly, she agrees to appear later in the week.

The purpose of her visit remains unknown. Clara claims she has come "t'visit friends."

*Tuesday morning, July 17.* Clara's first visit is not to a friend. When Mrs. William Earl Pearson answers her doorbell, Clara demands to know where her $30,000 went. "Don't darken my doorstep," Elizabeth Pearson replies, then slams the door in Clara's face.

Elizabeth Pearson is six months' pregnant.

*Tuesday afternoon.* Clad in red, white, and black lounging pajamas, Clara entertains local reporters in her hotel suite. They ask what she did during her train trip. She boasts that she read two books, Evelyn Waugh's *Vile Bodies* and Dora Mack's *Ex-Mistress,* and liked the latter better. Again they wonder why she has come to Dallas. She answers vaguely that she intends to "straighten things out" with "a boyfriend" before returning to Hollywood for a talkie remake of *Hula.* "The studio thinks I'm in Hawaii," she whispers conspiratorially. "They've been tryin' t'trace me."

The reporters are charmed by Clara. One writes that she possesses "a lack of pretense too convincing to have been studied."

After they leave, Fairfax Nesbit lingers. A crafty journalist with a thick Southern drawl, Nesbit casually mentions to Clara that a certain dashing doctor has just returned to Dallas from Europe. Has she seen him?

Clara clams up. "Ain't gonna talk about him," she says firmly.

"Come clean, Clara," cajoles Nesbit. "Aren't you here to pay Earl Pearson's wife $150,000?"

The ruse works. "That *bitch!*" explodes Clara. "I already gave her thirty grand, and I ain't payin' another cent!" Her mouth working faster than her mind, Clara divulges the real reason for her trip: in October 1928, her studio-controlled trust fund was forfeited to Paramount and another $30,000 was paid to Elizabeth Pearson. Then, last week, word reached her that Elizabeth Pearson had never accepted the money. She has come to Dallas to find out where it went.

Nesbit asks Clara whether she will steal Earl Pearson from his wife a second time. "Oh, I dunno," shrugs Clara. "I'm sorta changeable, and besides, there's another boy on the Coast I like awful well. His name's Rex Bell." She sighs. "Gee, he's a swell fella!"

Nesbit has a scoop and then some. She rushes off to write it.

That evening, Clara appears at Bagdad, a swanky nightclub outside Dallas. Her escort is Earl Pearson.

*Wednesday, June 18.* Nesbit's story, CLARA BOW AIRS LOVE SUIT, hits the local front pages. Elizabeth Pearson leaves Dallas, destination unknown. Her husband remains behind. "I don't see why my name should be used in any way in connection with Miss Bow's," he tells reporters. "I am in no way connected with the case and know nothing about it."

Clara is more forthright, blaming her original breakup with Pearson on his disapproving parents. "His folks didn't know me, see?" she says, smacking her chewing gum as she speaks. "They thought I was a terrible person 'cause they saw and heard me in the movies and I said 'ain't.' They didn't really know me." Clara claims neither she nor Pearson know where his wife has gone. Rumor claims she is in seclusion in Birmingham, Alabama.

Back in Hollywood, Ben Schulberg declines to comment on Clara's trip, calling it "a personal matter." Privately he is enraged. Clara has gone to Dallas without Paramount's knowledge or permission. Had he known, he would have forbid her to go or at least would have sent Teet Carle along as protection. Instead she traveled in secret, fell prey to Fairfax Nesbit, and has now undone everything done on her behalf twenty months ago. Back then Paramount had hushed up the Pearson affair swiftly and effectively. Why hadn't Clara let the studio handle this the same way?

*Thursday, June 19.* Wire services feed Nesbit's article to newspapers across the country. Headlines label Earl Pearson's bedside manner CLARA BOW'S LOVE BALM. None mention that his wronged wife is expecting a child. The story is already juicy enough.

Advertisements for *True to the Navy* picture Clara winking invitingly. "Bring on the gobs!" reads the copy. "Bring on the A.M.A.!" runs the joke it inspires.

In Hollywood, Paramount ponders how to work the publicity to its advantage. One executive suggests changing the hero's profession in *Hula* from engineer to physician and calling the film *Oh, Doctor!* Schulberg rejects the idea, feeling that the faster the incident fades from memory, the better for Clara's career and reputation.

Otherwise, Paramount is powerless. Clara has already violated her morals clause (and forfeited her trust fund), and her contract allows no further censure unless Will Hays intervenes. At this point it is quite possible he will do so.

From New York, a humiliated Richman calls Clara. "It's the bunk, Harry," she assures him of the rumor that she has come to Dallas to pursue Pearson. Richman does not believe her and wants his $5,000 engagement ring returned. Clara convinces him to let her keep it. "Harry's so sweet t'me," she gushes after she hangs up. "I don't think I'll ever marry him, but our engagement ain't officially broken."

Rex also calls Clara to ask whether she will marry Pearson when his divorce is granted. Again Clara denies it, then tells reporters it is Rex, not Pearson or Richman, whom she is "thinkin' of marryin'."

"This terrible thing hadda come along and might blow up my romance in California," she frets. A telegram to her father indicates that she still has not assumed responsibility for her actions:

JUNE 19, 1930

DEAREST DADDY:

DON'T BE ALARMED OVER PAPER STORIES, JUST DON'T SAY ANYTHING ABOUT ANYTHING IF YOU ARE ASKED BY NEWSPAPER MEN ABOUT ANY LAWSUIT. I DON'T KNOW HOW IT LEAKED OUT ABOUT THE WHOLE AFFAIR BUT IT DID SO THAT'S THAT.

THE STUDIO IS FURIOUS WITH ME BUT I COULDN'T HELP IT. I WISH YOU WOULD TELL THEM THAT I HAD NOTHING TO DO WITH IT GETTING OUT AND THAT THE STORY WAS PRETTY WELL KNOWN IN DALLAS ANYHOW. I WAS JUST AS MUCH SURPRISED TO SEE IT BREAK AS THEY WERE.

I AM TRYING TO GET IT STRAIGHTENED OUT BEFORE I COME HOME.

CLARA

*Friday, June 20.* "Keep your mouth shut until you get back here, and get back here quick," Schulberg commands Clara, who cannot resist one final press conference. "I hate t'think of explainin' this t'Will Hays," she admits. Hays has given her an ultimatum: marry Richman, break off her engagement to him, or retire from films. Clara chooses the latter. "My contract'll expire in a year and I don't think I'll sign a new one," she says. Until then, she will continue to work in movies. "I'm gonna be real quiet and orderly when I get back," she promises.

From Hollywood, Schulberg denies that Paramount dissolved Clara's trust fund after Elizabeth Pearson threatened to sue her for alienation of affections. "As I have stated before, the primary purpose for creating the trust fund was to have her get into the habit of saving," he lies, knowing full well that the trust fund substituted for a morals clause in Clara's contract. Schulberg also states that the studio did not retain the trust's $26,000 contents. This too is false.

Since the $30,000 earmarked for Elizabeth Pearson is still unaccounted for, Clara has caused a scandal for nothing.

*Saturday, June 21.* Disobeying Schulberg, Clara departs Dallas for New York and Richman. "I still love him with all my heart," she tells reporters.

Questioned about her disastrous stay in Dallas, Clara blames Fairfax Nesbit for the whole fiasco. "It all got started when a Dallas

reporter misquoted me," she explains. "I didn't go to Dallas to see
no doctor. I went for a rest."

"What a swell rest it was," she concludes sarcastically. "The
whole vacation was bum!"

*Monday, June 23.* Clara arrives in New York. Like her last visit
six months earlier, Richman and a huge crowd await her. But this
time Clara leaves the train at an outlying station. Now her fans
unnerve her more than ever. Now their stares seem like leers.

When Clara returned to Hollywood two weeks later, the mystery of the missing $30,000 was still unsolved. Paramount claimed
Elizabeth Pearson had received it. Elizabeth Pearson claimed she
had refused it. Clara didn't have the money. Who did?

The obvious culprit was Earl Pearson. By June, 1930 he had
returned to Texas, reconciled with his wife, started a family (William Earl Pearson, Jr., was born three months later), and achieved
his ambition: a private urology practice in the prestigious Medical
Arts Building in downtown Dallas. A relative who examined Pearson's accounts that year remembers wondering how, amidst an
unprecedented economic depression, an inexperienced doctor
could earn $30,000.

Neither his wife nor his mistress had suspected Pearson of
keeping the hush money for himself. Elizabeth Pearson realized it
when Clara came to her door but fled instead of telling her. Clara
learned the truth after her return to Hollywood. She never saw or
spoke to Earl Pearson again, but the consequences of her scandalous conduct could not be ignored. A stunning publicity portrait of
Clara in a bridal gown was "killed" because of the nasty cracks it
would no doubt inspire, as was an even more improbable shot of
her in a nun's habit. Formerly her most sympathetic allies, the fan
magazines also turned against her. "She disregards all laws of
convention and hopes to get away with it," editorialized *Photoplay.*
"She has no regard whatever for public opinion. She [has] paid no
attention to the modern adage, 'If you can't be good, be careful.'

"Clara, we are afraid you are on a toboggan!"

Paramount tried to halt her downward course. The *Hula* remake was replaced by *Her Wedding Night,* an appropriately racy

comedy with Clara playing a movie star with a hyperactive love life. "Clara Bow invites you to *Her Wedding Night!*" teased the advertisements. "I've had enough trouble with men without marrying any," declares her character as she lies nude on a massage table. The joke was on the star, but at least audiences were laughing with Clara instead of at her.

The success of *Her Wedding Night* suggested once again that, given roles which suited her reputation, Clara was still a strong draw. Thus the timing of her next scandal could not have been worse.

# 23

Despite her recent conduct, Rex Bell had remained devoted to Clara, accepting her actions and trusting her explanations for them. "Yeah, I'm crazy about her and she knows it," he admitted during her trip to Dallas, "but I don't figure to let her walk on me, if you get what I mean. I know she goes around with other guys, and that's all right if she tells me the truth about it." Never had a lover given her such leeway, and Clara came back to Hollywood convinced that Rex was her long-awaited dream hero. Here at last was a man whose unconditional love she could return.

Two months later Rex traveled to Lake Tahoe, Nevada, for *Lightnin'*, a Fox film starring cowboy-comic Will Rogers. Bored and lonesome, he called Clara every night and wired her every day. DEAREST SWEETHEART, began a typical telegram, BACK ON THE SET AGAIN TODAY. SURE WAS GOOD TO HEAR YOUR VOICE LAST NIGHT. SURE WILL BE ON THE FIRST TRAIN WHEN WORK IS FINISHED. DARLING BABY, I DO MISS YOU AND THIS IS ONLY A BEGINNING. BEST LOVE ALWAYS, REX. Clara read this and told Daisy to pack their bags for Tahoe. The drive took all night, and since Daisy despised Rex, she resented every minute of it.

To celebrate Clara's arrival, Will Rogers invited her, Rex, and Daisy to a casino in "Cal-Neva," an unincorporated strip of land on the California-Nevada border that was not subject to the antigaming laws of either state. Clara was delighted: with gambling legal and English spoken, Cal-Neva was even better than Caliente. She signed a blank check and was given a stack of chips just like the fifty-cent pieces at the Mexican casino.

Before Daisy left Clara at the blackjack table, she put her on a $200 limit. "Aw, pull in your neck," pouted Clara. "I'm only playin' with fifty-cent chips." Daisy relaxed. Not even Clara could lose four hundred chips in an hour.

An hour later, Will Rogers approached Daisy. "You'd better

get over there," he warned her. "Clara's signing another check."
At the blackjack table, Daisy learned that Clara had already signed
not one, but *three* more checks, and that casino owner James McKay
was demanding a fourth. Daisy asked why. McKay told her that
contrary to what Clara had assumed, her "fifty-cent" chips were
actually hundred-dollar pieces. Clara had lost 139 of them. She
claimed she owed $69.50. McKay wanted $13,900.

It seemed like a costly blunder by a reckless customer, but it
wasn't. Clara had money and a precarious reputation to protect,
and James McKay figured she would pay an extortionary amount
rather than risk the consequences.

He underestimated her. Enraged, Clara refused to "kick in" a
penny more than she owed. To prevent a public dispute, Daisy
wrote a fourth check for the full amount, dragged Clara from the
casino, made the long haul back to Hollywood for the second
consecutive night, dropped Clara off at her house, and, still sleepless, went straight to the bank to stop payment on the checks.
Thanks to Daisy, Clara's savings were still intact.

Two days later two of McKay's goons arrived at Bedford
Drive. No hack screenwriter could have written worse dialogue,
but these threats were not from any script. "Either you make that
check good tomorrow," growled one at Clara, "or you'll get acid
all over your pretty puss."

"Instead of 'the "It" Girl,' you'll be 'the "Ain't" Girl,' " added
the other.

Terrified, Clara called Ben Schulberg, who instructed her to
send the men to his office the following day. Then Schulberg called
Los Angeles District Attorney Buron Fitts, a Paramount-owned
politician accustomed to suppressing scandals involving stars. Fitts
dispatched detectives to Schulberg's office, where they hid behind
curtains as the two goons reiterated their threat: either Clara paid
McKay $13,900, or "Miss 'It' won't be worth shit." No sooner were
the words spoken than the detectives emerged from their hiding
place, arrested McKay's henchmen, and booked them for extor-
tion. Schulberg considered the matter closed.

Instead it burst wide open. Facing criminal investigation, Mc-
Kay announced that Clara had refused to honor her gambling

debts. CLARA BOW A WELCHER, charged headlines in Hearst papers, and though the epithet seems mild today, "at that time, it was worse than calling a woman a whore," says Teet Carle. As Carle and everyone else who had read the "Love Balm" stories knew, Clara's virtue had already been besmirched.

Paramount's publicity department was desperate. "We agonized about what to do," recalls Carle, "because even though Clara caused us one headache after another, we loved her more than any star on the lot." Finally Carle decided to make the incident look like a prearranged publicity stunt, so a new scene was written for "Winter Bow" in which Clara's character refers directly to her Cal-Neva mishap. "I was playin' with fifty-cent chips, and after I lost they told me they was worth a hundred dollars apiece," she fumes. "Can ya imagine that?" The film's original title was changed to *Lose Your Money,* then changed again (why remind audiences that Clara had almost lost a small fortune?) to the less obvious *No Limit.*

As anything but an excuse for Clara's conduct at Cal-Neva, "Winter Bow" was inexcusable, and at least one Paramount executive knew it. Calling *No Limit* "no story to make with Clara at a time in her career when only a great picture [will] save her," David O. Selznick opposed its production. He was overruled by Schulberg, who claimed he had no alternative. Once Clara's films had been derived from formula, but after Earl Pearson and *Her Wedding Night,* then Cal-Neva and *No Limit,* they were inspired by scandal. Since she could not stay out of trouble, Schulberg felt it a blatant but necessary strategy.

Selznick insisted that strong material would resuscitate Clara's career. Schulberg made an empty promise to find it for her.

By the time *No Limit* began shooting that October, Clara's value to Paramount had plummeted. No longer an economic boon, she was a scandal-ridden burden whom Schulberg derisively called "Crisis-a-Day-Clara." He owed his job to her yet felt neither gratitude nor loyalty, concentrating instead on a twenty-year-old actress named Sylvia Sidney. As refined as Clara was coarse, sedate as Clara was restless, and stage-trained as Clara was intuitive, Sidney quickly became Schulberg's protégée. Given his professional and social ascendance since his days at Preferred Pictures, his choice made sense. Then Schulberg had been a low-budget independent producer and outcast; now he was a powerful studio executive and pillar of the Hollywood community. As such, sponsorship of a nice Jewish girl like Sylvia Sidney was appropriate. Affiliation with a notorious tramp like Clara was not.

As Sidney left for Hollywood, Clara traveled to New York for location work on *No Limit.* During this trip, her third in 1930, the toll of two scandals in three months showed. Journalist Paul Jarvis was shocked by the change: once cheerful and confident, Clara seemed defensive and defeated. "The trouble with me is, I ain't no sneak," she said bitterly. "Why, I ain't done nothin' that everybody else in Hollywood ain't done. My big mistake's been that I was open and aboveboard about everythin'." It was all she would say.

"Clara is licked," wrote her listener. "She is pathetic."

Still she remained professional, enduring logistically night-marish exterior scenes which drew huge crowds. Clara avoided contact with everyone except children. At night she stayed in her hotel room, preferring to play poker with Daisy than play publicity magnet for Harry Richman. Spurned, he demanded (in public, of course) the return of his engagement ring, which he announced had already been accepted by Lina Basquette. Lina promptly reminded reporters that she was already married. "Harry Richman would do anything to get his name in the paper," she recalls with contempt. "Clara just about hit the ceiling until I explained it to her."

Upon her return to Hollywood, Clara tersely referred to her romance with Richman as "a mistake." She refused to discuss Rex.

Though her ability to speak and sing effectively was no longer in question, Clara's fear of dialogue during *No Limit* was paralyzing. All the negative publicity from Pearson and Cal-Neva seemed to strike with cumulative force, leaving her so lacking in confidence that any unfamiliar phrase could incapacitate her. The day the movie's climactic wedding scene was scheduled to shoot, Frank Tuttle, who had directed her in seven films and never seen a sign of temperament, was told that Clara would not leave her dressing room. Tuttle found her in tears inside it. "I can't make no sense outta what I'm supposed t'say," cried Clara. "Everybody's gonna think I'm a dumb jerk."

Tuttle was mystified. What was so incomprehensible about a simple marriage ceremony?

Clara shoved her script at him. "What does that mean?" she demanded.

Tuttle read her line aloud: "I, Helen, take thee, Douglas, to my lawful wedded husband." He smiled. "That's just an old-fashioned way of saying 'take you to *be* my wedded husband,' " he assured Clara. She nodded doubtfully, then tried repeating the line. To Tuttle's despair, she could not do so without stammering pitifully. "Her panic had completely inhibited her," he realized.

Thinking fast, Tuttle made Clara a proposition: if she did the scene, he would shoot actor Norman Foster's lines and not hers. All Clara would need to do was stand beside Foster at the altar.

Before she could object, Tuttle bolted from her dressing room and conferred with Foster and the real-life minister, who was donating his salary to his church. Tuttle told them both to get Clara through the mock ceremony any way they could. He could not cut the most important scene from the movie.

By now Clara's unprecedented delay had become the subject of speculation and rumor on the *No Limit* set. Fortunately a distraction arose when the most infamous man in America appeared with two dozen bodyguards in tow. Contrary to his fearsome reputation, the visitor was affable and awed, confessing excitedly that he had come all the way from Chicago to meet his favorite star and fellow Brooklyn native. Normally Clara's sets were closed to the public, but Paramount was not about to defy Public Enemy #1. So while the cast and crew awaited her anxiously, so did Al Capone.

Clara arrived on the set quaking with fear. Tuttle rushed to her, steered her past Capone (whom Clara was too distracted to notice anyway) to Norman Foster at the altar, and yelled "Roll 'em!" while still within camera range. Clara seemed so close to a breakdown that the director was afraid to waste time.

"And . . . *action!*" he called as soon as he was off-camera.

The minister spoke. Foster replied. Clara began to cry. It was not a scripted reaction.

Unfazed by her tears, the minister turned to Clara. "Repeat after me," he intoned gently. "I, Helen, take thee, Douglas . . ."

Behind the camera, Tuttle held his breath. The minister had given Clara her cue. What would she do?

To his astonishment, she responded without hesitation, repeating the vow in a soft, sobbing whisper which audiences would interpret as virginal modesty, not mortal terror: "I, Helen, take thee, Douglas . . ."

The reverent silence that followed was suddenly broken by a shriek of surprise and delight. "Jeez!" shouted Clara, turning to Tuttle and smiling through tears. "I *said* it!"

The cast, crew, and Capone burst into cheers and applause. "Cut!" said Tuttle. "Print it," he told cameraman Victor Milner. Then he grinned broadly. Clara had come through.

But it was only a temporary reprieve from a persistent affliction. Clara had overcome her fear—for today. What line of dialogue would undo her tomorrow?

# V

## "This Ain't No Life"

Miss Humpty Dumpty sat on a wall
    Miss Humpty Dumpty had a great fall
For all of her "S.A." and all of her "It"
    Just couldn't make her in talkies a hit . . .
                        – Anonymous verse (1930)


" 'She has a way of being crazy,' old Drogue said, 'that
photographs pretty well.' "
                        – movie director to son
                        *Children of Light*

# 24

By the fall of 1930, Rex and Daisy's rivalry for Clara had intensified into open combat. Aware of their mutual antipathy, she had kept her boyfriend and best friend apart, a short-term solution that promoted a longer-ranging problem: the less the two knew of each other, the more suspect each seemed. Rex distrusted Daisy's unorthodox bookkeeping, which consisted of paying Clara's bills with cash, then reimbursing herself from the "Special" account. In turn, Daisy attributed Rex's wishful tales of ranch life to his plot to obtain one from Clara. Superficially, both beliefs seemed valid. As a business manager, Daisy lacked experience and qualifications, while after Pearson and Richman, Rex did seem too ideal to be real. Yet both had Clara's best interests in mind, and had they been better acquainted, Daisy and Rex would no doubt have realized this. Since they weren't, they couldn't, and that fall their feud culminated in a battle to rid Clara of the weaker opponent.

Daisy considered the outcome a foregone conclusion. *"I wasn't sleeping with her,"* she says bluntly. "Bell had that edge on me."

Her worries were confirmed by Rex's offhand remark about a get-rich-quick counterfeit racket which required a $10,000 investment. Mistaking idle conversation for dire intrigue, Daisy went to the California Trust Company and ordered banker Benjamin Odell to rescind Clara's check-signing privilege on the "Special" account. Odell asked why. Daisy described Rex's counterfeiting scheme. "I just know he's going to get her to write a check," she said. *"I don't want her giving him any money."*

Regarding her curiously, Odell reminded Daisy that he had no control over a customer's account. Clara was entitled to spend her money any way she chose.

"Not while I'm around," snarled Daisy. Her vehemence took Odell aback, but Daisy didn't care. Rex had sex, "but I still controlled the purse strings," she recalls. Daisy had discovered her weapon: as long as she stood guard over the "Special" account, Clara was safe from swindle.

Relieved, Daisy returned to Bedford Drive. The house was deserted, so after working in the spare bedroom she used as an office, she took a nap. The sound of Clara's voice in the adjoining Chinese room awoke her. "I don't care," Daisy heard her say defeatedly. "If ya want her t'go, ya can tell her yourself, 'cause *I* won't."

"I'll tell her," Rex replied, adding that he was more qualified to handle Clara's finances than an ex-hairdresser without a high school diploma.

Daisy lay still, her mind racing. *So that's Bell's plan: to have me fired, then install himself in my place. Unless I stop him. I lose my job and Clara loses her money.* Silently she resolved to let neither happen.

Daisy did not stir until Clara and Rex had gone. Then she rose, approached the office file cabinet, and emptied its contents—the "Special" account checkbook, business documents, and personal correspondence from Pearson, Richman, and Rex—into a suitcase. Afterward she left the house, went back to the bank, and stored the checkbook in her safe-deposit box where it would be out of Rex's reach. She would hold on to everything else until she had warned Clara about him.

Ironically, an incident caused by Daisy's suspicions of Rex confirmed Rex's suspicions of Daisy. Each had been waiting for the other to make one false move, and now Daisy had done so. Unaware that she had overheard his plan to fire her, Rex mistook Daisy's motive as larcenous. "Clara, she's robbed you!" he cried when they discovered the ransacked file cabinet.

Clara denied it. Daisy was her best friend. She knew if she ever needed anything, all she had to do was ask. "You an' me're like sisters," Clara had often told her. "What's mine is yours." Besides, Daisy had recently caught Billy Bow, Clara's ne'er-do-well cousin, trying to jimmy the file cabinet lock. Afterward she must have transferred its contents to the house she shared with her lover, *Mantrap* and *Children of Divorce* cameraman James Wong Howe, for safer keeping. Whatever she did with them, Clara was certain that Daisy had a reason for it.

Daisy *did* have a reason, and the next day she went back to Bedford Drive to reveal it. When her key did not open the door, she rang the bell. The housekeeper told her that Clara was at the studio. Not wanting to disturb her during shooting, Daisy said she would wait. The housekeeper shook her head. She had been ordered by Rex not to let Daisy into the house. He had already had the locks changed.

Daisy was furious. A servant to whom she gave orders and paid wages was turning her out of the house which was her second home. She hated Rex more than ever.

That night, he answered the door. Daisy demanded to see Clara. Rex refused. Daisy said she could explain everything. "The checkbook's in the bank where you can't get your hands on it," she added triumphantly. Since she left without a glimpse of Clara, it was small consolation.

The confrontation between Daisy and Rex left each certain of the other's ulterior motive. Both were wrong.

The misunderstanding was gaining dangerous momentum.

Daisy felt helpless. Rex Bell had usurped her best friend and job, then cut off all contact between her and Clara. Appealing to Schulberg, who still held a grudge against her for refusing to spy on Clara, was pointless. Instead Daisy sought advice from studio attorney Henry Herzbrun. *"Mister* Rex Bell has gotten me in dutch with Clara," she complained bitterly. "What a dirty deal he's giving me." Assuming she expected more than an apology, Herzbrun referred her to W. I. Gilbert, the lawyer who had kept Clara out of Elizabeth Pearson's divorce suit two years earlier. Herzbrun assured Daisy that Gilbert would work out an appropriate settlement for her, too.

Daisy could not believe what she was hearing. For twenty-two months she had run Clara's house on budget and made weekly deposits into her trust fund. Indeed, Clara's bankbook was Daisy's best witness: when she was hired, its balance was $16,000; when she was fired, it had reached $249,000. A quarter of a million dollars gave Clara the financial independence she had always wanted. Now she really could afford to retire when her contract expired.

It was hardly the conduct of a disloyal employee or a false friend, yet Rex and Herzbrun had treated Daisy like both. Angry, hurt, and humiliated, she fought back with an unforgivable threat. "Tell Clara she can have her papers if she's willing to pay for them," she told W. I. Gilbert, the lawyer Herzbrun had recommended. "Otherwise I'm going to turn them over to the newspapers." Gilbert asked her price. "$125,000 and not a damned nickel less," replied Daisy, deciding that she was entitled to half the trust fund she had helped build. Gilbert wondered why Clara would pay such an exorbitant sum. "Because one more slam in the papers," warned Daisy, "and Clara is through in pictures." Schulberg had said so to Clara, who had repeated it to her.

The next morning a penitent Daisy appeared at Clara's to withdraw her threat. It was too late. All Clara knew was that her best friend had tried blackmail, and no explanation or apology would suffice. "Ain't it true ya went t'Mr. Gilbert and said I hadda pay ya $125,000?" she demanded when Daisy tried to explain. Daisy assured Clara she had not meant it. All she wanted was her job back.

"Are ya kiddin' me?" asked Clara incredulously. "You're tryin' ta shake me down for 125 g's and now ya wantcha *job back?*"

At this point, Rex wrapped a protective arm around Clara and ordered Daisy to leave. It was the third time he had banished her from Bedford Drive, and Daisy feared it would be the last. With foolhardy desperation she suddenly switched tactics, turning her heartfelt plea into a spiteful threat. "I've got some letters and telegrams that won't do you any good if I turn 'em over to the papers," she reminded Clara menacingly. *"I want my job back."*

Before Clara could reply, Rex slammed the door in Daisy's face. Then he called the police.

What had begun as a misunderstanding was now a criminal matter, and since it involved a Paramount star, the DeVoe case bypassed the usual channels and went straight to studio-owned District Attorney Buron Fitts, who gave it top priority. Accompanied by a police officer but not a search warrant (in the Fitts administration, a citizen's civil rights were immaterial), Rex raided Daisy's safe-deposit box and retrieved the "Special" account checkbook. Also confiscated were the rest of its contents, including a bow-shaped diamond and platinum pin that Daisy claimed Clara had given her as a birthday present. Clara swore she had never bought it.

"Of course she hadn't," says Daisy scornfully. "Clara had cheap taste and she knew it. I always picked out her gifts, even the ones for myself." Those who knew them both verify this.

It didn't matter. Over fifteen hundred "Special" account check stubs showed purchases made by Daisy and paid for by Clara, so on November 6, 1930, she was arrested and interrogated for twenty-seven straight hours. Refusing to sign a confession stating that she had stolen $35,000 from Clara, Daisy was thrown into jail. She had still not been formally charged with a crime. She was not allowed to contact a lawyer.

That night newlyweds Artie and Gloria Jacobson (whose wedding present from Clara, an elegant amethyst ring, had been chosen by Daisy) arrived in Hollywood from New York, where Gloria had worked as Clara's stand-in on *No Limit*. News of Daisy's arrest a day earlier had reached them en route, and Jacobson was worried. To him, the issue of her innocence or guilt was beside the point: one more scandal would finish Clara, and Daisy could cause it. "If she flaps her yap, all hell's gonna break loose," Jacobson told his wife.

The couple went directly from the train station to the county jail, where Jacobson promised the jailer a bit part in a Paramount movie for a chance to see Daisy. Though he did not know it, she had already given his name as a character reference anyway.

As Jacobson entered her cell, Daisy leaped from her cot and threw her arms around him. "How could she do this to me?" she cried. "Get me out of here!"

"I'll do what I can," replied Jacobson, "if you stop what *you're* doing, Daisy."

"I haven't done anything!" she protested. "It's all Bell's fault. He aced himself in and oozed me out. He poisoned Clara against me."

Her visitor knew better. "Rex was the nicest guy in the world, and crazy about Clara," he asserts. "He wouldn't do a thing to hurt her." As Jacobson was learning, Daisy would. "She'd always been a happy-go-lucky gal, but now I could see where she was so mad and vicious that she could cause Clara an awful lot of trouble."

After his visit to Daisy, Jacobson and his wife went to Clara's, where he "begged her on bended knee" to make Buron Fitts release Daisy. "Clara, you've got to drop this," he pleaded. "Daisy's fighting mad."

"So what?" snapped Clara. "She can't do nothin'."

"She can if she doesn't tell the truth. Please, Clara. Call Fitts and tell him to lay off."

Clara shook her head. "Nix. I'm gonna make that little bitch sorry." Blinded by fury, she could not seem to understand that her career was at stake.

Meanwhile Daisy struck back with a lawsuit of her own. After her degrading and illegal detainment in jail, she hired shyster lawyer Nathan Freedman. "Why didn't you come to me when you were still working for Bow?" he wailed when she explained her dilemma. "Then we could have *really* fleeced her." By now Daisy was wondering the same thing herself. Freedman urged her to file a false-arrest suit against Fitts, Rex, and Clara demanding the return of her property and $5,000 in damages. Daisy did.

It was bad advice and worse strategy, for it put Buron Fitts on the defensive. Faced with a false-arrest suit, the District Attorney called a Grand Jury hearing to bring an indictment against Daisy. Accordingly a case was prepared against her.

At this point only Ben Schulberg's intervention could have prevented Clara's third calamity in six months. Had Schulberg ordered Fitts to drop the DeVoe case, the entire matter might have met with the obscurity it deserved. Instead Schulberg did nothing. "Crisis-a-Day Clara" had caused trouble again, and this time Paramount would not protect her. This time she would fight her own battle.

Ultimately it wasn't even her battle to fight. Although Clara appeared as a witness for the prosecution at a secret grand jury session, the case now belonged to Fitts, who presented hundreds of canceled "Special" account checks Daisy had written to herself. In yet another instance of his inept, corrupt representation, Nathan Freedman allowed Daisy to appear before the grand jury. She claimed she had reimbursed herself for expenses incurred by Clara, who never carried money. Again those who knew them both believed her.

The grand jury did not. On November 25, 1930, an indictment for thirty-seven counts of grand theft was handed down against Daisy. Since each count carried a one- to ten-year sentence, she faced a prison term of thirty-five to three hundred seventy-five years.

It was an outrageous penalty for a dubious offense. Nonetheless a trial date was set for the following January.

Suddenly and belatedly, Clara realized that she had allowed Buron Fitts to turn a feud between best friends into a criminal case between sworn enemies. The fact that Fitts's case was flimsy and unworthy of prosecution (it was less a question of what Daisy had stolen than what Clara had given) had become irrelevant: what began as a misunderstanding would go to trial because a venal D.A. had manipulated a shortsighted star. Based more on emotion than evidence, this was a case where justice could not possibly be served.

As usual, Clara stood to suffer most. The thought of testifying in open court terrified her, while the trial itself seemed destined to become the final scandal in a career already tainted by too many. Aware of this, Nathan Freedman was advising his client that her best defense was a defamatory offense. Daisy obliged by dropping titillating hints about her impending testimony. "Embezzlement!" she sneered to reporters. "Well, I'll tell the world a few things about that when I get on the witness stand!" As Artie Jacobson had feared, Daisy DeVoe was going to "flap her yap." The results could only be disastrous.

*People vs. DeVoe* was billed in advance as the most sensational trial since the Arbuckle-Rappe "rape" a decade earlier. Given Clara's reputation, few doubted it, and as the sun rose above Los Angeles on January 13, 1931, crowds amassed outside its County

Courthouse. By nine A.M. thousands of people filled the streets, then besieged the building to secure ringside seats at the impending catfight. Those who could not squeeze into the packed courtroom jammed the courthouse corridors, where person-to-person, up-to-the-minute reports from within were dispatched down hallways like a human telephone line.

Inside the courtroom, Nathan Freedman whetted juror and spectator appetites with the promise of "a strange, fascinating tale of two young and lovely girls, a blonde and a redhead, who traveled a path strewn with the pleasures and excitement which money and fame can buy." As he spoke, the blonde in question basked in the attention, looking, noted one observer approvingly, "extremely fetching and chic" and acting "self-possessed and unruffled." Daisy's demeanor appealed to her audience. Hers did not seem like the conduct of a guilty woman.

Clara's did. In marked contrast to Daisy's stylish poise and brazen assurance, she entered the courtroom that morning clinging to Rex in mute terror. "She hates crowds," her lover told reporters as Clara held on to him silently. "She's scared to death to sit in the witness chair with everybody staring." No one disputed this, but his words did not help her case. Clara's fear seemed suspect in itself. If she was the victim and Daisy the villain, why worry?

The ensuing proceedings provided a dramatic answer. After damning testimony against Daisy from attorney W. I. Gilbert, who related her initial extortionary demand; from Rex, who witnessed her second shakedown attempt; and from banker Benjamin Odell, who called her story of Rex's counterfeiting scheme "wild" and "silly," prosecutor David Clark called the defendant to the stand. This was Daisy's big moment. Here was her chance to "tell plenty."

Whenever she could, she did. With an "icy calm" broken only by occasional, "sardonic half smiles," Daisy diverted attention from the charges against her to her character assassination of Clara. Questions were parried with slurs: referring to the ransacked file cabinet, Clark asked Daisy whether she had notified Clara that she was removing its contents. "No," she answered coolly. "Miss Bow was drunk, and if I had gotten into any argument with her she would have tried to kill me." A collective gasp swept the courtroom. "She had tried to once before," added Daisy quickly. It was a false and ugly accusation, yet everyone accepted it. From her front-row seat beside Rex, Clara shook her head miserably. Daisy's strategy was succeeding.

She had only just begun. Revelations of drunken rages gave way to accounts of all-night, high-stakes poker games, though under cross-examination Daisy was forced to admit that Clara played for a fifteen-cent limit and usually won. Grudgingly she estimated Clara's heaviest losses at "between four and five dollars."

After drinking and gambling came Daisy's list of lavish trinkets she had purchased for Clara's "boyfriends": a $3,000 wristwatch and $1,000 locket and chain engraved "E.P." (Earl Pearson), a sapphire ring for *Dangerous Curves* director Lothar Mendes, a $2,000 gold watch for Richman, and, in a gesture both touching and pathetic, a $10,000 engagement ring Clara had bought herself.

Testifying that she had secretly burned Gary Cooper's and Victor Fleming's love letters when she began working for Clara, Daisy produced eighty-five surviving telegrams from Pearson, Richman, and Rex. SWEETHEART, BE A GOOD GIRL AND DON'T STAY OUT TOO LATE WITH THE BOYS, the King of Broadway had begged when Clara traveled to San Francisco to promote *The Saturday Night Kid.* I LOVE YOU. I LOVE YOU. I LOVE YOU. Rex's were shorter but to the same point: THINK OF YOU ALWAYS, he had wired Clara in New York. HURRY HOME, BABY. BEST LOVE ALWAYS. However harmless in content, the overlapping dates of several such telegrams indicated that Clara was involved with at least two men at one time. To anyone who still harbored any doubt, it was conclusive proof of her promiscuity.

Daisy's final dig was her nastiest. Discussing Robert Bow's brief but profligate stint as Clara's business manager, Daisy claimed that Clara had retained records of his squandering for future reprisal. "He went through $25,000 of her money," she declared under oath, "and she wanted to keep those checks so if he wanted to start trouble she would have them." Every fan magazine reader was familiar with Clara's unwavering devotion to her strange and shiftless father. That Daisy would accuse her of black-mailing him was the unkindest cut of all.

Had she stooped to this level, Clara could have dropped a few bombshells of her own. While Daisy was in court casting asper-sions on Robert Bow, her own father was serving time in San Quentin prison for bootlegging. Clara never mentioned it. Even more explosive was Daisy's affair with James Wong Howe, who had come to Clara before the trial and beseeched her not to divulge their relationship. Although its exposure would have destroyed Daisy's reputation (and hence her credibility), Howe feared it would also ruin him. He was right: had Clara revealed that her nemesis was an Oriental man's mistress, Howe's career as a Holly-wood cameraman would have been endangered. Naturally she never said a word.

Noble acts did not help her in court. Called to the witness stand to refute Daisy's testimony, Clara tried to assume the same icy poise, but the facade cracked as soon as she spoke. "Well, she took my dough, see?" she began, unaware that a heavy cold and severe stagefright rendered her accent even more nasal than nor-mal. "Wuh-el, shuh tuhk muh duh, suh?" was what she sounded like, and spectators tittered when she said it. Embarrassed and even more nervous, Clara paused to apply and reapply a powder puff to her face, a stalling tactic that made her enemy smirk. "Ya needn't sneer at me like that, Daisy!" hissed Clara. "Yuh nuhduhnt snee-uh ut muh luck dee-at, Duh-suh," heard the crowd, whose titters turned to laughter. Daisy sat calmly, the smirk still on her face.

Thoroughly demoralized, Clara was now subjected to Nathan Freedman's tawdry cross-examination. Hadn't she ordered Rex to destroy even *more* love letters from *more* men? he demanded. Clara denied it. "Rex Bell *is* your private secretary, is he not?" persisted Freedman.

"No, he ain't!" snapped Clara.

"Doesn't he live on Bedford Drive?" asked the lawyer with a leer.

"No, he don't! How dare ya!"

She was rescued by prosecutor David Clark's furious objection to the question. Judge William Doran ordered it stricken from the record, then accused the defense of turning his courtroom into "a mudslinging carnival. To read an account of this case in the newspapers," fumed Doran, "it would be difficult for the layman to determine just who was on trial." His reprimand forced Freedman to address the actual charges, though the defense attorney's method of doing so was once again designed to impugn Clara, who was bombarded with picayune queries about business transactions. She freely confessed that she could not remember which checks went to pay what bills. "That's why I'm so sore," Clara added. "I trusted her. I never looked at the books." Freedman responded by mocking her unfamiliarity with her finances. "I don't get ya," said Clara. "Daisy handled it. She's the one that oughta know." Meanwhile Freedman thrust one "Special" account check after another into her face, demanding to know which she had and had not approved. "What're ya tryin' ta do, kibollix me all up?" cried Clara in exasperation. Again her words and accent were met with derisive laughter.

Clara was devastated. Here were her fans, openly jeering her tale of betrayal. Now her "emotions began rocketing dangerously." Her powder puff reappeared, her gestures became more manic, and her voice rose to an even shriller pitch.

Finally she lost control altogether. Describing Daisy's blackmail threats, Clara burst into tears. "She was my friend—my best friend—my best friend in the world," she gasped between brokenhearted sobs. "I'm sorryta be cryin', but I can't help it." Her abject apology was repeated again and again. "I can't help it. I can't help it. I can't help it. I c-c-c-c-*can't* . . ."

Spectators watched in horrified silence. Clara was breaking down before their eyes.

Daisy showed neither pity nor remorse. "Yeah, I know, she gave it to me hot and heavy when she got on the witness stand," she told reporters as Rex escorted an inconsolable Clara from the courtroom. "But that's Clara. She staged the fireworks only because she's got to be the main drag. This is my trial, but she had to be the center of it just the same."

She was wrong on both counts. First, it was Daisy's trial in name only. As the presiding judge pointed out, *People vs. DeVoe* put "the 'It' Girl" on trial, and the case against her reflected the recent moral and economic shifts in America. When the court convened that January in 1931, the grim effects of "Black Thursday" were finally being felt nationwide. A month before the trial, four hundred thousand depositors saw their life savings vanish when the Bank of the United States folded, the largest in United States history to do so. The Depression had begun.

Poverty, hunger, and hopelessness were rampant that January in 1931, and as a result, all that "the 'It' Girl" once represented was now seen as obscenely and unforgivably profligate. CLARA BOW'S SPENDING ORGIES! shrieked headlines detailing "how two Hollywood girls spent $350,000 in a giddy whirl lasting less than two years." This figure was so impossibly exorbitant that not even Daisy would have dared cite it. But the nation wanted, *needed* to believe the worst about its fallen idol, and although *People vs. DeVoe* was literally Daisy's trial, an angry America charged Clara with frivolity and excess—traits praised during the previous decade—and found her guilty of each.

Retribution was swift. The day after Clara's courtroom breakdown, *No Limit* opened to abysmal business. The idea of its star playing a virtuous heroine offended some, amused others, and fooled no one. "If the producers [i.e., Schulberg and Paramount] insist on pulling the 100% pure and demure [act] throughout her pictures while audiences think it's different on the outside, they're not doing much to prevent what looms as one of Hollywood's chief professional catastrophes," warned *Variety*. It was a shrewd but belated observation, since many audiences avoided *No Limit* not by choice, but law: that month, towns in Texas and California banned Clara's movies.

Contrary to Daisy's second claim, Clara hardly wanted "to be the center" of the trial. Although the proceedings lasted for another week after her testimony, she never appeared in court again. Instead Rex attended without her, explaining that Clara's cold had confined her to bed. Paramount knew otherwise. "Bow in hysterical condition due to strain of trial," reported a confidential studio memo. Under doctor's orders to rest for at least a month, she experienced a crushing disappointment: the movie meant to save her career would shoot without her. In a last-ditch attempt to rescue her films from formula, Schulberg had assigned *City Streets* to the studio's ranking talent: director Rouben Mamoulian, writer Dashiell Hammett, and Gary Cooper, now Paramount's most popular leading man. *City Streets* was a stark drama with all the makings of a hit, and Clara wanted desperately to do it. From her sickbed she called herself "broken-hearted. It was my biggest opportunity, the one I been waitin' for. A big dramatic part, not the sorta thing I been doin' at all." She was replaced by Sylvia Sidney, whom Schulberg pronounced "a sensational screen discovery." He did not add that she was also his mistress.

*City Streets* began production the day *People vs. DeVoe* ended. Within three hours of their dismissal, the jury had returned four times to inform Judge Doran that they could not reach a decision. Doran ordered them to resume their deliberations. Word spread that several were doing so with their fists.

Sensing a hung jury, Daisy's confidence soared. In the courtroom, she thumbed through fashion magazines and chatted with the crowd, all of whom seemed to have taken her side. Neither Clara nor Rex were present.

Forty-eight hours later the jury returned with a verdict. It was Friday, January 23, 1931. The courtroom was "packed to suffocation," and bailiffs tried in vain to restrain spectators from clambering atop courthouse benches for an unobstructed view of Daisy, who sat ramrod straight in her chair, clearly expecting acquittal on all thirty-five counts. Instead she was found "Not guilty" of thirty-four and "Guilty" of one, an $825 "Special" account check dated October 29, 1930. Clara had testified that Daisy told her the check was for income tax, then had used it to buy herself a fur coat.

Now it was Daisy's turn to break down. As flashbulbs popped and outraged spectators booed, she screamed and fell to the floor in a dead faint. Once revived, her steely composure was replaced by prostrate sorrow. "I can't stand it, I can't stand it!" she moaned. "I can't be guilty of one charge and innocent of all the rest. In God's name, why did they do this to me?" Sobbing bitterly, she was led from the courtroom. Female jurors wept openly. A New York

*Times* correspondent wrote that nearly every other woman in the courtroom cried with them.

Clara also cried when she heard the verdict. "For Daisy's sake I hope the judge'll be lenient," she said. "I'm sorry it all hadda happen." Against everyone's advice, she sent Buron Fitts a plea for mercy. "I would never have called the matter to your attention if Daisy had not threatened to blackmail me, and I knew of no other way to protect myself," she wrote Fitts. "I wish you would tell the judge about this letter."

Fitts did not. The DeVoe trial had become a political embarrassment, and after fighting for a conviction on all counts, the ambitious D.A. did not intend to see Daisy go free on one. Neither did Judge Doran. Still enraged by her sleazy but successful mudslinging, Doran delivered a blistering reproach to Daisy during a subsequent hearing. "Miss DeVoe, the evidence in this case discloses that you conducted a systematic raid on funds that were entrusted to you. There are no extenuating circumstances that appeal to me. The jury was quite generous and evidently quite sympathetic because they only found you guilty of one count. That was their prerogative, but certainly the evidence was abundant and sufficient to support a conviction on all counts." Ignoring the jury's recommendation for probation, Doran sentenced Daisy to eighteen months in the County Jail.

One question remained: was Daisy guilty? Jurors admitted that after twenty ballots, they had compromised by picking one count at random and convicting her of it. The fact that their choice was a check she had not written obscured justice even further. In a specious finish to a senseless trial, Daisy went to jail for a check that Clara had signed.

*People vs. DeVoe*'s catastrophic effect on Clara's career was obvious. Less manifest but more insidious was its psychic toll. As Adela Rogers St. Johns had realized, "the thing she likes best about her success is the admiration of people." Clara called these people "my wonderful fan friends," and when they turned against her during the trial, she could not bear the betrayal. Stunned and bewildered, her self-esteem nonexistent, Clara believed their defection her fault. *I made 'em hate me,* she brooded. *I drove 'em away.* To a woman who derived her personal identity from her public image, disfavor had brought self-loathing and despair.

Clara had no emotional fortitude left. She could not recover without it.

Clara's convalescence ended in mid-February of 1931, when she returned to Paramount to begin *Kick In.* It was a sign of her new, lowly stature at the studio that although she remained on salary throughout her sick leave, Paramount did not add any time to her contract. Equally indicative of her worthlessness was that, unlike Dashiell Hammett's original story for *City Streets,* the source material for *Kick In* was a Broadway play first produced in 1914. Busy grooming Sylvia Sidney for stardom, Schulberg had relegated Clara to a rotten theatrical chestnut despite David O. Selznick's repeated protests that only a fresh start in a great film could save her.

By this time she appeared beyond salvation. Three scandals in six months, a courtroom breakdown, and the failure of *No Limit* had obliterated Clara's confidence to the point where she could barely function in front of a camera. Director Lothar Mendes coped with her fear by shifting *Kick In*'s focus from its nominal star to leading man Regis Toomey. When Schulberg learned that Clara was playing a supporting role in "Spring Bow," Mendes was replaced by Richard Wallace. Washed up as she was, Paramount still paid Clara $5,000 a week, and in the words of one executive memo, the studio had every intention of "extracting the last ounce of value out of Bow before letting her go."

Known as a kind man who adored Clara, Richard Wallace was nonetheless unable to relax her. In desperation he sought Regis Toomey's help. A stage veteran, Toomey had never met Clara prior to *Kick In,* though tales of her promiscuity preceded her. "She had a reputation of being 'easy,' " he recalls. "The big joke was that Clara laid everything but the linoleum." Instead Toomey was surprised to encounter "a scared little girl who was falling apart because she couldn't handle dialogue."

Like everyone who worked with her, Toomey took an instant

liking to Clara. "I talked to her like an old Dutch uncle and discovered the problem: if she had a dramatic scene, she was very good, but a matter-of-fact scene threw her into hysteria." On *No Limit*, only unfamiliar phrases had panicked her; on *Kick In*, even simple ones were torturous. One scene between Clara, Toomey, and supporting player Paul Hurst involved a lengthy, heated argument between the two men. All Clara had to do was interject, "You can't do this to us!" amidst it. You-can't-do-this-to-us. One six-word, six-syllable sentence.

Clara could not say it. Again and again she missed her cue, muffed her line, or stammered it in terror. Each blunder exacerbated her guilt and embarrassment until she became so agitated that Toomey took Wallace aside. "Forget it," he advised. "We'll play the scene without her saying anything. You can shoot a close-up and cut it in later." Wallace agreed. Although the solution necessitated a clumsy interruption of a climactic scene, there was no other choice.

Her dread of dialogue was followed by her worst case of mike fright yet. Now it no longer mattered if Clara had a line in a scene; whether speaking or reacting, her eyes would involuntarily travel upward in the direction of her offscreen enemy. "She couldn't keep her eyes off it, she hated it so," sighs Artie Jacobson, who worked on *Kick In* and witnessed what happened after she had botched several takes by "throwing" her eyes up at the mike. Wallace asked Clara to try it once more. She did but could not control her gaze. "Cut!" called the director wearily. He did not need to elaborate. Clara knew she had failed again.

It was more than she could take. As Wallace, Jacobson, and the rest of the crew watched in horror, "Clara blew her top. She became completely hysterical." Screaming in agony and swearing in frustration, she reached up, grabbed the mike, and began pummeling it with her fists. "Hoist the mike, hoist the mike!" shouted Wallace. A grotesque tug-of-war between Clara and a technician followed. Finally he wrested the mike from her bloodied fists and she ran off the set, still shrieking and cursing hysterically. Wallace sent Jacobson after her, but by the time he reached Clara's dressing room, she was gone. Borrowing a studio security guard's car,

Jacobson chased Clara all the way to her Malibu cottage, where he calmed her down, called a doctor, and put her to bed. Standing above her prostrate, whimpering form, he could not help comparing the lively girl he had once loved to the piteous wreck stretched out before him.

As if she had read his mind, Clara opened her eyes. "This ain't no life," she murmured miserably. "The fun's all gone." Then she began to cry.

Jacobson held her in his arms until the doctor arrived.

It did not seem as if anything worse could befall Clara, yet within a week it did. On March 28, two days after *Kick In* finished shooting, the latest issue of a self-proclaimed "political weekly" called the *Coast Reporter* appeared. EXTRA! its banner headline proclaimed. CLARA BOW "IT" GIRL EXPOSED! That Saturday and for three successive weeks, the *Coast Reporter* proceeded to do just that, libeling Clara in graphic detail. Even by today's standards, these so-called "facts of the blushless love life of Clara Bow" remain shocking. The *Coast Reporter* denounced her as "the brazen mistress" of stuntman Jimmy Dundee, Earl Pearson, film technician John Rinehardt, Harry Richman (with whom, claimed the *Coast Reporter,* she often had sex in public), and Rex Bell, a "cowboy lothario" she liked best because he was "ambidextrous in the saddle."

It was only the beginning. The *Coast Reporter* asserted that Clara's trips to Agua Caliente were taken not to gamble, but to consort with a Mexican croupier who joined her on a drunken spree to Tijuana. There the two spent the night in a brothel, where Clara initiated a threesome between herself and two whores while her Mexican lover watched. When his wife discovered this, the croupier murdered her, then killed himself. The *Coast Reporter* claimed Clara felt no remorse.

Returning to Hollywood, she seduced Herbert, her chauffeur, and Billy Bow, her cousin. When there was no available man around, Clara resorted to Tui Lorraine and servant Dorothy Carlson; when there was no available *woman* around, she turned to animals. A pet koala bear was "preferred to a man." So was Duke, the huge dog Harry Richman had bought her. According to the *Coast Reporter*, Clara was "as well satisfied with the Great Dane, her frequent boudoir companion, as with creatures of her own kind."

The wages of such sins was incarceration at Sylvan Lodge Hospital, where Clara was treated for a "social disease caused by her sexual excesses." There doctors warned "that eventually she would suffer disintegration of the brain cells as the result of such excesses. Clara laughed at such predictions and [said] she would rather 'die young and be a beautiful corpse' than live without enjoying every thrill prompted by her degenerate desires." Surgery left her hooked on morphine, although she still drank three highballs before breakfast every morning.

The *Coast Reporter* was not without its own twisted sense of compassion. Attributing her behavior to heredity, the exposé's anonymous author concluded that it would have been better for Clara if, during one of her deranged attempts to kill her daughter, Sarah Bow had succeeded.

Promiscuity and exhibitionism, kinkiness and incest, lesbianism and bestiality, drug addiction and alcoholism, venereal disease and family insanity . . . no movie star had ever been vilified in such an obscene and brazen manner. Copies of the *Coast Reporter* were given free to newsboys for door-to-door distribution. "Hand it on!" urged each issue. "Do not break the chain!" Men were hired to hawk the paper outside Paramount's main gate. When Clara saw a copy, she ran back to her dressing room and vomited.

The novelty of accessible pornography with a world-famous protagonist made the *Coast Reporter* an instant sensation, for an ingenuous public reasoned that if a newspaper dared to print such stories, it must have proof of their veracity. Those who knew Clara knew better, but the rest believed what they read. In a cruel mockery of one *Coast Reporter* revelation, bisexual Broadway star Libby Holman bought a Great Dane of her own and christened it Rex. Meanwhile a new rumor raged through Hollywood: Paramount would fire Clara not because her career was flagging, but because she had been seen screwing Duke at a party.

Emboldened by his success, *Coast Reporter* editor and publisher Frederic Girnau made two mistakes. First, in apparent forgetfulness of his editorial credo ("We are opposed to blackmail, and have kept clean," pledged the *Coast Reporter;* "we may be poor, but happiness is wealth itself"), Girnau sent two men to Malibu with a proposition: if Clara purchased his paper, its series would cease. The price: $25,000.

Girnau's second mistake was to mail *Coast Reporter*s to Will Hays, Superior Court Judges, and local PTA officials, thus violating Section 211 of the United States Penal Code, which prohibited "mailing, transporting or importing anything lewd, lascivious, or obscene." Three years later a commensurate statute would be overturned in a landmark case known formally as *United States v. One Book Entitled "Ulysses" by James Joyce,* but on April 23, five days after the fourth and final installment of the *Coast Reporter*'s series, Girnau was arrested by federal agents. He defended himself by producing an affidavit from Daisy DeVoe granting him exclusive rights to her account of life with Clara. "I modified it about three hundred percent before I printed it," Girnau bragged. From her jail cell Daisy denied any association with Girnau, whose prior conviction of criminal libel was discovered. Coincidentally, his victim in that case had been District Attorney Buron Fitts.

Although Schulberg had defended Clara during her latest crisis (calling her "morally unfit" to act in movies, the *Coast Reporter* had demanded that Paramount fire her), he had no intention of allowing it to disrupt the studio's production schedule. With the brutal bad timing which plagued her, Clara was supposed to start rehearsing her next film, *The Secret Call,* the same day as Girnau's arrest. Although she was gratified by the government's action, the thought of testifying at yet another trial, especially a federal case whose evidence sickened and defamed her, was unbearable. Nor could she bear to face people at Paramount, many of whom gaped at her with curiosity or contempt. Once Clara had lived to work; now she hid at home in terror and shame.

Schulberg was furious. WE HAVE TRIED TO GET YOU ON THE TELEPHONE FOR SEVERAL HOURS WITHOUT SUCCESS, he wired her on April 24. [*The Secret Call*] COMPANY HAS BEEN WAITING FOR YOU SINCE YESTERDAY NOON. I EXPECT YOU TO SNAP OUT OF IT AND COOPERATE WITH US AS YOU CERTAINLY SHOULD. This veiled threat was followed

by a blatant one: IF YOU FAIL TO REPORT TODAY, WE WILL BE FORCED
TO TAKE EVERY LEGAL AND FINANCIAL SAFEGUARD TO MINIMIZE THIS
LOSS. YOU WILL BE TAKEN OFF SALARY AND TIME WILL BE ADDED TO
THE END OF YOUR CONTRACT.              .

As usual, Clara faced the situation squarely, composing an
extraordinary letter to Schulberg which he immediately suppressed. Unseen for six decades, her apologetic, articulate, often
repetitive but always heartfelt (and heartrending) plea reveals a
woman broken in health and spirit.

April 24, 1931

Dear Ben:

I was just finishing a letter addressed to you when I received
your telegram. After reading it I tore the letter up. I will not tell you
why, except that it was a heart to heart letter explaining many things
and telling you of my high regard for you and Paramount.

I will tell you why you couldn't reach me to-day. My phone
number was being changed and the men just finished a little while
ago, hence the failure to reach me. I am not trying to dodge the
studio and I don't take off receivers to avoid being reached by anyone.

I didn't come to the studio yesterday because I was at the beach
house and didn't receive the message to report until four o'clock,
which was rather late to start in and rehearse.

The other reason was the more important though. The truth of
the whole matter is that I am a very sick girl. My physician tells me
there is only one cure and that is a complete rest regardless of
anything else. If my career must be sacrificed, I can't help it. My
health comes first and you know it. I have been through so much the
past year including the last vicious attack by Girnau, that my system
can stand it no longer. I'm on the verge of a nervous breakdown and I
don't intend to have one if I can help it. In the past I have always tried
to do my best for Paramount and play square, thinking only of my
employers, but the time has come when I am forced to think about
myself first. The only reason I am not at the studio is because I am ill,
please believe that. I told you once before that if I didn't work for
Paramount I wouldn't care to make any more pictures. Paramount is
my home, and if anything should happen to prevent my working
there anymore, I would give up pictures altogether.

I want you to know I appreciate all you have done for me in the
past and the hard work you and others have put in to this latest

production for me. I think it is a corking story and a swell part, and I am just as disappointed as you in not being able to do it. I am not being tempermental [sic] or anything like that, you know me well enough to appreciate that. I am very sorry that I have caused you to worry, but you see I can't help it. I must obey my doctor's orders or suffer the consequences. Please don't be angry with me and try to understand my feelings. I am sick in heart as well as body and I am only going away to try and regain my health. I will be back as soon as I am able to resume my work at the studio, that is if you still want me. If you don't, well, thats [sic] up to you to decide.

You say in your telegram, you will be forced to take legal and financial safeguard[s] to minimize your loss, well Ben go ahead. What little money I have is in a trust fund and the only property I have is my little home and the lot next door to it. If you take those two things away from me, I will have nothing left, but I guess I can take it with my chin up. I have been through so much trouble, I guess I can take a few more knocks without squawking. I have always tried to be decent and nice to everyone and I think the people who know me well understand the real Clara Bow.

By the time you receive this letter I will be far away. In case you care to know where I am, you can find me c/o Woolf Ranch, Nipton, California, seeking mental peace and rest, trying to get well again, far away from people's lies, and their efforts to destroy my reputation and health. I have found out that nothing else except happiness and health count in this life. I have never had much of either, but I am going to find them both.

In your wire you asked me to snap out of it again. You know I have in the past, and if I could at this time, don't you think I would, Ben? It is just physically impossible. Please let me hear from you, as I would not want anything to interfere with our friendship of eight years, and as for suing me, you know that isn't necessary. You can have the little I have without going to law.

I know that any industry must keep going regardless of anything, or anybody, still a human mind and body can only stand so much punishment, and if you will just sympathize with me for a moment, you will realize my condition. It is needless to say that the last vicious attack on me by Girnau was the last straw. Please understand, and don't be angry with me.

Clara

Schulberg never responded. Concealing her letter, he ordered studio attorney Henry Herzbrun to handle Clara as he would any employee in breach of contract. Herzbrun gave her one last chance. WE ARE ABOUT TO DISBAND COMPANY AND CANCEL PRODUCTION OF YOUR NEXT PICTURE, he cabled Clara at the ranch where she had fled with Rex. FEEL YOU ARE PICKING JUST WRONG MOMENT TO JEOPARDIZE YOUR ENTIRE FUTURE. IF YOU WISH TO RETURN TO WORK WIRE AT ONCE. Beset by guilt and doubt, Clara caved in and wired Herzbrun that she would be back by the end of the week.

Paramount was triumphant. "We have prevailed upon Bow to return," began a confidential, self-congratulatory executive memo. "While this will give us only eleven weeks, we think, by making terrific effort in production we can still make release date." Having lured her back, Paramount now planned to rush Clara through a breakneck shooting schedule. It was exactly what she could not endure.

True to her word, Clara returned to Hollywood on Friday, May 1. The next day was devoted to wardrobe fittings; then she and Rex spent a quiet evening at home. On Sunday afternoon director Stuart Walker came to Bedford Drive for a private rehearsal. Impressed by her reading, Walker was more eager than ever to work with Clara, who still considered *The Secret Call* "corking" and her role within it "swell." That night she promised Rex she would try to sleep before her six A.M. call. He kissed her goodnight and went to his mother's apartment.

A half hour later, the housekeeper awoke to the sound of screams so bloodcurdling that at first she thought Clara was being beaten. Instead she found her weeping hysterically. "I can't do it, I can't do it," sobbed Clara again and again. "I can't, I *can't* . . ." Unable to calm her, the housekeeper called Rex, who hurried over, assessed Clara's condition, and realized that this crying jag was singular even by recent standards. He carried her to his car and drove to the Glendale Sanitarium. En route, all Clara could say was, "Poor Stuart—he wanted me t'be in the picture an' I can't do it, I can't . . ."

Doctors diagnosed a case of "shattered nerves" and prescribed what Clara had already told Schulberg she needed: a respite from films. "It would be dangerous for her to make a picture at this time," they concluded emphatically. "Her trouble can only be overcome by absolute rest." To prevent Paramount from bullying their patient, the sanitarium staff refused to allow anyone from the studio near her. Stymied, Schulberg recast *The Secret Call* with Peggy Shannon, a redheaded Ziegfeld Follies showgirl who had arrived in Hollywood a week earlier.

Paramount executives were left to ponder the riddle of Clara's future. Any hope of renewed support from a sympathetic public (naturally Clara's latest collapse was front-page news) was dashed by *Kick In*, which opened that month to poor reviews and empty theaters. Again Clara's fans had abandoned her, and Paramount acted accordingly. "With wretched showing of last two Bow pictures, we question the advisability of proceeding with additional starring vehicles with her even if her health and state of mind are such that she can return to work," wrote the studio's Hollywood executives to their New York counterparts. On May 27, officers from both coasts met in Denver "to negotiate a settlement with Bow."

It was a risky business. Under the terms of her contract, absences from work were tacked onto its existing expiration date. Thus Clara would be within her contractual rights (and Paramount would be bound by its contractual obligations) to take a six-month hiatus before completing her service to the studio. In an industry defined by inconsistency, a six-month absence from the screen was a chancy move for even a popular star; for a pariah like Clara, it was professional suicide. Besides, Ben Schulberg was tired of her traumas. Clara had become more trouble than she was worth, and Schulberg was eager to rid himself of her forever. But discharging her now meant paying her $5,000 a week for three more months. Unless Clara requested a release from her contract, Paramount was stuck for a $60,000 settlement.

Schulberg did not intend to spend a dime. Clara's letter had assured him that she wanted a release as much as he did, and now he used her candor against her, announcing at a press conference in Denver that "there is a big chance the girl will never make another picture." Asked to elaborate, Schulberg feigned guilt for holding Clara to her contract, confessing that, if not for its concern for her "shattered nerves," the studio would release her right away.

What sounded altruistic was actually a well-laid trap, and Clara fell right into it. "I don't wanna hold Paramount to no contract," she told columnist Louella Parsons. "I ain't been able t'fulfill my obligations." By publicly admitting her inability to do so, Clara had handed her studio the escape hatch it needed. "I euchred her," gloated Schulberg to Herzbrun, "by my Denver statement into making the statement she made to Parsons." Gleefully he told Herzbrun to draft a release for Clara exonerating Paramount of any further financial responsibility to her.

Having just saved the studio $60,000, Schulberg could afford to be emotionally magnanimous. "Dear Clara," he wrote, enclosing copies of her release, "this ends a long and successful motion picture affiliation, one of the longest and most successful in the annals of the industry. It had its worries and anxieties for you and ourselves, but it has never been my good fortune to have anyone as sweet, as loyal, as conscientious, and as courageous to work for or with as yourself. If ever we wished anyone good fortune, we wish you the best there is in the world and blessed with good health and happiness." Six weeks earlier she had begged for both. Schulberg had not answered her letter.

One day in early June, Clara returned to Paramount to pack her belongings from her dressing room (which Schulberg had already reassigned to Sylvia Sidney) and bid farewell to her fellow workers. As the biggest star on the lot, she had been everybody's pal; stripped of her rank and reputation, few bothered to stop and say goodbye. One who did was Teet Carle, the devoted publicist who had weathered all her scandalous storms. Carle had been transferred to temperamental Nancy Carroll, and the contrast left him downcast. Without Clara, it felt as if a pioneering era of artistry, dedication, and fun had ended forever.

As he was leaving her dressing room, Clara drew near to Carle and kissed him. "That's for all ya done for me," she said softly. Carle blushed and departed. He did not want Clara to see him cry.

That evening Clara left Paramount for the last time. Discarded and disgraced, the most popular star in movie history had become an obsolescent has-been with a legendary past and obscure future.

She was twenty-five years old.

# 26

The week after Clara's departure from Paramount, Rex invited Artie and Gloria Jacobson, Buddy Fogelson, and a few others to dinner at Bedford Drive. The evening began as a casual gathering of close friends, all of whom had remained loyal to Clara and were relieved to see that the most marked change about her was her hair, which she had bleached blonde to avoid recognition during her rare ventures from home. Although she seemed subdued, her guests attributed this to recent troubles and felt optimistic that Clara's vivacity would return in time.

After the meal, Rex rose for what his audience assumed was a toast. "We have an announcement to make," he began. "This is the last time you're going to see Clara." Before his stunned listeners could protest, Rex continued. "I'm taking her out of this town, and she's not coming back. I'm going to save her life."

For several moments the room was still. Finally Artie Jacobson turned to Clara. "Do you agree with all this?" he asked her. She nodded silently. Jacobson stood up, approached his first love from Brooklyn, and kissed her. "Then God bless you," he said. "Good health and good luck." One by one, the other guests followed suit. They neither knew nor asked where Rex was taking Clara. All they could hope was that wherever it was, she would finally find the happiness she deserved.

Rex could not have chosen a more remote getaway. Two hundred and fifty miles from Los Angeles, straddled between the California-Nevada border, lay 300,000 acres of desert dotted with cacti and dry alkali lakes. This was the land which Daisy DeVoe had been certain Rex was trying to finagle from Clara, who did indeed purchase the ranch at his instigation. But Daisy had been only half right; contrary to her suspicions, Rex sought a haven from Hollywood for Clara's sake, not his own. By now he had heard so many

snide references to himself as her "private secretary" that he swore
not to marry her until he could support them both. "Rex was afraid
the world would say he married me for my money," recalled Clara
with amusement. "Imagine, t'be afraid of gossip as mild as that
after what had already been said about me!" Nonetheless she knew
better than to blab about their "understanding" to the press. "I'll
never announce any engagement again," she admitted, " 'cause all
I get outta one of those is a lotta wisecracks from smart people."
Instead Clara lived with her lover at the ranch she owned and he
ran.

Rex called their residence "the Shack." The title was not
quaint, for this Shack was just that: a ramshackle, unpainted
wooden building with a corrugated tin roof and no electricity,
telephone, running water, plumbing, heating, or cooling. For illu-
mination, the Shack had stinking kerosene lamps; for sanitation, a
primitive outhouse; and for bathing, an outdoor shower stall with
freezing-cold water from a nearby well and a rusty water pipe as its
spigot. Clara, Rex, and his ranch hands all drank from the same tin
cup attached to the Shack's sole water pitcher. The sun scorched
her skin, the wind chapped her lips, and the 3,800-foot altitude
gave her nosebleeds.

She thought it paradise. With the nearest neighbor thirty-five
miles away, her new home on the range provided Clara with the
peace and privacy she needed. Each day shared the same welcome
routine: rising at eight, she would join Rex, who was always up with
the sun, and the ranch hands for a breakfast of ham and eggs,
bacon, baked beans, and cracked wheat bread. Although canned
milk was staple ranch fare, Rex insisted on fresh milk for Clara
from his herd of 1,200 cattle.

To him a hearty appetite was a sure sign of recovery, and Clara
obliged with gusto. "Gosh, how I could put away the grub!" she
discovered. "I ate like a horse!" Within a month she had put on
twenty-five pounds. Delighted, Rex nicknamed her "Punkin."

After breakfast Clara donned a sweatshirt and riding breeches
and took Duke, the Great Dane made notorious by the *Coast Reporter,* and Diablo, a spaniel she had found abandoned on a desert
road, on a hike amidst her vast acreage. On these morning consti-

tutionals Clara, Duke, and Diablo encountered every type of local wildlife, including mustangs, mountain sheep, deer, coyotes, jackrabbits, Gila monsters, and the long-tailed, fleet-footed cuckoo birds known as "road-runners."

By the time she had returned from her hike to the Shack, it was 108 degrees in the shade. Exchanging her riding breeches for see-through white jersey slacks, Clara and Rex, who wore overalls, boots, and a Stetson hat whatever the weather, ate a light lunch, then drove to Searchlight, the former Nevada gold-mining town that was their closest contact with civilization. Since Searchlight had no movie theater, its 130 citizens had no preconceived notion of Clara, who immediately endeared herself to them. "I never seen her in the movin' pitchers," declared the toothless proprietress of Searchlight's one and only general store, "but she's a right nice girl. She acts real nacherel. She and Mr. Bell orter settle down and raise a pack o' kids."

From the general store where they bought fresh vegetables, the couple continued on to the post office, where Clara picked up fan letters forwarded from Bedford Drive. "To the Greatest Actress on the Screen," began a typical one from Iowa, "when you quit the films, I quit going to them. Don't believe all you hear, Clara. Your best friends are silent." Clara read each letter aloud, surprised and touched by the sentiments expressed within them. Apparently her "wonderful fan friends" had forgiven but not forgotten her.

If Rex had business in town, Clara passed the time playing baseball with local children, a frontier version of her stickball games on Brooklyn streets. Afterward Rex gave her shooting lessons. Under his tutelage, she had become a crack shot whose favorite targets were bottles and buzzards. She refused to hunt any other animals, and when ranch hands butchered a calf she considered a pet, Clara burst into tears and vowed to become a vegetarian. The smell of veal stew that night changed her mind.

Back at the Shack, Rex and Clara rode Lucky and Andy, their favorite horses, to the base of the McCullough Mountains to watch the spectacular desert sunset together. It was her favorite time of day.

Dinners were prepared on the Shack's wood-burning stove, and occasionally she and Rex would return to Searchlight to play poker (Nevada had legalized gambling that March) or socialize at a town square dance. Otherwise they were asleep by eight o'clock in a bed whose dilapidated iron frame was a far cry from Clara's made-to-order model. Her one concession to luxury was a golden satin bedspread she had brought from Bedford Drive.

Clara's only public appearance after leaving Paramount occurred on July 4, 1931, when she and Rex hosted an Independence Day rodeo in Searchlight. Continuing a tradition he had begun at Hollywood High School, Rex and his cowboy buddies demonstrated their horse racing, bronco busting, roping, and bulldogging skills. Clara rode Andy and joked with visiting reporters about her transition from film queen to cattle queen. Pressed about her future plans, she grew serious. "I don't know what's gonna happen t'me," she admitted. But of one thing she was sure: "Nobody ever again can make me do what I don't wanna."

"For the first time in her life," wrote one journalist, "she is genuinely happy."

To her immense relief, Clara was not needed at Frederic Girnau's trial. Government prosecutors convinced Federal Judge Harry Hollzer that the *Coast Reporter*'s contents were too obscene to enter into the trial's transcript, thus preventing the defense from defaming Clara further. On July 31, 1931, two days after her twenty-sixth birthday, Judge Hollzer rendered a scathing verdict, calling Girnau "a character assassin" and the *Coast Reporter* "verbal garbage unfit to be fed even to swine." Girnau received an eight-year prison sentence.

That winter Trem Carr Productions offered Rex a starring role in ten low-budget westerns for $500 a week. It was one-tenth of what Clara had earned, but enough to support her. As soon as he signed the contract, the couple drove seventy-five miles to a small Nevada town called Las Vegas. On December 3, 1931, the same day that Girnau's prison term began, Rex and Clara were married.

Although the groom persuaded the justice of the peace to wait a month before filing the marriage license, within a day the wedding was international news. The first trans-Atlantic telephone call in Las Vegas history came from London's *Daily Mail,* which wanted Clara to confirm or deny the ceremony. Robert Bow, who had just opened a local diner with his daughter's money, took the call, and since he still hated Rex, he was happy to pretend she had not married him. Undeterred, the press descended upon the Shack, where Rex stubbornly maintained that no wedding had taken place. So did his bride until the constant scrutiny unnerved her. "Give us a break and let a coupla honeymooners alone," she pleaded.

Once Clara had started, she did not stop. She and matrimony had always been incompatible, she explained, because "I didn't know how I'd wear in marriage. I had so little of the Rock-of-Gibraltar sorta thing in my life. I was afraid." Now she declared that Rex had given her grim fairy tale a happy ending. "He's given me the only unselfish devotion I ever had," sighed Clara. "When I was so sick and blue last spring, and he was so good t'me, I fell for him like nobody's business." The fact that Nevada had passed a bill requiring only six weeks' residency to become eligible for divorce did not faze her. "No Nevada divorces for me," she grinned. "Y'see, this state's where I got my man!"

Having shown the world that she had salvaged herself, Clara proceeded to do the same with her career. Her impetus was "Where Now, Clara?", a *Photoplay* article which claimed she had "done a complete humpty-dumpty" and was languishing in enforced exile like Trotsky and Negri. Though the first reference was lost on Clara, the comparison to Pola Negri riled her. She felt her undoing in talkies had not been her voice, but her material; given its formulaic derivation, it was remarkable that the public had remained so loyal for so long. Indeed, the fact that fans urged her to "come back" was both touching and tantalizing: if she had thrived for five years in inferior movies, what might she achieve in worthwhile ones? To find out and prove *Photoplay* wrong, Clara resolved to return to Hollywood.

Her intention generated widespread interest. A stage revue called *Earl Carroll's Vanities* offered her $20,000 a week for one skit per show, a deal Clara considered "too good t'pass up" had she not feared the prospect of seven live performances per day. In Hollywood every studio except Paramount vied for her services. Warner Brothers wanted her under long-term contract, but bitter past experience had taught Clara not to commit herself for an extended period. Metro-Goldwyn-Mayer considered her for a racy comedy called *Redheaded Woman* but cast platinum blonde Jean Harlow, whom Clara had befriended on *The Saturday Night Kid* and whose contract the studio had just purchased from millionaire aviator-producer Howard Hughes. Hughes's plan to sign Clara failed when she declined his three-picture offer. The message was clear: this time Clara was being careful. This time she would set her own terms.

Other studios were willing to meet them. She was offered Universal's *Impatient Virgin* and United Artists' *The Greeks Had a Word for Them* but rejected both as exploitative. A more intriguing proposal came from David O. Selznick, who had left Paramount for R.K.O. and hired Adela Rogers St. Johns to write a "sensational vehicle" for Clara's comeback. Adela did, then visited her ex-protégée at the Shack and told Selznick to forget it: Clara was fat, happy, and in no rush to change either condition. Selznick cast Constance Bennett instead and filmed Adela's story as *What Price Hollywood?* Later it would be remade as *A Star Is Born*.

Eventually Clara narrowed her choices to Columbia and Fox, two studios willing to grant her script, director, and cast approval. Her final decision was economic: Columbia's $100,000 offer for one film was exceeded by Fox's $250,000 for two. Clara had not intended to commit herself to more than one movie, but this was a staggering salary amidst the Depression. Besides, Rex's ten-picture deal would require the newlyweds to live in Hollywood for a while anyway. She signed with Fox.

Her return could not have been more triumphant. In June, 1932, exactly one year after fleeing Hollywood in disgrace, Clara came back with a quarter-million-dollar contract and creative control over her movies. For the first time in her career she would be one of Hollywood's highest-paid stars.

But not even a fortune could assuage her mike fright. Admitting that the prospect of acting below one still terrified her, Clara demanded a closed set on her comeback vehicle. Fox went a step further, reopening its unused Western Avenue studios for the shooting of *Call Her Savage,* a bestselling novel it had bought for Clara. John Francis Dillon, the director who had made Colleen Moore a flapper icon in *Flaming Youth,* was hired with her approval, and after testing Joel McCrea as a favor to Rex, she chose Gilbert Roland for her leading man. As the world once knew (and the Fox publicity department hastened to remind it), Roland and "Clarita" had fallen in love and, if not for her father's fierce opposition, would have married during *The Plastic Age* seven years earlier. To preclude speculation that history would repeat itself, Roland and Rex fraternized on the first day of shooting while Clara paced the set nervously, cracking a long black bullwhip used as a prop in her first scene. "Rex taught me how t'do this on the ranch," she explained to an electrician. Her forced chatter fooled no one. Clara was frantic.

She looked lovely anyway. A crash diet had dropped the twenty-five pounds gained at the Shack, while her "blondined" hair had been redyed flame red and restyled with bangs which accentuated her cheekbones and profile. Her nipples visibly erect beneath a sheer organdy blouse, her riding breeches tight and tailored, and her black bullwhip cracking with recently acquired expertise, Clara mustered her courage and signaled to Dillon that she was ready. He called "Action!" and witnessed a startling transformation as the panic-stricken star became the consummate trouper, enticing and then whipping Roland because, her character informs his, she must practice for marriage.

It was only the beginning of perhaps the strangest, most perverse film of its period. Starved for strong material, Clara had approved a story with enough melodrama for three movies. Consider *Call Her Savage*'s lurid plot: after the introduction to Clara's character, Texas heiress Nasa Springer, and Roland's, a brooding half-breed named Moonglow, Nasa writhes on the floor with a gigantic Great Dane (a blatant, tasteless reference to the rumors about Clara and Duke) and is sent to finishing school by her father. Two years and many scandals later she elopes from her debutante party with a rake who marries her to spite his mistress. Disowned by her family and abandoned by her husband, Nasa seeks revenge by gambling away a fortune. Her spree ends when she is summoned to New Orleans to confront her estranged spouse, now destitute and deranged from syphilis. Nonetheless he tries to rape her.

Pregnant and poor, Nasa moves to a tenement and bears her child in a charity hospital. When her baby falls ill, she sells herself to buy medicine, entrusting the infant with a little girl next door who runs away when a drunk attempts to molest her. The drunk drops a lighted match, the tenement catches fire, Nasa's baby dies, and she returns to New York, enriched by her father's death and determined "t'get even with life." This means a new lover, a reunion with her miraculously recovered husband, and a slugging match with his mistress. After dinner at a Greenwich Village restaurant where two mincing waiters sing a tender duet about sailors, Nasa's lover jilts her. She goes on a bender, recovers, reforms, returns to Texas, and discovers that her real father was a redskin chieftain. Since her "savage" nature is hereditary, Nasa realizes that fellow half-breed Moonglow is the only man for her. Naturally he has loved her all along.

Not surprisingly, *Call Her Savage* was condemned for having "hardly a thought above the navel." It was complimented for the same reason. "Turning Clara Bow loose in a wild woman role was the only device necessary for a clean-up in acclaim and box office," proclaimed *Variety*. "Bow's greatly improved acting technique is an added element of strength. She is abundantly capable of holding any audience's attention." Actually it was not Clara, but her role that had improved. Histrionic as *Call Her Savage* was, Nasa Springer possessed an emotional depth which Clara's formula heroines had not. "The 'It' Girl" was finally playing a woman.

*Call Her Savage* proved that Clara was still a star. New York's 6,200-seat Roxy, the largest movie theater in America, had its highest-grossing week since its reopening after renovations. In other cities the stampede for tickets caused box offices to close early.

Nowhere was the poetic justice of her comeback more apparent than at Paramount. While *Call Her Savage* played to huge crowds, the studio that had considered Clara's career finished went into receivership following a $15 million deficit, a far financial cry from its $18 million profit in 1929 when she had been its biggest draw. Blamed for Paramount's downfall, Ben Schulberg was fired and forced to make a humiliating and ultimately unsuccessful return to independent production. Instead of reveling in her former adversary's professional and personal misfortune (Schulberg had left his family for Sylvia Sidney), Clara visited him at his home. There the two shared a bottle of Moët-Chandon and toasted to olden times.

As a reward for *Call Her Savage*'s success, Fox sent Clara on a two-month tour of Europe. With the exception of location work in New Bedford, Massachusetts, for *Down to the Sea in Ships* in 1922; San Antonio, Texas, for *Wings* in 1926; a few weekends in Agua Caliente in 1929; one week in Dallas in 1930; and afternoons in Searchlight, Nevada, during the past year, she had never been anywhere but New York and California. Now she and Rex sailed for England, France, Switzerland, and Germany to enjoy the honeymoon they had never had. Once abroad, the first sight Clara insisted on seeing was Elinor Glyn, pushing seventy but still as doggedly modern as ever. On *It,* Clara had referred to "Madame" as "that shithead"; in London she presented her with a signed portrait. Its inscription: TO ELINOR GLYN, WHOM I RESPECT AND ADMIRE MORE THAN ANY WOMAN IN THE WORLD.

Prior to the Parisian leg of her trip, Clara bought a travel journal. "I wanna write down the names of places and how to pronounce 'em and all that," she explained excitedly. Instead its entries chronicled her warfare with a foreign tongue. "Can't ya understand me?" Clara would cry in exasperation after her attempts to communicate in French had failed. "Gee, these French are dumb clucks," she wrote. "Started reading my order from the menu and the *garcon* just stood there with his mouth open." Gallic culture also left her cold. "Lots of old-fashioned pictures," reported Clara of the Louvre. "Some of the colors are wonderful, but you get so tired walking down miles of dingy corridors. I'll take my art in small doses after this." On the *risqué* Folies Bergère revue: "Well, all I can say is: 'Was my face red!' Oh boy, Will Hays ought to come over here. He'd never be so hard on poor Hollywood after that!" Relieved to leave Paris, she loved the skiing and sledding in St. Moritz. In Berlin a starstruck Adolf Hitler presented her with a signed copy of *Mein Kampf.* FOR MY MOST ESTEEMED FRIEND CLARA, he wrote, WITH THE WISH THAT SHE DERIVES THE SAME PLEASURE READING THIS BOOK AS I DID WRITING IT. ADOLF.

"Madness," wrote Clara, adding that the best thing about Berlin was its zoo.

Clara's sole trip to Europe left a single and lasting impression. "The one thing I love here is the *freedom,*" she concluded wistfully. "Nobody asking any questions. Everybody minding their own business. They don't give a darn what you do over here. That's the only way to live."

Returning home on the ocean liner *Rex,* she learned that Fox had still not found a suitable follow-up vehicle to *Call Her Savage.* By now Clara had no desire to work again anyway, but contractual obligations kept her and Rex in Hollywood. In another break with the past she sold 512 Bedford Drive, moving temporarily into the Bel-Air mansion of producer Louis Lewyn while she and Rex house-hunted. Lewyn's wife, the former Marion Mack, had been Buster Keaton's leading lady in *The General,* and she and Clara became close friends. But Marion Lewyn's affection for Clara did not extend to her relatives, who followed her from Bedford Drive to Bel-Air. As weeks stretched into months, Marion Lewyn found herself cooking, cleaning, and caring for Clara's father, her cousin Billy, and Billy's ten-year-old twin brother and sister. While she tended the Bows, Clara recovered from a night's insomnia with a day's rest. She rarely rose before three P.M.

Once awake, she invariably redeemed herself by turning Marion Lewyn's annoyance into amusement. "Clara had a great sense of humor," her hostess recalls. "The way she used to act out the stories she told was adorable." When fellow cowboy star John Wayne took Rex to dinner and brought him home drunk, Clara gave her husband a tongue-lashing, sent him to bed, and forced Wayne to dance the hula with her until he passed out. "No more drinkie-poo for you!" chanted Clara as she skipped around his inert form. The sight of the six-foot, four-inch Wayne felled by a

Above, a break during shooting
of *The Wild Party*, Clara's
traumatic first talkie.
She stands in front of Jimmy Dundee
and Fredric March, with her hand on
Artie Jacobson's shoulder.
Dorothy Arzner (in white fedora)
crouches behind "dialogue
director" Robert Milton.

Right, a fat and weary "It" Girl
visits Coney Island in 1929
with "Slapsy Maxie" Rosenbloom
and Harry Richman.

Fearing the wisecracks it would inspire, Paramount never released this publicity portrait.

# Los Angeles Examiner

*AN AMERICAN PAPER FOR THE AMERICAN PEOPLE — THE GREAT NEWSPAPER OF THE GREAT SOUTHWEST*

VOL. XXVIII—NO. 35    LOS ANGELES, THURSDAY, JANUARY 15, 1931    Two Sections—Part One    M    PRICE FIVE CENTS

# CLARA BOW NEAR COLLAPSE AT DAISY DE VOE TRIAL

## imee's Name Enters Shuler Quiz

### tress Chokes and Sobs Describing Final Meeting

gizes to Court
ence, Then
wders Away
Her Tears

ary Was Best
d,' She Says
ies Rex Bell
n Employ

xes and choking sobs
made her second
appearance yester-
he trial of her former
and companion, Daisy
whom Clara charges

ear collapse of the
al actress as she sat
itness stand came as
ght of the proceedings
erday before Judge
y Doran.

had been recalled
news stand by Deputy
Attorney Dave Clark
portions of the testi-
had given Tuesday.
to disclose the alleged
by Miss De Voe to
our down to the tune

motions Rise

calm at first under
tion of the deputy
, but her emotions
ly as she took up the
regarding her final
with her former com-
panion. She said at
after November 1

there, in the presence
, demanded that she
ed to her former posi-

you kidding me?' I
isy. 'No,' she said.
t some letters and
, and that won't do
all if I turn them
the papers,' said
I want my job
Miss Bow testified.

rst in Tears

pint Clara burst into
would not resume her
for several minutes
family is worried
red her words, pausin
she came slowly

friend—my best
, I asked,—
re not kidding me?'
e went up to W. I.
and I had to pay
23,000. Isn't it true,
hat you're trying to
the actress testified.

#### Here's Statement of Actress' Ex-Aid

Following are the highlights of
the Daisy De Voe's statement in the
District Attorney's office, when she
was questioned on Clara Bow's
charges and after her confession
story. The statement is dated November 6, 1930.

She said, after "thinking a second," that she was 26 years old and
came from Louisville, Ky. She
couldn't remember where she lived
in Louisville, because she was "a
child" when she left there; that at
25 years old, she admitted a moment later.

Briefly sketching her first em-
ployment as a beauty operator, she
said she made Miss Bow's acquaintance when she "took care of her
hair in a picture. At the time she
was working for Paramount in
1928."

Q.—What was the arrangement
in connection with Miss Bow?

A.—She asked me if I would like
to come and work with her because from there I was dissatisfied with
Bogart Rogers, who was the person
charge of her affairs. I studied it
over a day or two, because everyone said Clara was a kind of hard
girl to work for and I didn't want
to lose my job.

Q.—What would you say your
salary was then?

A.—I don't think I made less than
$60 a week. As I decided to go with
Clara, she wanted me to go to New
York about two days after I went
in her papers, and I refused, because my home was in a

very bad condition and I asked the
Daisy she didn't think it would be
for me to stay and get everything
straightened out.

Q.—Had your particular capacity
been designated at that time?

A.—Clara said she wanted me to
come and work for her as her secretary and later on as her business
manager.

Q.—Had you had any experience
either as a secretary or business
manager prior to your association
with Miss Bow?

A.—No, I didn't and she knew it.
I told her.

Q.—And can you think of any

*(Continued on Page 4, Column 1)*

#### Agua Caliente Results

### DRYS CHARGE MAIL ORDER LIQUOR RING

**Three Arrested in Alleged $5,000,000 Business; Death of Banker Starts Inquiry**

NEW YORK, Jan. 14.—An al-
leged $5,000,000 mail order rum ring,
whose steadily mounting sales were
made in every state in the Union,
was reported uncovered today by
prohibition agents under Chief
Agent Horace J. Simmons.

In the offices of "The Brothers
Agency," here, they arrested Dan-
iel E. Lefkowitz, Vautine Paris and
Benjamin Williams.

"The Brothers Agency," it was
said by officials, was the name
used to mask the illegal business
of the ring, which supplied high
quality liquors, wines and cor-
dials to the wealthy persons in the
Middle West and the South.

**Form Letters**

The dry agents found thousands
of copies of form letters in the office, with a partial list of the ring's
select clientele.

One letter had been addressed to
Buffalo.

"Dear Sir," it read, "your order received, for which we
thank you. We are mailing you
price list under separate cover.
The merchandise is the finest
obtainable in the New York market, and if you intend ordering
would advise you to do so at
once so as to take advantage of
new shipments now on, and hoping to be of further assistance
to you and your friends."

**Death Starts Probe**

The downfall of the ring came,
officials said, because of the death
of one of his best customers, a
banker in the Middle West.

The execution of his estate, ex-
amining his papers, found correspondence with the banker's boot-
leggers and notified the Prohibition
Bureau. Simmons was put on the
trail.

To get evidence, the Government
agents had a case of liquor shipped
to Buffalo and was arranged to
purchase five cases in New York.
United States Commissioner Gar-
rett J. Cotter held the three pris-
oners for hearing February 16.
Lefkowitz in bail of $2000, Williams,
$1500 and Miss Paris, $500.

**Motorship Northland Beached in North**

SAN FRANCISCO, Jan. 14.—
Bound for Ketchikan, Alaska, the
motorship Northland, carrying 21
passengers, was beached off the
mouth of the Salmon River after
she tore a hole in her starboard
side when she crashed into a reef
off Helmcken Island, according to
word received here early today by
the Mackaye Radio Company.

#### From Farmer to Congress

BY ARTHUR "BUGS" BAER

From behind each fence and
barnyard wall
The farmers answered bawl for
bawl.

Letter written by relieved
farmer to Congress:

To those whom it may dis-
concert: Just wrote to our Con-
gressman, who is an old frenzy
of mine, and told him he didn't
have to worry about that relief.

Things is tighter than a rope
at a lynching. We burned the
barn down to get rid of the mice.
The cows ain't mooing any more.
They is broadcasting like wolves.

Just went through the pockets
of the scarecrow to see if he was
holding out on us.

The sheep is so thin you can
use them for college diplomas
right now.

The old hoss is working up a

*(Continued on Page 8, Columns 5-3)*

### GOLDEN LEADS WITH 70 AT CALIENTE

**Ed Dudley, Mortie Dutra One Stroke Behind Ryder Cup Veteran for First Day**

BY MAXWELL STILES

AGUA CALIENTE, Mex., Jan. 14.
—Ten thousand silver dollars dang-
le like a string of fish before the
eyes of sturdy, stocky Johnny
Golden as these lines are written
down here in the rainswept valley of The Juans.

Flying Fish, mebbe, but anyway
the veteran Ryder Cup player from
Stamford, Conn., can just get a
glimpse of the pot of gold as, with
a sterling 70 to his credit today, he
leads the field in pursuit of the
$10,000 first prize in the second an-
nual Agua Caliente $25,000 Open
golf championship.

Whether all of those silver coins
are to sprout wings and whirl away
beyond his vision, and beyond recall, depends entirely on what
Johnny Golden himself does over
those high-powered and lengthy
three days to come.

**Stroke to Spare**

Johnny came marching home today with a stroke to spare over Ed-
gar Ed Dudley of Wilmington, Del.,
and Mortie Dutra of the Virginia
Country Club at Long Beach, who
also cracked par with a pair of rat-
tling good 71's.

Tied for third, and even with par
at 72, were MacDonald Smith and
Horton Smith, those two hardy son-
ny of this biggest of all money
tournaments a year ago; "Light-
horse" Harry Cooper and Agua Caliente's own professional, "Captain
gap Leo" Diegel.

There were a number of 73's of
which that made by Abe Espinosa
seemed to be the most obvious,
while Walter Hagen and George
Von Elm were numbered among the
74's and are very much among those
present and in the running for the
money.

Scanning the lists of the real
tournament campaigners today, it
is found that Al Watrous and Al
Espinosa each had a 75 along with
Craig Wood and "Wiffy" Cox.
Frank Walsh and Joe Turnesa had

*(Continued on First Page Page)*

### 'Broadcaster's Accusations Are Untrue'

ELWOOD de GARMO

### QUAKE ROCKS MEXICO CITY

MEXICO CITY, Jan. 15.—(P)—A
sharp earthquake, one of strongest
felt in years, rocked Mexico City at
6:16 o'clock tonight (8 p. m., Eastern
Standard Time), shaking
buildings for more than ten
minutes and darkening lights. It
was not known immediately if any
damage resulted, but the city was
in great confusion.

Residents evacuated buildings
frantically.

SANTA CLARA UNIVERSITY,
Cal., Jan. 14.—(P)—An earthquake
of "considerable intensity" was recorded on the University of Santa
Clara seismograph tonight. The
record began at 5:30 p. m. (Pacific
Standard Time) and continued
more than three-quarters of an
hour. It indicated the temblor was
centered 2300 miles to the south-
east or southwest.

DENVER, Jan. 14.—(P)—Father
A. W. Forstall, seismologist at
Regis College, reported a severe
earthquake was in progress at 5:15
p. m. (Mountain Standard Time)
tonight. The seismograph at the
college was still registering a dis-
turbance at that time.

Father Forstall said the quake
was where of first or second degree
intensity.

**Alleged Kin of 'Legs' Diamond Arrested**

VIENNA, Jan. 14.—John Diamond, allegedly the brother of notorious Jack "Legs" Diamond of
New York, was arrested in the Austrian town of Steinbach today at
the request of American authorities
in connection with bootlegging
charges.

**Austrian Munitions Blast Kills Two**

VIENNA, Jan. 14.—Two workmen
were killed and eight others seri-
ously injured today in an explosion
at the Hirtenberger munitions factory. Two more were reported missing.

### EVANGELIST AID DENIED BY JURIST

**Pastor's Charges He Warned Grand Jury Foreman, 'Abso-lutely False,' Says Keetch**

Superior Judge Arthur Keetch
yesterday accused the Rev. R.
P. Shuler of broadcasting lies
about him in connection with
the jurist's abrupt dismissal of
the 1926 grand jury.

Shuler's accuser was called as
a witness before Examiner El-
lis Yost of the Radio Commission at the hearing to determine
whether or not Shuler's station,
KGEF, shall stay on the air.

Trinity Church's loudspeak-
ing pastor was not credited
with originating alleged un-
truths, but of putting on the
air statements that he attributed
to E. J. Nagle, foreman of the
1926 grand jury.

**'Absolutely Untrue'**

Respecting these broadcast decla-
rations, Judge Keetch quietly but
emphatically branded them.

"Absolutely, unqualifiedly untrue."

And, later in the afternoon, at
his dismissal of the inquisitorial
body was gone into at length, the
jurist summed up the charges Shuler said were made by heatedly de-
claring:

Evangelist Aimee Semple. Mc-
Pherson's name rang through the
hearing room several times.

Shuler, assertedly quoting Nagle,
told his radio listeners that
the grand jury had discussed
grand jury doings with Nagle and
ordered him to "lay off the Aimee
McPherson investigation" because
she had many followers.

Judge Keetch, denying this, declared:

"That is utterly absurd. I never
spoke to Nagle about that case or
any others. I did not know what
was pending before the jury. In
fact, the whole Nagle statement is
an unqualified lie."

**Flatly Contradicts**

The witness flatly contradicted
Mr. Shuler's broadcast inferring that
impeachment proceedings against
himself had been instituted before
the State Legislature.

He insisted that charge as
"utterly false," and read a letter
from Harry F. Sewall, chairman
of the Assembly judiciary committee, assuring him that no such
action was taken or contemplated.

All of the charges to which Judge
Keetch entered specific and em-
phatic denial, Shuler said were made
by Nagle; that Nagle had discussed
a gathering of citizens in a downtown hotel and that a stenographer
was present who transcribed
Nagle's remarks.

A transcript of Nagle's speech
was furnished to Shuler, he had
said, adding that they were supported by affidavits, which he had
broadcast on a previous evening.

The Nagle accusations, in addition to those already recited, as
Shuler sent them over the air, were
to the effect that Judge Keetch had
visited the county's Big Pines
recreation camp, with a party of
examinites, new evidences of law
violations, and came home with
leaving the members of the grand
jury at the camp.

That the grand jury had under
investigation charges that $2,590

Daisy De Voe as she appeared yesterday on trial for grand theft.—Examiner photo.

The *Kick In* set moments before Clara's crackup. She sits between Regis Toomey and Paul Hurst.

"He's my man and I worship him": Mr. and Mrs. Rex Bell in 1932, a few months after their wedding.

Above, *Call Her Savage*,
Clara's lurid comeback vehicle,
began with her bull-
whipping Gilbert Roland.
Promiscuity and
prostitution followed.

Right, in costume
for a 1933 Hollywood party.

Clara, Tony, Rex, and baby George in 1938. She was devoted to her sons and tried desperately to be the ideal mother.

A rare appearance at a Las Vegas restaurant in 1948.

A family reunion in 1960.

Father and daughter in 1957.

nimble woman one foot shorter reduced Marion Lewyn to tears of laughter.

Occasionally she carried her antics too far. A penny-a-point bridge game between the Bells and the Lewyns ended when Clara, enraged by Rex's absentminded playing, ran into the kitchen, returned with a pot of spaghetti, and dumped it over his head. Though comically reminiscent of her food fights with her father and Harry Richman, this incident did not occur in Clara's homes on either Hollywood Boulevard or Malibu, nor was the couch which cost the Lewyns $750 hers to ruin. As much as she liked Clara, Marion Lewyn awaited the day when she returned to work.

Clara dreaded it, but in the summer of 1933 Fox found a story for her. By now a year had passed since *Call Her Savage,* an inexcusable delay if her follow-up film was to sustain the momentum of her comeback success. Even more inexplicable was Fox's choice, a Broadway play called *The Barker* that the studio retitled *Hoopla.* Clara hated her role as the amoral cooch dancer regenerated by love for a carnival barker's son, but rejecting the script meant postponing her second movie. Eager to end her commitment to Fox, she approved *Hoopla.*

Clara was sure critics would dislike *Hoopla* as much as she did. She was wrong. "A more mature performance which shows an improved actress," noted *Variety* approvingly. "Quite a long gap since her last release, but she looks and photographs extremely well. Bow seems ripe to come back strongly and this performance will help plenty." In other words, the year-long gap between *Call Her Savage* and *Hoopla* had not mattered. Clara's career was in excellent shape.

It was also over. "I've had enough," she announced, refusing all offers with a finality that convinced even cynics. "I don't wanna be remembered as somebody who couldn't do nothin' but take her clothes off. I want somethin' real now." For a woman who had never faced reality before, it was a formidable prospect. Clara was about to tackle the most difficult roles of her life: housewife and mother. She could not rely on experience or instinct for either.

# VI

## Mrs. Beldam

"Marriage means the fulfillment of everythin' for me. This sounds like the bunk, I know. But I mean it. Else I wouldn't say it."

– Clara Bow (1933)

"She has been exceedingly unhappy at the ranch and sees nothing but hopelessness and ruin ahead of her . . ."

– psychiatric report of Clara Bow Beldam (1940)

# 27

By definition, a housewife and mother require a home and child. Within a year of her retirement Clara had both.

First came the construction of Rancho Clarita, a two-story, twelve-room hacienda with a pair of steer horns mounted above its front door for an address. Hot and cold running water had been piped thirty miles across mountain and desert at a cost of $18,000, the cavernous fifty- by thirty-foot living room had a twelve-foot high fireplace built from a dozen varieties of desert rock, there was a fully equipped screening room, and a special "gaming room" with a rail bar, roulette wheel, slot machines, and billiard table. In the backyard a pine-pillared ramada deflected the desert sun onto a landscaped rock and cacti garden with a century-old Joshua tree at its center. Rancho Clarita also had a spring water swimming pool and its own electric-light plant.

The only modern convenience Clara's new home lacked was a telephone, but seclusion from the outside world suited her fine. "My desert paradise," she sighed of her dream home. "My desert of love."

Before she had accustomed herself to it, she was back in Hollywood, where an obstetrician performed a dilatation and curettage, scraping her uterus to precipitate fertility. Six months later she was pregnant.

Because of her family history of fatal childbirths and medical history of female problems, Clara and Rex rented a house in the exclusive Hancock Park section of Los Angeles. This way she could consult her obstetrician regularly and lead the inactive life he advised. Bored and nervous, she began binge-eating and ballooned to two hundred pounds, nearly twice her normal weight.

On December 16, 1934, Rex rushed an unrecognizably obese Clara to Santa Monica Hospital where, after medically induced labor and a high-forceps delivery that left her baby's temples bruised and left arm broken, she gave birth to a son. Christened Rex Larbow Beldam and nicknamed "Tony," the flaxen-haired, blue-eyed baby already looked just like his father. Apprised of this, Robert Bow refused to visit the hospital. He was not interested in a grandchild who resembled Rex.

After Tony's birth the family remained at the rented house in Hancock Park, returning to Rancho Clarita only when Rex, who insisted on supporting his wife and son, was not working in low-budget westerns. Clara passed the days playing bridge with other Hancock Park matrons, many of whom had assumed the worst about their neighbor only to encounter a modest housewife whose auburn hair and ample girth hardly recalled the infamous "It" Girl of a few years earlier. In fact, Mrs. Beldam never even mentioned her historic career, nor did she resent the ascendance of "Blonde Bombshell" Jean Harlow, even though Harlow's midwestern twang made Clara's Brooklynese sound cultivated by comparison. But since her retirement, shifting public tastes and vast strides in sound technology had turned distinctive voices and accents into assets. Besides Harlow, two other top female stars of the thirties were Jean Arthur, who had been told to leave Hollywood after *The Saturday Night Kid* because of her foghorn voice; and Carole Lombard, formerly Janie Peters and Clara's Garden of Allah guest, whose breathless delivery and half-swallowed words would have recorded as gibberish in early talkies.

Clara did not envy her successors, but when her second pregnancy ended with the spontaneous miscarriage of a two-month-old male fetus, she was devastated. To assuage her grief Rex encouraged her to return to work, and in September, 1937 the couple opened the "It" Cafe on the corner of Hollywood Boulevard and Vine Street. Thin and glamorous once again, Clara informed reporters that she would be a constant presence at her restaurant, supervising the chef (though her only specialty was stewed prunes) and greeting customers.

Two weeks later she was pregnant again. Warned by doctors that this child would be her last and terrified of another miscarriage, Clara took to bed. The "It" Cafe closed shortly thereafter, but on June 14, 1938, George Francis Robert Beldam was born by

Caesarean section. Clara had wanted a daughter but was grateful for a healthy baby. Meanwhile Rex informed his father-in-law that, unlike Tony, this grandson had the brown eyes and auburn hair of a Bow. Immediately a delighted Robert visited the hospital.

Clara showered her sons with the love and affection her own parents had denied her. Both were as feisty and rambunctious as she had been, but unlike their mother, Tony and George were never punished for their personalities. When Clara did discipline them, she invariably apologized all the while. "You're lucky ya didn't have *my* father," she told Tony amidst a spanking that seemed to hurt her more than him. What riled her most was waste and rudeness. Having gone hungry in her own childhood, she was infuriated when her sons hid unwanted food behind the dining room curtains. Likewise, "sassin'" an elder enraged her. Jean Harlow's sudden death at twenty-six had upset Clara deeply, and she subsequently made a point of befriending Betty Grable, the "Pin-Up Girl" who had replaced the "Blonde Bombshell" (who had replaced "the 'It' Girl") as reigning sex icon. When Grable paid a visit to June Street one day, Tony welcomed her by shouting, "HIYA, BETTY!" from the second-floor landing. "Well," he recalls, "when Mother heard that, she turned right around, charged upstairs, dragged me into my room, and spanked the hell out of me!" Again Clara's anger derived from past experience. Disrespected during her own career, she forbid her son to treat "Miss Grable" the same way.

Following George's birth the family returned to Rancho Clarita, where Clara planned to raise her dream family in her dream home. Since she was developing an aversion to everyone except her family, the isolation appealed to her more than ever. Rex also loved ranch life but remained an extrovert, enjoying the camaraderie of fellow cowboys and cattlemen. Affable and charming yet serious and singleminded, he was an ideal spokesman for his fellow ranchers, who elected him director of his grazing district, then member of the National Grazing Committee. It was a job which entailed frequent travel throughout the area, and since distances were great, hotels were scarce, and roads were poor, often Rex did not return from a meeting until the following day. Clara resented her husband's overnight trips, pointing out that they were not necessary to his profession. But he enjoyed the work and was extremely able at it. Constituents called Rex a born politician.

Since his wife did not welcome strangers in their home, Rex held business conferences in Las Vegas. The more he was gone, the angrier Clara became. Finally she decided he had spent the night away once too often. When Rex returned to Rancho Clarita the next morning, Clara emerged with a rifle and shot out his tires.

A marital rift had begun, and each spouse blamed the other for it. Rex felt Clara unfair: she wouldn't socialize with him and she wouldn't let him socialize without her. He also disapproved of her irregular hours. Throughout the night Clara would battle insomnia with sedatives, then fall asleep at sunrise and awaken in a drugged stupor that afternoon. Rex felt his wife ought to rise with her family, not spend the day in bed. The fact that she expected him to keep her company until five A.M. seemed equally unfair. Rex had a huge ranch to run, as well as his Grazing Committee business, sponsorship of a local Boy Scout troop, involvement with the Las Vegas Chamber of Commerce, and volunteer work for the Nevada Christmas Seals drive, Parent-Teachers Association, and YMCA. Compared to his activities, Clara's routine seemed abnormal and selfish.

Clara's perception of the problem indicated how hypersensitive she had become. In her mind, her mother's credo had come true: she had sacrificed her independence to a man (just as Sarah had for Robert), and now that man was abandoning her (just as Robert did to Sarah). Neither the fact that Rex was rarely gone more than a day nor the knowledge that his business trips truly were business pacified Clara. She felt that if he really loved her, he would never go anywhere; after all, *she* didn't. And if he really loved her, he would stay up at night, keeping her company and telling her what she needed to hear: that she was a good wife and mother, that he loved her and so did their sons. But Rex never did. Easygoing and confident, he did not realize that his wife needed constant validation of her worth, and Clara blamed him for the oversight. Her former dream hero, she concluded bitterly, was "a stupid cowboy" who was not sensitive to her needs. Likewise, her former "desert paradise" had become, in Clara's agitated opinion, a hell on earth. "She now despises the ranch," a doctor would soon report, "and everything connected with it."

Clara reacted to her domestic situation exactly as she had seen Sarah Bow do thirty years earlier. Suddenly she began to suffer from various ailments—chronic backaches, headaches, toothaches, menstrual cramps, and constipation—which left her bedridden. It was the same controlling tactic that Sarah had used on her errant spouse: believing that Rex had abandoned her at home, Clara now confined herself there as an invalid, becoming both his burden and responsibility. Of course, Sarah really had been deserted. Clara had not, yet so convinced was she that the husband who loved her would leave her that she felt it necessary to fill Rex with fear and guilt about her condition. At least that way she knew he would return.

At first her strategy worked. Troubled by her infirmities and barbiturate dependency of five Nembutals a night, Rex consulted a Las Vegas doctor, whose examination of Clara revealed nothing. Mystified, the doctor recommended the Mayo Clinic in Rochester, Minnesota, where specialists might be able to discover a neurological factor for her illnesses and insomnia.

On December 17, 1939, Rex took Clara to Rochester. The train trip gave her such severe claustrophobia that while her husband slept soundly beside her, she lay rigid in their berth, wide awake and gasping for air.

Clara spent two weeks at the Mayo Clinic and was again given a clean bill of health. "Needless to say, I found Mrs. Bell a very delightful and cooperative patient," wrote Dr. Frederick Moersch, adding that Clara's incredible life story "should be related by a master of fiction rather than a humble doctor." Having emphasized this point, Dr. Moersch moved on to the matter at hand, dismissing Clara's "physical complaints [of] very little consequence" as less significant than the fact that "she has come to feel thwarted at every turn" by Rex and, though she did not express it directly, by life itself. His conclusion: the basis for Clara's insomnia and other ailments was not physiological, but "a personality problem." The sooner she sought professional help for it, the better for herself and her marriage.

The diagnosis perplexed Rex. His wife said she suffered physically, yet here was a specialist prescribing psychiatry. Did Dr. Moersch suspect Clara of lying about her condition? Was she ill in body or mind?

Clara insisted on the former, and though she rejected Dr. Moersch's opinion to the contrary, she went directly from the Mayo Clinic to the Kimball Sanitarium in Los Angeles. Four months later she returned to Rancho Clarita, feeling better but still maintaining that her problems were physical. With her came Robert Bow, who proceeded to crown himself "King" and refused to answer to any other title. Soon those meeting "King Bow" for the first time assumed it was his real name.

Her father's presence provided Clara with a full-time companion. When Rex was away on business (and King Bow preferred him that way), father and daughter played poker all night. While she slept all day, he puttered around the ranch. One of King Bow's favorite chores was to shovel horseshit from the stables into a wheelbarrow. As soon as it was full, a pet mountain sheep who seemed to know and hate him would charge, butting the wheelbarrow until it had overturned. Cursing, King Bow would begin shoveling all over again.

Because George resembled a Bow and Tony a Beldam, the former was as beloved by his grandfather as the latter was reviled. "You're just like your father," Robert would tell Tony with disgust. "You look like him and you act like him." The terrified boy often hid in a cottonwood tree to escape his grandfather, whose beatings usually began with the same command he had used on Clara. "Don't look at me in that tone of voice," King Bow would snap, then slap Tony hard across the face. If Tony neglected to clean his room, his grandfather would wait until the middle of the night, then jerk him awake violently and order him to do so.

By 1941 Rex's ranch had grown to 600,000 acres, making him one of the largest landholders in the state. But World War II made labor scarce, so he sold the northern half of his property to foreman Al Marshall and retired from films. Now Rex spent even more time in Las Vegas, where in addition to his various activities he had become a leader of the local Republican party.

One night while his father was away in January 1942, Tony spotted black smoke billowing from Table Rock mountain and ran to tell his mother. "Somethin's wrong," said Clara as she and her son surveyed the fumes from her bedroom balcony. Though they did not know it, Rex was already proceeding to the site with a search party. There they discovered the wreckage of a plane whose passengers had included Carole Lombard. Later Rex comforted Clark Gable, Lombard's grieving husband.

On July 29, 1942, Rex threw a huge thirty-fifth (recently Clara had subtracted two years from her true age) birthday party for his wife at Rancho Clarita. *Call Her Savage* was shown in the screening room, a band played outside, and a barbeque fed Rex's friends, business associates, and political cronies, as well as servicemen stationed at a nearby training camp. Intended as a gesture of his love, Clara considered the celebration yet another example of her husband's insensitivity. She had refused to go out in public, so he had brought the public to her. The fact that Rex neither appreciated nor understood her feelings reinforced Clara's view of herself as his victim. She had put her faith, love, and trust in her husband, and he had disappointed her. Her mother had been right. The ideal man she had dreamed of did not exist.

It was a crushing disillusionment. Clara had sacrificed her sexual autonomy and professional achievement for marriage in the belief that it would be her reward and salvation. Instead it had become her punishment and undoing.

Her worst fears were confirmed the following year, when Rex announced his candidacy for Nevada's sole congressional seat. Clara felt betrayed: her husband knew the role of political wife was abhorrent to her, yet he was running for office anyway. Faced with a public life much like movie stardom and possible relocation to Washington, her insomnia and accompanying ailments recurred with a vengeance. Again she emulated her mother's example, becoming a shrewish invalid who tormented her husband with embittered, self-pitying harangues. Beleaguered, bewildered, but ever patient, Rex coped with Clara's tirades by ignoring them.

But he could not overlook her bizarre behavior. At dinner one night with her husband, sons, father, and mother-in-law Daisy Beldam, Clara suddenly turned upon eight-year-old Tony. "Who d'ya like best," she asked him intently, "ya Grandma or ya Grandpa?"

Tony did not hesitate. "I knew my grandmother loved me and my grandfather didn't," he recalls. "So I told the truth and said I liked Grandma best." Hearing his response, Clara slapped her son's face so hard that he fell to the floor. While she watched dully, Rex carried the sobbing child from the room. "That wasn't a fair question to ask you," he told his son. "It wasn't right. I'll talk to her."

Instead nothing further was said of the incident, though in retrospect Rex should have regarded it as a warning sign. By the time he did, it was too late. One afternoon while their father was off campaigning, Tony and George decided to serve their mother breakfast in bed. Carrying a tray into Clara's room, her sons found her lying supine in bed with one arm drooped over it. "Mom?" whispered Tony. Clara did not stir. Tony raised his voice. Still she would not wake up.

Sensing trouble, Tony ran to foreman Al Marshall's house. "Do you know how to read a thermometer?" he asked Marshall's wife Marge. "My mother's sick." Following Tony to Clara's bedroom, Marge Marshall found five-year-old George applying both a heating pad and ice packs to his unconscious mother while stepping carefully over the empty bottles of barbiturates that littered the floor beneath her outstretched arm.

It was a heartbreaking sight. "She was dying," Marge Marshall realized. "And there were her two little boys, telling her to wake up so they could feed her."

Fighting panic, Marge Marshall sent Tony and George downstairs, then ran home and told her husband to drive into town for an ambulance. When she returned to Rancho Clarita, Tony showed her a note he had found in his mother's bedroom. In it, Clara told Rex she preferred death to public life.

An ambulance arrived and a doctor pumped Clara's stomach. "She'll live," he assured Marge Marshall. "But she's lucky. If you'd swallowed what she did, you'd be dead by now." Clara's high tolerance had saved her life. By the time the ambulance took her away, she was coherent enough to ask for a cigarette.

Clara viewed her rescue as a futile twist of fate. With her sons sent to live with their grandmother and her husband still pursuing his political career, her sense of worthlessness was overwhelming. She had failed as a wife and Rex had left her. She had failed as a mother and her sons had been taken from her. She had even failed to kill herself.

There was one consolation: a stunned, guilt-ridden Rex lost his election.

Eighteen months after their mother's suicide attempt, Tony and George returned to Nevada. Rex compromised with Clara by moving the family to Las Vegas so he could come home at night. She would sacrifice her isolation, but that was the trade-off. Left with no other choice, Clara accepted it.

By now Las Vegas bore little resemblance to the frontier town where Rex and Clara had married fifteen years earlier. Its population had quintupled to 25,000, its saloons had been replaced by opulent hotel-casinos, and its reputation as "America's Playground" was promoted nationally. A self-proclaimed "oasis of pleasure" where even prostitution was legal, Las Vegas had become a magnet for movie stars, gamblers, gangsters, and tourists eager to observe them. To outfit them all with appropriate ostentation, Rex opened a Western Wear store stocking the "Las Vegas look": custom-tailored cowboy suits, shirts with snaps from cuff to elbow, rhinestone-studded belts, and ten-gallon hats.

Few men wore such clothes as well as Rex. Tall, well proportioned, and still disarmingly handsome, he was an ideal model for his merchandise, and his store soon became an essential stop on every tourist's itinerary. The fact that movie-star cowboys like Joel McCrea, Tex Ritter, and Bob Steele were regular customers enhanced its prestige even further.

His 1944 congressional defeat had not diminished Rex's political ambition. A rear room in his store served as unofficial headquarters for state Republicans, all of whom were impressed by their host's rugged charisma and larger-than-life personality. Still, Rex knew he could never run for office. The risk of a candidacy upon Clara was too great.

In an incessantly social city like Las Vegas, her reclusiveness appeared more pronounced than ever. Clara rarely left the family's house on Goldring Avenue, waiting instead for her husband and sons to return from work and school. Aware that his father-in-law hated him and abused Tony, Rex forbid King Bow to live with the family, so Clara's father rented an apartment a few blocks away. Each day he would walk uptown to visit his daughter wearing only a bathrobe, boxer shorts, slippers, socks and garters, and a pork-pie hat. As usual, a stogie was stuck in his mouth.

During one of these visits Tony tired of his grandfather's blows and hit King Bow back. Informed of this, Clara brought her father and son into the living room, handed each a pair of boxing gloves, and ordered them to start sparring. Within seconds Tony had knocked his opponent down. "Had enough, Daddy?" asked Clara. King Bow nodded sullenly. Satisfied, Clara retrieved the boxing gloves. The fact that she had pitted her twelve-year-old son against her seventy-two-year-old father did not faze her.

This time Rex recognized a warning sign but had no idea what to do about it. He had tried all he knew already.

> "Two o'clock and all's well,
> Who it is I cannot tell,
> Queen has her king, it's true,
> But not her ribbons tied in blue."

So ran the rhyme murmured by "Mrs. Hush," mystery guest on NBC's "Truth or Consequences" radio show in January 1947. During the next eleven weeks, 730,000 listeners guessed at "Mrs. Hush"'s' identity based on the clues in her quatrain. Shirley Temple? Margaret Truman? The Duchess of Windsor? All were tried but none were correct. Finally a team of three housewives broke the code: in nautical time, "two o'clock" was four bells, meaning Rex, Clara, Tony, and George; "who it is" was "the 'It' Girl"; "her king" was Rex; and "ribbons tied in blue" made a Bow.

The irony of Clara as "Mrs. Hush" was obvious. In her heyday she had been a star who was seen and not heard; in 1947, exactly twenty years after *It*, she had become a historical souvenir who was heard but not seen. The title also seemed woefully suited to Mrs. Beldam's self-imposed silence and seclusion.

Clara had consented to play "Mrs. Hush" because the contest's proceeds benefited the March of Dimes, the leading fund raiser for polio research, and because she was a fan and friend of "Truth or Consequences" host Ralph Edwards. But as much as she wanted to help—and she did, raising $550,000—the prospect of speaking into a radio microphone petrified her. As the contest dragged on from week to week, her dread of each live broadcast increased until she had become so frantic that Ralph Edwards decided to record her voice and use the playback. That week she was rescued by the right answer, only to face the barrage of publicity that followed.

Thrust back into the spotlight, Clara mustered her courage and cooperated with journalists eager to relate the fate of the Jazz Age's hottest jazz baby. Their conclusion: the "It" Girl had graduated from flapper to housewife and was blissfully content in her new role. Clara wished it were true, but in reality the "Mrs. Hush" contest precipitated her inability to function either in public or private. Unwilling to leave her home and unable to function within it, she allowed Rex to enroll nine-year-old George in a Southern California military school. When they went to visit him, her fear was so paralyzing that she stayed drunk the entire time.

Rex had run out of patience. While physicians pronounced his wife healthy despite her complaints to the contrary, his political career had stalled and his sons had been deprived of maternal care. A prominent Los Angeles neurologist-psychiatrist named Karl von Hagen advised institutionalization, and though she still attributed her troubles to sleeplessness, Clara consented. "I'm gonna get shock treatment so I can sleep right," she told Tony, omitting the fact that such therapy would be accompanied by intensive psychiatric evaluation. Only through the latter would doctors discover what was suppressed within her subconscious.

# 28

Founded in 1822, the Institute of Living in Hartford, Connecticut, was one of the first psychiatric hospitals in the United States. By 1949 it was also the most prestigious. A thirty-seven-acre retreat whose swimming pool, putting green, and Tudor cottages evoked an exclusive country-club ambience, the Institute had won international renown for its progressive philosophy and treatment of mental illness, which a United States Government report had just cited as the number one public health problem of the postwar era. Fifty percent of all hospital beds were occupied by mentally ill patients, many of whom had returned from wartime service with psychoneurotic disorders. Such statistics lessened the stigma of a condition once considered cause for shame and disgrace.

The Institute's "campus" housed four hundred "guests" treated for ailments ranging from depression to dementia. It was not uncommon for a recognizable face to appear among them, and on October 3, 1949, one such celebrity arrived with her husband after what she called an "exhausting" cross-country train trip. Subjecting the admitting physician to an "interminable list of physical complaints" which currently included leg pains, tenseness over her eyes, pressure in her eyeballs, and a skull ache, the new arrival submitted to an examination which made it "quite apparent that there is a large hypochondriacal element to her vague and ill-defined symptoms."

A routine search of her luggage followed. When the doctor found nothing, the guest "took a childlike pleasure" in producing a supply of sleeping pills from her cosmetic case and swearing she had not purposely hidden them.

"She is," her listener concluded, "the actress at all times."

Once ensconced at the Institute, Clara followed a regimen of diet, exercise, psychiatric consultation, and electroconvulsive ther-

apy. Reluctant to leave her $125-a-week private room and refusing
to socialize with fellow guests, she devoted her spare time to painting and drawing classes, as well as a four-year correspondence
course in Remedial English in which, to her surprise and delight,
she earned straight-A's. When not preoccupied with her various
aches and pains, Clara proudly told psychiatrists of her academic
achievement and read them a story she had written. Titled "Nocturnal Visitor," her tale concerned a lonely woman living in the
desert with her husband and two sons. Late one night—the woman
has insomnia and her husband is, as usual, away on business—she
listens with rising hysteria to what she believes is a homicidal
prowler but is actually a stray cow. The discovery ought to come as
a relief, yet the narrator's tone remains desperate and grim. "If I
ever hear heavy but stealthy footsteps in the future," she concludes
in the last line of the story, "I'll firmly believe they belong to a cow,
or even a horse, but what if they should really be a human's, a *real*
menacing nocturnal visitor? What then?"

Meanwhile a battery of psychological tests began. As expected, Clara scored abnormally in every category. Her most
marked aberrations included "Hypochondriasis," a result which
confirmed the imaginary basis for her incessant physical complaints, and "Psychopathic Deviate," a condition involving "an
inability to profit from past experience" and "a disregard for social
mores." Of course, anyone who read a fan magazine or newspaper
in 1930 could have figured as much.

More revealing and even more abnormal was a massive "Depression" factor caused by her retirement almost twenty years
earlier. As her doctors now discovered, Clara's personal identity
derived entirely from her professional activity: without work, she
was without an identity. Acting allowed her to escape from reality;
marriage and motherhood required a firm grip on it. It was a
daunting prospect for a person who felt certain that, off-camera,
she did not exist as an actualized personality.

"Off the screen, she disappeared like an overexposed negative," wrote Louise Brooks of her idol. "The only thing she was was
this *image* they had made for her." Unconsciously aware of this,
Clara had made her work paramount. She had to: her persona

provided the only personality she had. *It* had made her so dependent upon an illusory identity that when she retired from films, she felt lost and frightened without them. Movies had manufactured her image and retirement had taken it away, depriving her of her career and hence her sense of self. And though Clara could not articulate this in such abstract terms, she did feel that life had played a cruel trick on her. She had pictured marriage and motherhood as an ideal, idyllic existence and instead had found it even more stressful than stardom. As usual, she blamed her dilemma on herself, and these feelings of failure as a wife and mother accounted for her high "Depression" score.

Doctors found her sexual profile fascinating. Like much else about her, Clara's sexual "Interest" score was a function of her mother's embittered emotional legacy. As a child she had been taught by Sarah Bow that men would exploit, humiliate, and abandon her if she let them. A woman's only weapon, ranted Sarah to her impressionable daughter, was her sexual favors, which she must grant not to express love for a man, but to secure freedom from him. Using her own wretched life as an example of what befell those who failed to do so, Sarah raised Clara to regard sex as combat and deploy her wiles accordingly.

Sarah's death reinforced her teachings, convincing her grief-stricken daughter that she must follow her mother's advice or risk a similar, horrible fate. That her own nature was sensual and romantic did not matter: "The 'It' Girl" used sex for power, not pleasure. Equating promiscuity with independence and monogamy with commitment and thus surrender to a male, she paradoxically kept one man away by keeping many close. Had Clara been as cold and calculating as Sarah, her strategy might have succeeded; since she wasn't, her overwhelming love needs lacked congruence with her strictly professional sexuality. The result was piteous. For all her brazen affairs, her crude comparisons of cock size, and her status as liberating role model for her flapper generation, Clara remained a confused and frustrated woman who found no fulfillment from sex.

"Of all the movie stars I've ever known," wrote Budd Schulberg, "and I've known some famous birdbrains, Clara Bow was an easy winner of the Dumbbell Award." Beset by feelings of ineptitude and worthlessness, she would have agreed even though an "Intelligence Quotient" test at the Institute of Living proved otherwise. Certainly no one was more amazed than Clara that her I.Q. fell well within the "bright normal" range. But her Conceptual Quotient (C.Q.) did not, indicating that her behavior, which Budd Schulberg and others attributed to a lack of intelligence, was actually caused by an incapacity to reason. On a scale which rated a C.Q. below 77 as abnormal, Clara's 53 score confirmed a "serious impairment in abstract thinking ability," a characteristic closely associated with one particular mental illness. Immediately Institute doctors tested her for it. The result: on a scale of 1–100 with a mean-normal of 50, she scored a definitive 91.

The doctors made their diagnosis: Clara was schizophrenic. Her symptoms included an inability to reason, poor judgment, and inappropriate or bizarre behavior, while her family history read like a textbook case for the disorder. Like her mother and sisters, all of whom were committed to asylums, Sarah Bow was probably born schizophrenic, though her condition was complicated further by epilepsy, poverty, grass widowhood, and motherhood. Ravaged by both genetic and environmental factors, Sarah never stood a chance against mental illness. Raised by a schizophrenic-epileptic with whom she shared the same genes and environment, neither did Clara.

Schizophrenics cannot tolerate stress and are counseled to avoid it, since a highly charged emotional environment and exposure to critical evaluation are often perceived as worse than they actually are. One need not belabor the point that as a movie star of unprecedented fame, then unprecedented infamy, Clara endured overwhelming amounts of both intense emotion (her trade skill) and criticism (her occupational hazard). Yet it was not her movie career, but marriage and motherhood which exacerbated Clara's schizophrenic condition. Constant responsibility to a husband and children places enormous stress on a schizophrenic who feels she must devote all her energy to her own maintenance. Since Rex and her sons comprised the family Clara never had and always wanted, she was wracked by guilt over her failure to be a better wife and mother to them. It is worth noting that Clara surmounted her illness during her stardom, which allowed for artistic expression, but was undone by domesticity, which suppressed it.

As the weeks, then months passed, Clara's psychotherapy at the Institute of Living grew more intensive, more painful, and more revelatory. Psychological testing had determined what ailed her, and now her subconscious memories surfaced to reveal why. An initial schizophrenic "break" usually occurs in late adolescence as the result of severe stress. According to yet another Institute test, Clara's had happened at age 16.7, or February, 1922, the month her mother tried to kill her and was committed to an asylum.

Once this emotional dam had burst, Clara spared her doctors no details. "There are rough days when the material she is discussing obsesses her," they wrote as she described two events suppressed since adolescence. Together they completed the Institute's inventory of her tortured psyche.

The first memory was one of Clara's earliest, preceded only by Frederick Gordon's fatal apoplectic fit while he pushed her on the indoor swing. Afterward Sarah Bow had been left to fend for herself and her four-year-old child, and Clara now recalled that her mother's routine rarely varied: each evening she would leave their tenement room, returning later with a stranger whom she introduced as her daughter's "Uncle." Then Sarah would lock Clara in a cupboard-sized closet, warning her not to make a sound until "Uncle" had gone. Crouched in the darkness amidst roaches, rats, and stale air, her eyes shut tight and her fists in her ears, the child retreated into an imaginary world where the strange, scary noises her uncles and mother made on the bed could not be heard.

Nonetheless Clara liked her uncles, because after one came, she and her mother always had enough to eat. She also felt proud to be part of such a big family, and when spiteful girls mocked her stammer, Clara fought back by boasting that she had more uncles than them all. Later—too late—she would learn the difference between a relative and a trick.

If the memory had ended there, perhaps Clara could have understood and accepted her mother's actions for what they were: the sole means of survival available to an impoverished, unstable woman. But the more Sarah's mind degenerated, the more warped her beliefs and their effect on her daughter became. Grappling helplessly for a reason why her mother, who really *had* prostituted herself, would call her a "hoor" and then try to kill her for it, Clara invented an excuse she clung to for the rest of her life. *She did it for me,* Sarah's traumatized daughter told herself and her doctors. *She did it because she loved me.*

It was the same with her father. Robert Bow's extended absences from home and the brutal beatings his daughter received upon his return made no difference to Clara, whose loyalty to her father seemed as inexplicable as it was steadfast. Although abused children often idealize abusive parents, Clara and Robert's relationship had a more sinister aspect. Whether "shockingly jealous" of his daughter's lovers, openly hateful of Rex and the grandson who resembled him, or assuming a royal title like his son-in-law (if Robert could not be Rex Bell, he would be "King" Bow), Clara's father seemed less a parent than a rival of other men in her life.

Evidently his attitude was also shaped in February of 1922. With Sarah in an asylum, Robert Bow found himself in a domestic situation with a sixteen-year-old girl who, despite her stricken state, cooked his meals, washed his clothes, and cleaned their tenement room without complaint. Since her father was the only person left in her life, Clara did all she could to please him. In return she sought tenderness and love.

Instead Robert Bow raped her.

The shift from psychotic mother to sexually abusive father was more than Clara could stand. Betrayed by a parent once again, she reinterpreted reality once again, accepting incestuous rape as her father's expression of affection. *He did it for me,* she told herself. *He did it because he loves me.* Thirty years later she still believed it.

Following these harrowing but cathartic sessions, Clara seemed close to acknowledging the actual basis of her insomnia. "She has spontaneously grasped the idea that she did not sleep at night because she was afraid of the thoughts that might come on her," an Institute of Living report noted approvingly, "and she felt she had to remain on the alert and to foᴄus on something outside for fear she would think too much." After years of hypochondriacal excuses, it was a significant step in the right direction.

Her progress did not last long. To her doctors' dismay, Clara's defense mechanisms proved impenetrable, and reports which had once predicted a breakthrough soon ended with the same refrain: "she continues to resist deep therapy and insists there is a physical cause for her vague, hysterical symptoms." Clara could discuss the emotional traumas of her childhood but not relate them to her current physical complaints. Shock treatments had not helped, and she remained dependent on sleeping pills. Doctors had reached a therapeutic dead end.

On July 27, 1950, two days shy of her forty-fifth birthday, Clara Bow Beldam left the Institute of Living unescorted. She had spent ten months and $5,000 to learn why she could not sleep, then rejected the reason as incorrect and absurd. "The problem of chronic insomnia is still unsolved, but I'm an optimist," she wrote actress-turned-gossip columnist Hedda Hopper just before her departure. "It goes without saying that I'm lonesome for my boys and Rex, and my old Dad." The statement shows how little self-awareness she had. Though her family life had been fraught with emotional tension and her father had brutalized and exploited her, here she was, happily anticipating her return to both.

By now Rex knew better than to believe it, and when Clara arrived in Los Angeles en route to Las Vegas, he took her back to see Dr. Karl von Hagen, the neurologist-psychiatrist who had recommended long-term therapy at the Institute. "I found no evidence of organic disease of the nervous system," states Dr. von Hagen today, "so [I] applied what might be called 'supportive psychotherapy' with no hope of relieving her major symptoms. She obviously was schizophrenic, so there was little reason to try to get her to acknowledge the actual basis of her hypochondriasis. Many of her symptoms were probably delusions so by definition not subject to logical analysis."

A devastated Rex made a difficult but necessary decision. "I can't let her come back," he told his sons. Whether or not she was willing to admit it, Clara was mentally ill.

Accustomed to extended separations from their mother (four months in 1940, eighteen months in 1943–45, and ten months in 1949–50), Tony and George were not upset by this development. Both agreed to attend military school near Los Angeles, where Clara would also live so she could be near Dr. von Hagen. Rex would rent an apartment in Las Vegas. Rancho Clarita, the "desert paradise" built in expectation of her ideal life with an ideal man, would be sold.

Informed of her husband's intentions, Clara was angry and hurt. "He won't let me come home," she told fifteen-year-old Tony bitterly. It was an understandable reaction, for Rex had inadvertently fulfilled Sarah Bow's dire prophecy. Clara felt she was being abandoned by a man just as her mother had predicted. Now she was back where she started: alone.

# 29

Separation from Rex and relocation to Los Angeles in 1950 made Clara consciously aware of what instinct had already taught her: solitude meant safety. Relieved of responsibility to her husband and children, financially independent from her trust fund, and buoyed by Dr. von Hagen's self-described "supportive psychotherapy," she could finally negotiate an existence tolerable to her schizophrenic terms. Had her grandmother and mother been able to achieve a similar state of independence, perhaps their lives would not have ended so horribly. Certainly Clara's didn't. Seclusion was her salvation.

For a year she resided at the Los Altos Apartments in downtown L.A.'s fashionable Wilshire District, then moved to the Gramercy Apartments nearby. But apartment living did not provide enough privacy for a woman who dreaded even casual encounters in lobbies, stairways, and elevators, so Clara left the Gramercy and rented a cottage in Santa Monica. When living alone proved equally difficult, Dr. von Hagen committed her to the Southern California Sanitarium. There Clara was weaned from barbiturates but not insomnia. Reluctantly Dr. von Hagen prescribed sedatives once again. Still she could not sleep.

Nonetheless Clara "worshipped" her doctor, and to his credit Karl von Hagen believed in a neurological basis for schizophrenia three decades before medical research would indicate one. At the time his most famous patient was not Clara, but Doris Day, who, contrary to her cheerful screen image, suffered from incapacitating anxiety attacks. Dr. von Hagen put both women on the same regimen: reading, swimming (the dead man's float was considered a complete relaxant), a careful avoidance of stressful situations, and absolutely no socializing, drinking, or drugs. Likewise, each was told to list all her aches and pains, which Dr. von Hagen would then relate to underlying emotional tension. In the case of an overworked star like Doris Day, the routine ended in a full recovery; for a schizophrenic like Clara, it provided at least a degree of relief. It wasn't much, but it was more than she had known in twenty years.

Upon her release from the sanitarium, Clara rented a two-bedroom stucco bungalow at 12214 Aneta Street near Dr. von Hagen's Culver City office. Estella Smith, a trained nurse who had attended Rex's mother until her recent death, joined her as a live-in companion, a position Clara had expected her husband to fulfill. Now she required professional care.

Although Clara only left home for her weekly consultations with Dr. von Hagen, word soon spread that the fifty-year-old former "It" Girl was back in Los Angeles, a shattered fragment of her former self. "Upset to no end" by such gossip, Clara defended herself in a letter to Hedda Hopper. "Rumors of me being an alcoholic, insane, etc. are absolutely bosh," she declared. "I retired from public life in 1933. All I've ever wanted since then is a small bit of privacy." To those familiar with her hermitic existence, it was quite an understatement.

Clara spent her days swimming, painting, and reading. Undaunted by her seventh-grade education, the woman who had read no more than a dozen books in her life now read as many in a week, preferring nonfiction to novels and plowing through historical volumes from *The Decline and Fall of the Roman Empire* to *The Rise and Fall of the Third Reich.* The more informational the book, the better Clara liked it, and for the same reason she devoured the Los Angeles dailies, turning to Louella Parsons and Hedda Hopper's columns first, then poring over the rest of both papers from cover to cover before moving on to *U.S. News & World Report.* "She was totally current and had opinions about everything," discovered Tony when, to his amazement and delight, Clara showed up for a big football game at his military academy, cheering from the stands like the proud parent and avid sportsfan she was. When Tony matriculated at Notre Dame, Clara was thrilled but refused to root for the Fighting Irish over the Trojans, still her favorite college football team. The U.S.C.–Notre Dame rivalry became the subject of affectionate teasing between mother and son.

It was moments like these which made it hard for Tony and George to believe that their mother was mentally ill. As far as her sons could tell (and based on what Clara told them), all she needed was privacy and sleep. Otherwise she appeared healthy, and Tony resented Estella Smith for treating her otherwise. "I don't want you boys upsetting her," she would lecture him and George. "You must be extremely careful not to hurt her feelings."

It was a frustrating command. "We knew the rules, but no guidelines were given," explains Tony. "And because Mother would never act upset at the time, George and I wouldn't find out until later that we'd done anything wrong." Clara's mood swings made it more difficult, for what she found funny one day might offend her on another. After hearing her joke about the weight she had gained since moving to Los Angeles, Tony sent his mother a postcard of an obese woman. The next time he visited, she would not allow him in the house.

Clara was happiest at Christmas, her favorite holiday and the one which reunited her family in her home. Though the prospect of entering a crowded store would have unnerved her at any other time of the year, she delighted in the annual ritual of choosing gifts for her father, husband, and sons. During these expeditions she wore heavy makeup and dark glasses, but her anonymity never lasted long. "Why, you're Clara Bow!" came the inevitable cry from middle-aged fans. Clara was gracious but discomforted by the attention. It was one more reason to stay home.

Still, the goodwill which pervaded the holiday season made the world more appealing to her than it usually was. Christmas cards from friends she no longer saw were displayed throughout her house, while her own printed greetings were designed from a motif of four bells (Rex, Clara, Tony, and George) for a large mailing list that included Louella Parsons and Hedda Hopper, Ralph Edwards, Bob Hope, Artie and Gloria Jacobson, Louis and Marion Lewyn, Groucho Marx, publicist Teet Carle ("Remember me?" scrawled Clara inside the first card she sent him), Harry Richman, Barbara Stanwyck, and former leading men Richard Arlen, Jack Oakie, Buddy Rogers and Gilbert Roland. Year after year, recipients of Clara's Christmas cards tried to call or visit her, but Estella Smith always dissuaded them.

Two former lovers persisted. Now a forgotten old man with dyed hair and a facelift, Harry Richman was trying to have his life made into a movie musical starring Frank Sinatra. Amused by his bluster, Clara enjoyed Richman's company until he decided that the film should "tell all" about their affair. Clara felt Richman had exploited her enough. She refused his offer, then his visits.

Gilbert Roland's were welcomed. "Still handsome and still my favorite actor," Clara would sigh, and besides her family, Estella Smith, and Dr. von Hagen, only Roland saw and spoke to her regularly. The tender, spiritual quality of a letter written from a film location indicates why:

Hello Clarita Girl;
    I am truly sad that you don't feel well. Sometimes when I go to church and I think of you, I say a prayer. It will be heard. God hears everything.
    You tell me you long for your boys. I share your feelings. My daughters are with their mother in Wiesbaden, Germany. And there is nothing I can do, except cry a little once in a while.
    I hope someday they show *The Plastic Age*. It would be wonderful to see that dancing scene, you and I. It would be pleasant seeing how I looked when I was your beau, and you were my dream girl. It would be pleasant seeing that. And then it might be very beautiful, and suddenly it might be very sad.
    It seems you are in my thoughts.
    It's good to feel that way.
    It's good I have never forgotten you.
    God bless you.

                                                             Gilbert


Though Roland remained her favorite actor, Clara followed every move in the careers of current stars. Wary of theaters, she and Estella Smith would attend drive-ins where, within the privacy of her car, Clara would watch a movie with intense concentration, then compare its stars to her peers. By the mid-fifties she had found an actor she liked as much as Roland; when she learned that he idolized *her*, Clara was so honored that she broke her cardinal rule and invited him to her home. Apparently the ensuing meeting was enjoyed by both, and a few days later a signed portrait arrived. Its inscription: FOR CLARA BOW BELL, A MEMORABLE PERSONALITY WHO HAS GIVEN SO MUCH TO SO MANY, WITH SINCERE RESPECTS, MARLON BRANDO. Clara cherished it.

Her admiration for her favorite actress, Marilyn Monroe, was accompanied by feelings of kinship and protectiveness. The affinity was obvious: both Clara and Monroe had mentally ill mothers and maternal grandmothers, all of whom were committed to asylums; both suffered physical and emotional abuse in childhood; both had been catapulted to oppressive fame, then underpaid for their services and underrated for their talent; and both had been endowed with, then entrapped by the same sexual-vulnerable, womanly-babyish, stupid-shrewd image. When *Life* magazine assigned photographer Richard Avedon to shoot Monroe as Clara, the blonde donned a red wig and decided to portray her predecessor in a movie. Clara was flattered but would not permit a "biopic" about herself in her lifetime. She did, however, make her casting preference clear: "I slip my old crown of 'It' Girl not to Taylor or Bardot, but to Monroe," she wrote Hedda Hopper and Louella Parsons. It was Clara's way of returning Monroe's compliment, for the two women, both so brazen on film, were too insecure to meet each other in person.

Bolstered by the straight A's she had earned in Remedial English and proficient at speed-typing from lessons taken at the Institute of Living, Clara became a voluminous correspondent, communicating with the world while remaining apart from it. The star who had received the most fan mail in movie history wrote humble fan letters to everyone from President Dwight Eisenhower to *Twilight Zone* creator Rod Serling. Eisenhower responded with an invitation to his inauguration, while Serling assured her that "I needed no reminder of 'the "It" Girl' or who she is. I hope you'll note the tense used here. You happen to have given a vitality, a beauty and an excitement to our industry that no one has ever duplicated."

Clara treasured such letters yet could not fathom why she was still remembered, let alone admired. Eager to praise others, she did not feel deserving of praise herself, and her response to a biography of Elinor Glyn by Glyn's grandson indicates her continued lack of self-esteem. In a letter extolling both Anthony Glyn and his grandmother, Clara recalled how "I was in a hospital recovering from surgery [actually, her 1943 suicide attempt]when I read she had passed on. I cried bitterly and felt the world had lost a truly great person when she left it." Then Clara credited Madame Glyn for her success in *It.* She could hardly credit her own talent if she did not believe it existed.

In 1957 Robert Bow moved from Las Vegas, where he worked as a shill for the Thunderbird Hotel casino, to his daughter's home in Los Angeles. Two years later he died. He was eighty-four years old.

Clara had feared his death for years. "If, God forbid, my father should pass on during my stay and Dr. von Hagen does not wish me to know it, *please,* Mr. Jaco, carry on for me and see to it that my Dad has a nice funeral," she had begged her trust officer before her commitment to the Southern California Sanitarium. With Robert dead, Rex on a business trip, and Tony and George in the Air Force and Marines respectively, Clara spent Christmas of 1959 without her family. It was a lonely and upsetting experience, and a letter she wrote Hedda Hopper the following day says as much about her state of mind as her politics. "You really showed up [choreographer] Agnes DeMille for what she is, a pro-Communist," congratulated Clara. "I have no use for anyone or anything Communistic. They are knawing [sic] away at our vitals at this very instant."

"Hedda, if you print any of the above," she added in a postscript, "please leave out the part concerning Agnes DeMille, because she might sue me in court and demand *proof* of what I think and say about her. You *know how clever* all the *Commies* are, and it's *almost impossible to prove their guilt.*" [Italics are Clara's.]

With an attitude like this, it was not surprising that she supported arch-conservative Arizona Senator Barry Goldwater, whom she hoped would defeat incumbent President John F. Kennedy in the 1964 election. So did Lina Basquette, and the two sexual rebels turned political reactionaries corresponded about their views. "The old saying of 'power corrupts and absolute power corrupts absolutely' seems to be gripping the President and his advisers," declared Clara to Lina and others. "Our dollar has shrunk to a dollarette and people run around seeking more pleasure, less work, more pay. The Fabian Socialists are ruining us."

Not even Barry Goldwater could compare to Clara's favorite elected official: her husband. After their separation, Rex had been free to pursue his political career, and absolved of any campaign participation, his wife supported him wholeheartedly. So did Nevada voters, for Rex Bell exuded charisma long before it became compulsory for a candidate. Clad in a custom-tailored cowboy suit, white ten-gallon hat, and hand-tooled leather boots from his Western Wear store, Rex stole the show at state parades and Republican rallies by appearing astride a magnificent white stallion, the epitome of movie-star presence in a political setting. It was an enormously appealing image, and Nevadans responded by crossing party lines to vote for this film star-turned-politician. Elected lieutenant governor in 1954, he received twice as many votes as his gubernatorial running mate, and although a Democratic sweep ousted every other Republican from office four years later, Rex was reelected by a huge majority. "He had a universal appeal," explains Grant Sawyer, a Democratic opponent. "People didn't care whether he was a Democrat or a Republican. If they liked him, they were for him."

Equally extraordinary was Rex's candor about his reclusive wife. Despite the stigma of mental illness and its potential embarrassment to his political career, Rex described Clara's condition with relative frankness. "The emotional strain of her early years was just too much for her," he told a reporter. "She has to live a different life. She needs the constant care of a doctor."

Rex concluded with a simile any Westerner could understand. "It's like training horses," he said. "Sometimes when you're starting thoroughbreds, you break 'em in too early, while you take a saddle horse and bring him along easy." The implication was clear:

since Clara's traumatic youth had made a normal adult life impossible, her husband did what he could to make it tenable.

What Rex had also done, as he admitted to friends, was fall in love with someone else. A blond divorcee a decade younger than Clara, Katie Jenkins accepted Rex's refusal to divorce his wife. His was not an easy decision, for Clara, like Sarah Bow before her, could turn vicious and paranoid, tormenting her husband with accusations and insults. No man had treated her as lovingly and loyally, yet Rex often endured bitter harangues from Clara by mail. "I am going to make this letter short and to the point," began a typical diatribe. "Rumors have been spreading that I am an alcoholic and I cannot imagine why [they] persist unless you have in a subtle way suggested [it] to other people to excuse your own actions.

"You have made a fool of me in Las Vegas with that woman. I certainly do not enjoy the gossip you have aroused by appearing in public with this Katy [sic] and perhaps other women as well.

"I only see you on Xmas Day for a few hours and I know you only put in an appearance because of our two sons and this whole business is a mockery. You are not fooling the boys and you are not fooling me."

Clara was devoted to her sons, who had grown into respectful and respective versions of their parents. Blond-haired, blue-eyed and fair-skinned like his father, Tony Beldam stood 6'5", though the cowboy boots he always wore increased his height another three inches. By contrast, George Beldam was all Bow, with his mother's brown eyes, auburn hair, and 5'9" height. George married in 1960 and Tony the following year, and although Clara did not attend either wedding, she thought her daughters-in-law "lovely" and "wonderful." The birth of Charles Robert Beldam in 1961 also delighted her. "I'm a grandma now!" Clara proclaimed to Marion Lewyn in a rare phone conversation.

"George hasn't been married too long," wondered her listener aloud. "What was it, a preemie?"

"Naw, ya fool—it was shotgun!" giggled the new grandmother. For a moment, Marion Lewyn was reminded of her irrepressible houseguest of thirty years ago. For a moment, Clara had not changed a bit.

On July 4, 1962, thirty-one years after the rodeo he and Clara had hosted in Searchlight and two weeks after filing his candidacy for governor, Rex Bell attended an Independence Day rally to introduce his running mate and protégé, neophyte politican Paul Laxalt. Afterward Rex returned to Katie Jenkins's home and collapsed from a fatal heart attack. He was fifty-eight years old.

Since his certain victory had precluded any intraparty rival, Rex's sudden death threw state Republicans into turmoil. Clara was also frantic, for virtually every obituary of her husband speculated on whether she would emerge from seclusion to attend his funeral.

In Las Vegas, seven hundred mourners gathered to pay their last respects to Rex Bell. His widow was not among them.

In Los Angeles, a second service was held at Forest Lawn Memorial Park, where Rex would be buried. Fifteen minutes before it began, a black limousine pulled up to Forest Lawn's Church of the Recessional and a fifty-six-year-old woman in a billowing black silk dress, black picture hat, and dark glasses emerged from it. Immediately Tony and George Beldam rushed to their mother's side, shielding her from reporters, cameramen, and fans. Clara managed a wan smile and brief wave. It was her first public appearance in fifteen years.

During the eulogy, Clara sat stoically beside her sons and tried to ignore the sobs of Katie Jenkins nearby. Afterward she rose, approached the casket, and planted a farewell kiss on the forehead of her husband, who had been laid out in his trademark western wear. Then she left.

Past experience had led Clara to associate exposure with humiliation, and this latest instance proved no exception. In his will, Rex split his estate between his sons and bequeathed his interest in both Western Wear stores (besides the original Las Vegas location, Tony ran a second store in Reno) to Katie Jenkins. His widow was left nothing.

The press interpreted it as a betrayal from beyond the grave, and Clara obliged them with an indignant reaction. "I was stunned that I had been left out of my husband's will," she wrote Hedda Hopper, well aware that her words would reappear in Hopper's column. "In my will he would have received half of my estate and my two sons the other half." Actually, her will left everything to her sons, and unlike her late husband, whose estate was $100,000, astute investments and interest income had increased Clara's trust fund to $450,000. She was much wealthier than Rex, and her exclusion from his will was due to economic, not personal factors. His sons and lover needed the money. Clara did not.

Whether she had overlooked this or was just saving face in her letter to Hopper was beside the point: in Clara's mind, she had ventured into the world and been punished for it. Doctor's appointments and Christmas shopping excepted, she would never leave home again.

Her hypochondriacal ailments had convinced Clara that she would predecease her husband. When he died first, she grew certain her end was near and began preparing herself and her sons for it. "I'm gettin' everythin' together for you boys," she told Tony and George as she catalogued her huge collection of photographs, newspaper clippings, correspondence (including copies of her own letters), contracts, and fan mail from as far back as 1926. She also planned her funeral in meticulous detail, choosing the clergyman, text, pallbearers, casket ("the lining should be in either satin or silk of a pastel shade, preferably in apricot or egg shell"); clothing ("a flattering negligee also of pastel shade but not to conflict with the lining of the casket"); hair and makeup ("Helena Rubinstein's color lift in bright auburn; brown eyebrow pencil, eyeshadow, and false eyelashes; lips a shade of red that is most flattering, and my mouth made fuller than the natural lines"). To assist the mortuary beautician, Clara provided stills of herself in *Call Her Savage* and *Hoopla* "to help make me look as lifelike as possible." She did not find this at all morbid.

Ready to die, she saw no reason to make even minor household improvements. Again and again Tony urged his mother to replace the dingy thirty-year-old curtains she had brought from

Rancho Clarita. Clara refused. She would rather leave her money to her sons, she said, than spend it on herself.

Exactly one month after Rex's death, Marilyn Monroe committed suicide. If any woman could empathize, it was Clara, and although she had survived stardom and her successor had not, the loss left her desolate. "She was so lovely and too young to die. God bless her," she wrote of her favorite actress. Nonetheless Monroe's instant martyrdom struck Clara as extreme, for compared to the trials in her life, her successor's tribulations seemed minor. "She was never in the position that I was caught in," Clara noted. " 'Hot copy,' yes, we were both that—but mine was *bad* hot copy. She never had to go through quite the horrible things that happened to me."

The distinction did not lessen her compassion. "I never met M.M., but if I had, I would have tried very hard to help her," concluded Clara wistfully. "A sex symbol is a heavy load to carry when one is tired, hurt, and bewildered."

In 1957 the George Eastman House, a film and photography museum in Rochester, New York, asked silent film directors, actors, and cameramen to name the greatest artists of their era. As expected, the actress most often cited was Greta Garbo. Unforeseen was her stiffest competition, which came not from Mary Pickford, Lillian Gish, or Gloria Swanson, but Clara, who ran a close second to Garbo and far ahead of everyone else.

The tabulations left Louise Brooks triumphant. Now a Rochester resident and silent film scholar, Brooks had taken to interrupting interviews about her own career to proclaim her idol "the most neglected and underrated of all film actresses." When her peers voted their agreement, a colleague of Brooks's urged Paramount to distribute its prints of Clara's silent movies to revival theaters and college film societies. The studio refused, so the movies continued to sit in warehouses, ignored and untended. Such carelessness would soon have serious consequences.

While her silents languished, her talkies were licensed to television. Clara was furious at Paramount for denying her royalties (she would not be compensated, the studio had informed her, for a medium which her contract did not mention) and mystified by the public's enthusiastic response to these long and, in her opinion, deservedly forgotten films. "I cannot understand why fans still write me," she wrote friends with genuine befuddlement. "Of course, I'm pleased to no end that they still remember me. I even hear from young teenagers wanting pictures and autographs. This is very puzzling to me." Renewed fame brought new fans, who descended upon Aneta Street, knocking on doors to learn where Clara lived. Fond of the quiet neighbor who allowed their children to swim in her pool, the predominantly Japanese community would protect Clara's privacy by bursting into feigned gibberish whenever strangers inquired about her. Those who found the house anyway were rewarded for their persistence: Estella Smith would answer the door, take the photograph proffered of Clara, and return with an inscription upon it. All were signed the same way: CLARA BOW, "IT" GIRL OF THE SILVER SCREEN, 1925–32. No fan ever saw or spoke to the star herself.

Neither did Rudy Behlmer, whose 1963 encounter with Clara was nonetheless unique. Assigned to document her career for *Films in Review,* Behlmer wrote his subject and asked for an interview. Several requests and no replies later, he sent his completed manuscript to Clara to elicit her opinion of it. The results were remarkable: Belhmer's manuscript was returned promptly, its margins jammed with corrections and comments in Clara's shaky scrawl. A lengthy, typed letter providing additional information followed.

Unconventional as it was, the exchange constituted the first interview Clara had given in thirty years and as such was invaluable if not always accurate. Like any living legend, Clara sought to control her lore, though by now her life was so steeped in denial that she undoubtedly believed hers here. "I never paid any woman $30,000 or 30,000 cents," she declared of the Elizabeth Pearson settlement despite incontrovertible proof to the contrary. "And I never cursed a microphone, how silly!"

At the end of her letter, Clara apologized to Behlmer for her reluctance to cooperate further. "I've had many offers for the story of my life, but so far I've turned them down," she admitted, adding that if she ever changed her mind, her memoirs "will be a shocker in more ways than one." On that tantalizing note, Clara explained why she wouldn't: "I adore my two sons and their wives and my grandson, and I think they are the real reasons I'll never write the book. There are many things in my life that might possibly cause them embarrassment, and for all the money in the world I could not do this as I love them too much. Roger and out."

On Sunday evening, September 26, 1965, Clara prepared for her nightly bout with insomnia by watching a telecast of *The Virginian,* a 1929 western starring Gary Cooper and directed by Victor Fleming. A nurse substituting for Estella Smith sat in a chair beside her.

At six minutes past midnight, Clara's head slumped suddenly against her pillow. In someone else the motion might have been mistaken for sleep, but her nurse knew better. For once and forever, Clara Bow would rest in peace.

# EPILOGUE

The autopsy report revealed that Clara had been suffering from severe heart disease for years, and that her final, fatal seizure had not been her first. Apparently a minor heart attack had passed unnoticed by a woman preoccupied with hypochondriacal aches and pains.

Following his mother's instructions, Tony Beldam asked the Reverend Kermit Kastellanos of the All Saints Episcopal Church to preside over her Forest Lawn funeral service. Reverend Kastellanos read the Twenty-third Psalm from the Episcopal Book of Common Prayer, and Ralph Edwards read from Kahlil Gibran's *The Prophet* as Clara had planned. Also chosen in advance were her pallbearers: ex-leading men Richard Arlen, Jack Oakie, and Buddy Rogers (Gilbert Roland was on location in Europe); former heavyweight champion of the world Jack Dempsey; and Los Angeles *Times* columnist Paul Coates. She was buried beside Rex.

In 1964 British writer Kevin Brownlow visited America to interview silent filmmakers and actors for a book on their era, and four years later *The Parade's Gone By* was published to international acclaim. Clara was not mentioned once.

From Rochester, Louise Brooks (who rated an entire chapter in *The Parade's Gone By*) was outraged. "You brush off Clara Bow," she wrote Brownlow, "[for] some old nothing like Brooks.

"The more I think of it," fumed this self-described old nothing, "the madder I get. You writing about some old fucks and not even mentioning Clara Bow's name. Clara made three pictures which will never be surpassed: *Dancing Mothers, Mantrap,* and *It.*"

Though Brooks soon forgave Brownlow, she still bemoaned the neglect her idol was receiving. The publication that same year of a comprehensive volume called *Hollywood in the '20s* appeased her somewhat, since Clara graced its cover and was characterized within as "insolent, beautiful, and distinctly talented [with] a positive, aggressive sexuality." Now Paramount was deluged with requests for her movies and its warehouses were scoured for them. What was found was tragic: one storage vault after another yielded not reels of film, but handfuls of powder. The studio had allowed its silent movies to disintegrate into dust.

Incredibly, Paramount did not seem to care. As museums and movie archives searched frantically for surviving prints of Clara's films, the studio refused to fund their quest, even though it would legally own whatever films were found and hence receive any profit made from them. Fortunately their lack of cooperation did not deter preservationists, who located prints of, among others, *Dancing Mothers, Mantrap,* and *It.*

The losses were still staggering. Though preservationists never abandon hope (to this day, missing movies turn up in attics, salt mines, and even mislabeled studio vaults), the official list of "lost" films constitutes eighty percent of all silent movies. Among them are all Clara's 1928 releases, including *Ladies of the Mob,* her one attempt at drama; and *Red Hair,* which opened with a reel of Clara in Technicolor.

Most of her talkies were saved by television broadcasts, which necessitated striking new prints before irreparable decomposition had occurred. Yet to this day, prints of *True to the Navy,* the only film to feature Clara and Rex together, and *No Limit,* the movie modeled on her Cal-Neva gambling scandal, sit idly in archives, unsaved and, unless funds are raised, awaiting imminent oblivion.

The publication of *Hollywood Babylon* in 1975 and a lurid, book-length exposé of "the 'It' Girl" a year later defamed Clara almost five decades after the *Coast Reporter* had first done so. Though the dead have little legal recourse against libel, her sons considered a lawsuit but decided not to call attention to stories that did not merit any. But the damage was done: Clara became a fixture of volumes like *The Intimate Sex Lives of Famous People.* Likewise, 512 Bedford Drive became an obligatory stop of Hollywood tour buses, whose passengers still gawk at the site where, their guide claims, a slut with "It" took on a squad of Trojans.

Curiously the advent of music videos helped restore Clara's reputation. So enchanted was Prince that his 1985 album *Around the World in a Day* featured her on its cover and included a song, "Condition of the Heart," with a lyric about her. So enthralled was Madonna (whose manager proclaimed her "the 'It' Girl of the '80s") by *Mantrap* that, like Marilyn Monroe a generation earlier, "the Material Girl" announced her desire to portray "the 'It' Girl" in a movie.

Current showings of silent films on cable television and their availability on videocassette has widened Clara's audience beyond film-buffs and rock stars. One spellbound viewer was her son, who saw *It* for the first time in 1987, sixty years after its initial release. "If I ever saw Mother, I saw her in that movie," says Tony today. "The tremendous facial expression . . . It brought back so vividly what she was like." Actually, "the 'It' Girl" was who Clara *wished* she were like. With her films as her legacy, that wish has finally been granted.

# AFTERMATH

---

After his father's death, **Tony Beldam** changed his legal name to Rex Anthony Bell and attended law school. In 1986, Rex A. Bell was elected District Attorney of Clark County, Nevada, a jurisdiction which includes Las Vegas. He lives there with his third wife and two children.

**George Beldam** also lives in Las Vegas. He is divorced.

**Billy Bow** served under General George S. Patton in World War II. He died in 1955 from injuries sustained in combat.

The outbreak of World War II trapped **Tui Lorraine Bow** in Australia, where she had been traveling. She never returned to America, though she did continue her acting career. Recent appearances include supporting roles in *The Earthling* with William Holden and *Heatwave* with Judy Davis.

**Lina Basquette** married seven times, then retired from movies to breed Great Danes. She still judges at dog shows across the country.

**Louise Brooks** died of emphysema in 1985. **Teet Carle** celebrated his eighty-ninth birthday in 1988. **Gary Cooper** died of cancer in 1961. **Jimmy Dundee** died of leukemia in 1954.

"I had a ball," says **Daisy DeVoe** of her eighteen-month jail term. "I was the pet of all the prison wardens, 'cause I did their nails." After her release in 1933, Daisy worked in the aviation industry, remarried three times, and retired in 1968. Still energetic and independent, she lives alone and enjoys her anonymity.

During her trial, Daisy confronted her prosecutors. "You two are railroading me, and you'll both come to a bad end because of it," she told them. Four months later Assistant District Attorney **David Clark** was charged with double murder. District Attorney **Buron Fitts** committed suicide in 1973.

In 1934 **Victor Fleming** impregnated his best friend's wife and reluctantly married her. The birth of daughter Victoria turned the confirmed bachelor into a doting father and devoted husband until his 1948 affair with Ingrid Bergman. On a family vacation in Arizona the following year, Fleming suffered a fatal heart attack. He was sixty-five.

True to his word, **Buddy Fogelson** returned to Texas and struck oil. He and his wife, former actress Greer Garson, divide their time between a Dallas mansion and New Mexico ranch.

**Artie Jacobson** was assistant director of dozens of movies, including *A Farewell to Arms* with Gary Cooper and Helen Hayes, *Miracle on 34th Street* with Edmund Gwenn and Maureen O'Hara, and *Camelot* with Richard Harris and Vanessa Redgrave, the final film of his fifty-year career. Widowed in 1969, he turned eighty-seven in 1988.

**Sam Jaffe** founded The Jaffe Agency, whose clients included Humphrey Bogart, Lauren Bacall, Fredric March, and Barbara Stanwyck. Now retired, he lives in Beverly Hills.

After Rex Bell's death, **Katie Jenkins** never remarried. She lives in Las Vegas and remains a close friend of his sons.

Rex's running mate and protégé **Paul Laxalt** was elected lieutenant governor of Nevada in 1962 and governor four years later. In 1974 he won a seat in the U.S. Senate and served two terms. He now practices law in Washington and is considered one of President Ronald Reagan's closest friends.

Still making movies at the Marathon Street studios where Clara worked, **Paramount Pictures** (a subsidiary of the Gulf & Western Corporation) continues to dominate the film industry. Domestic grosses on such 1987 releases as *Beverly Hills Cop II, Fatal Attraction,* and *The Untouchables* exceeded $600 million. Studio founder **Adolph Zukor,** the man who brought Clara to Paramount in 1925, attended board meetings until his death in 1976 at age 103. To this day actors who work for Paramount or any other movie studio must sign contracts with morals clauses.

After bilking Clara of $30,000 and fathering a second son, **William Earl Pearson** divorced his wife and became an alcoholic vagrant. He died in 1970.

The year after Clara's death, **Harry Richman**'s memoirs were published. One chapter was entitled "I Love You, Clara," though had she read its contents, she would not have returned the endearment. The book was not a success. Alone and destitute, Richman died in 1972.

In 1937 **Buddy Rogers** married Mary Pickford, who had divorced Douglas Fairbanks a few months earlier. The couple lived at Pickfair until her death in 1979. Now remarried, Rogers lives in Beverly Hills. So does **Gilbert Roland.**

**Adela Rogers St. Johns** turned ninety-four in 1988. She lives in Southern California near daughter **Elaine.**

Estranged from his family for his suicide attempt over Clara fifty years earlier, **Robert Savage** died in 1977. He never married.

**B. P. Schulberg** never reattained the prestige he had known at Paramount. After his ignominious departure from the studio, he produced a series of unsuccessful films starring **Sylvia Sidney** and gambled away his fortune. Sidney left Schulberg after she found him in bed with two prostitutes. He died in 1957. Thirty years later, Sidney was nominated for an Emmy award for her performance in *An Early Frost,* a made-for-television movie about AIDS. She also played Juno, "social worker" for the dead, in the 1988 movie comedy hit *Beetlejuice.*

In 1941 **Budd Schulberg** wrote *What Makes Sammy Run?,* a classic Hollywood novel. Thirteen years later he won an Oscar for his screenplay of *On the Waterfront.* He lives on Long Island, New York.

Though team captain **Morley Drury** worked in finance, many **U.S.C. Trojans** of 1927 joined the film industry after graduation. **Jesse Hibbs,** the All-American tackle whose thumb was broken by Clara, became a successful film and television director whose credits included *To Hell and Back* and *F Troop.* Beginning as an extra in John Ford's *Salute,* the 1928 film which also featured ex-Trojan **John Wayne** and Rex Bell, **"Racehorse Russ" Saunders** became a production manager, a position he held for fifty years on movies like *Bonnie and Clyde* with Warren Beatty and Faye Dunaway and *Stripes* with Bill Murray. Drury lives in Southern California. Hibbs died in 1985, Wayne in 1979, and Saunders in 1987.

# SOURCES

## PART ONE: INTERVIEWS

Clinton Anderson, Jean Arthur, Edward Ashley, Lew Ayres, Baby Peggy (Diana Serra Cary), Solly Baiano, William Bakewell, Lina Basquette, Rudy Behlmer, Rex A. Bell, John Bennett, Sally Blane, Priscilla Bonner, Helen Bow, Millicent Bow, Tui Lorraine Bow, Helene Rosson Bowman, Cab Calloway, Teet Carle, Lita Grey Chaplin, Virginia Cherrill, Helen Cohan, Gertrude Cohn, Henrietta Cohn, Dorothy Colbert, William "Buster" Collier, Veronica Cooper, Joseph Depew, Daisy DeVoe, Dr. John Donnelly, Morley Drury, Harry Edelson, Douglas Fairbanks, Jr., Victoria Fleming, Wynne Gibson, Dr. Karl von Hagen, John Hampton, Ruth Hiatt, Arthur Jacobson, Sam Jaffe, Julanne Johnston, William Kaplan, June Lang, Arthur Lake, Marion Mack Lewyn, Mary Anita Loos, Dorothy Mackaill, Rouben Mamoulian, Joseph L. Mankiewicz, Lowry McCaslin, Joel McCrea, Roddy McDowall, Mary Louise Miller, Patsy Ruth Miller, Muriel Montrose, Colleen Moore, Lois Moran, Florence O'Dell, William Earl Pearson, Jr., Gil Perkins, Grace Peschelt, Aileen Pringle, Esther Ralston, Dorothy Revier, Charles "Buddy" Rogers, Albert S. Rogell, Frank Ross, Elaine St. Johns, Russell Saunders, Nicholas Savage, Budd Schulberg, Irene Mayer Selznick, Charles Starrett, Bob Steele, Blanche Sweet, Regis Toomey, Rudy Vallee, Fredrika Tuttle, Helen Tuttle, Fay Wray, Henry de Ybarrando.


## PART TWO: ARCHIVES

*United States*

### CALIFORNIA

Academy of Motion Picture Arts & Sciences Library, Beverly Hills (Sam Gill)
> Clara Bow files (miscellaneous)
> Edith Head Collection
> Hedda Hopper Collection
> Paramount Pictures Collection
American Film Institute Library, Los Angeles
> Harold Rosson Oral History
Bison Archives, Beverly Hills (Marc Wanamaker)
California Bureau of Vital Statistics, Sacramento
California State Bar Association, San Francisco
> Membership Records

Director's Guild of America, Los Angeles (David Shepard)
    David Butler Oral History by Irene Kahn Atkins
    Henry Hathaway Oral History by Polly Platt
    Arthur Jacobson Oral History by Irene Kahn Atkins
U.S. Federal Court Records, Los Angeles branch
First Interstate Bank of California, Los Angeles
    Personal Trust Division (William Medley, Frederick Whitmore, Kathleen Briley)
Los Angeles County Archives (Hynda Rudd)
Los Angeles County Clerk's Office
Los Angeles County Record Center
Los Angeles Hall of Administration
    Assessor's Office
Los Angeles Registrar Recorder's Office
Mariposa County Recorder's Office
Motion Picture Country Home, Woodland Hills
    Social Services Department
National Archives—Los Angeles Branch (Diane S. Nixon)
Riverside County County Recorder's Office
St. Vincent's Hospital, Los Angeles
    Medical Records (Barbara Jenkins)
San Bernardino Department of Vital Records
Stanford University
    Sports Information Office
Superior Court of California, Mental Health Division (David A. Ziskrout)
University of California—Berkeley
    Sports Information Office
University of California—Los Angeles
    Film, Radio & Television Archives (John Tirpak)
    Special Collections
    University Research Library (Audrey Malkin)
University of Southern California
    Alumni Records
    Archives (Paul Christopher)
    Doheny Library:
        Special Collections (Ned Comstock)
        Regional Cultural History Collection (Lana Beckett, Gary Bryson)
        Sports Information Office

CONNECTICUT

Institute of Living, Hartford
    Medical Records Department (Deborah C. Johndro)
    John Donnelly, M.D.
Yale University, New Haven
    Alumni Records

DISTRICT OF COLUMBIA

Department of Vital Records
Federal Bureau of Investigation
    Freedom of Information Act Office
Library of Congress
    Motion Picture Division
National Archives
    Civil War Records Division
National Republican Senatorial Committee

ILLINOIS

American Medical Association
Bureau of Vital Statistics, Chicago

KENTUCKY

Frankfurt Bureau of Vital Statistics (Shirley Martin)

MARYLAND

Epilepsy Foundation of America, Landover (Marie Ormsby)

MASSACHUSETTS

Boston University Mugar Memorial Library (Margaret Goostray)

MINNESOTA

Mayo Clinic, Rochester
    Medical Records Department

NEVADA

Clark County Library (Toby Sulenski)
Las Vegas County Bureau of Vital Records
Las Vegas County Clerk's Office
University of Nevada, Las Vegas
    Special Collections (Susan Jarvis)

NEW JERSEY

Princeton University Firestone Library (Greta Fitzell, Jean Preston)
    John Peale Bishop Papers

NEW YORK

American Museum of the Moving Image, Astoria (Richard Koszarski)
Brooklyn City Register
Brooklyn Historical Society (Clara Lamers)
Brooklyn Public Library (Elizabeth White)
Columbia University—Butler Library
George Eastman House, Rochester (Caralee Aber, Barbara Galasso)
    Evergreen Cemetery, Brooklyn

Greenwood Cemetery, Brooklyn
International Film League, Rochester (James Card)
Kingsboro Psychiatric Center, Brooklyn (Jackie Bouyea)
King's Park Psychiatric Center, King's Park
Lincoln Center Archives of Recorded Sound (Tom Owen)
Moravian Cemetery, Staten Island
Museum of Modern Art Film Stills Archive (Mary Corliss)
New York City Board of Education (Dick Riley)
New York City Bureau of Vital Records
New York City Marriage License Bureau
New York City Municipal Archives (Renee Daniels)
New York Genealogical Society
New York City Public Library
    Genealogy Division
    Map Division
New York State Archives, Albany
New York State Library, Albany
    Humanities Division (Melinda Yates)
Phototeque (Howard Mandelbaum)
P.S. 52, Sheepshead Bay, Brooklyn (George Greco)
Silver Mount Cemetery, Staten Island (Arlene Antonucci)

OHIO

Center For Human Sexuality (Stephen Levine, M.D.)
    University Hospital, Cleveland

TEXAS

Baylor College of Medicine, Houston
    Alumni Records
Brazos County Clerk's Office
Dallas County Medical Society (Robert Heath)
Dallas *Morning-News* (Martha Muse)
Institute of Texan Cultures, San Antonio (Clare Bass)

WISCONSIN

University of Wisconsin Film Archives, Madison (Maxine Fleckner
    Ducey)

WYOMING

University of Wyoming, Laramie
    Special Collections (Gene Gressley, Emmett D. Chisum)

GREAT BRITAIN

Borough of Tower Hamlets Library, London
Thames Television, London (Kevin Brownlow)
    (interview transcripts of Dorothy Arzner, Cedric Belfrage, Lou-

ise Brooks & Anita Loos from *Hollywood: The Pioneers,* produced for
Thames Television by Kevin Brownlow & David Gill)

SOVIET UNION

Gosfilmofond, Moscow (Mark Strotchkov)


PART THREE: NEWSPAPERS & PERIODICALS

Brooklyn *Daily Eagle, Coast Reporter,* Dallas *Evening Journal,* Dallas
*Morning-News, Films In Review, Fortune,* Hollywood *Citizen,* Hollywood *Re-
porter, Image, Liberty, Life, Look,* Las Vegas *Age,* Las Vegas *Review-Journal,* Las
Vegas *Sun,* Los Angeles *Evening Express,* Los Angeles *Examiner,* Los Ange-
les *Herald,* Los Angeles *Mirror,* Los Angeles *Times, Manhattan,inc., Motion
Picture Classic, Motion Picture Magazine, Movie Classic, Nevada, Newsweek, New
Yorker,* New York *Times, Photoplay, Picture Play,* San Antonio *Light, Shadow-
land, Show, Time,* Toronto *Telegram, Variety*


PART FOUR: BIBLIOGRAPHY

American Film Institute, *Index of Feature Films: 1921–30.*
Anderson, Clinton, *Beverly Hills Is My Beat.* Prentice Hall, 1960.
Anger, Kenneth, *Hollywood Babylon.* Straight Arrow Books, 1975.
Anger, Kenneth, *Hollywood Babylon* (banned edition). Associated Profes-
    sional Services, 1965.
Arce, Hector, *Gary Cooper: An Intimate Biography.* Morrow, 1979.
Asbury, Herbert, *The Gangs of New York.* Knopf, 1928.
Behlmer, Rudy (editor), *Memo from David O. Selznick.* Grove, 1972.
Blumer, Dietrich (editor), *Psychiatric Aspects of Epilepsy.* American Psychiat-
    ric Press, 1984.
Bow, Tui Lorraine, *The Mourning After: Memories of a Star-Crossed Spirit.*
    Unpublished manuscript.
Braceland, Francis J., M.D., *The Institute of Living: The Hartford Retreat,
    1822–1972.* The Institute of Living, 1972.
Bradshaw, Jon, *Dreams That Money Can Buy: The Tragic Life of Libby Holman.*
    William Morrow, 1985.
Briggs, Isaac G., *Epilepsy, Hysteria, and Neurasthenia.* Methuen, 1921.
Brownlow, Kevin, *The Parade's Gone By.* University of California Press,
    1968.
Brownlow, Kevin, and Kobal, John, *Hollywood: The Pioneers.* Knopf, 1979.
Brundidge, Harry T., *Twinkle, Twinkle, Movie Star!* Dutton, 1930.
Cantor, Eddie, as told to Freedman, David, *My Life Is in Your Hands.* Blue
    Ribbon Books, 1932.
Chierichetti, David, *Hollywood Costume Design.* Harmony Books, 1976.
Eames, John Douglas, *The Paramount Story.* Crown, 1985.
Eells, George, *Hedda and Louella.* Putnam, 1972.

Engstead, John, *Star Shots: Fifty Years of Pictures and Stories by One of Hollywood's Greatest Photographers.* Dutton, 1978.

Etherington-Smith, Meredith, & Pilcher, Jeremy, *The "It" Girls: Lucy, Lady Duff Gordon, the Couturière "Lucile," and Elinor Glyn, Romantic Novelist.* Harcourt Brace Jovanovich, 1987.

Fitzgerald, F. Scott, *The Pat Hobby Stories.* Charles Scribner's Sons, 1962.

Fountain, Leatrice Gilbert, with Maxim, John R., *Dark Star: The Untold Story of the Meteoric Rise and Fall of the Legendary John Gilbert.* St. Martin's, 1985.

Glyn Anthony, *Elinor Glyn.* Doubleday, 1955.

Glyn, Elinor, *Romantic Adventure.* Nicholson & Watson, 1936.

Graham, Sheilah, *The Garden of Allah.* Crown, 1970.

Harmetz, Aljean, *The Making of the Wizard of Oz.* Knopf, 1981.

Haver, Ronald, *David O. Selznick's Hollywood.* Bonanza Books, 1980.

Head, Edith, & Calistro, Paddy, *Edith Head's Hollywood.* E.P. Dutton, 1983.

Hecht, Ben, *A Child of the Century.* Simon & Schuster, 1954; repr. Donald I. Fine, 1986.

Hotchner, A. E., *Doris Day: Her Own Story.* Morrow, 1976.

Kael, Pauline, *5001 Nights at the Movies.* Holt, Rinehart & Winston, 1982.

Kaminsky, Stuart, *Coop: The Life and Legend of Gary Cooper.* St. Martin's, 1980.

Kobal, John, *People Will Talk.* Knopf, 1985.

Lewis, Sinclair, *Mantrap.* Harcourt, Brace, 1926.

Moore, Colleen, *Silent Star.* Doubleday, 1968.

Oakie, Jack, *Jack Oakie's Double Takes.* Strawberry Hill Press, 1980.

Parker, Dorothy, *The Constant Reader.* Viking, 1970.

Perrett, Geoffrey, *America in the Twenties.* Simon & Schuster, 1982.

Phillips, Gene D., *Fiction, Film and F. Scott Fitzgerald,* Loyola University Press, 1986.

Ralston, Esther, *Some Day We'll Laugh.* Scarecrow Press, 1985.

Richman, Harry, and Gehman, Richard, *A Hell of a Life.* Duell, Sloan & Pearce, 1966.

Riis, Jacob, *Children of the Tenements.* Macmillan, 1904.

Riis, Jacob, *How the Other Half Lives.* Scribner, 1901.

Robinson, David, *Hollywood in the Twenties.* A. S. Barnes, 1968.

Rosen, Marjorie, *Popcorn Venus: Women, Movies and the American Dream.* Avon (paperback), 1973.

St. Johns, Adela Rogers, *Love, Laughter, and Tears: My Hollywood Story.* Doubleday, 1978.

Schickel, Richard, *The Men Who Made the Movies.* Atheneum, 1975.

Schlessel, Ken, *This Is Hollywood: An Unusual Movieland Guide.* Southern California Book Co., 1978.

Schulberg, Budd, *Moving Pictures: Memories of a Hollywood Prince.* Stein & Day, 1981.

Seeman, M. V., M.D.; Littmann, S. K., M.D.; Plummer, E., R.N.; Thornton, J. F., M.B.; and Jeffries, J. J., M.B., *Living and Working with Schizophrenia.* University of Toronto Press, 1982.

Server, Lee, *Screenwriter*. Main Street Press, 1987.
Shipman, David, *The Great Movie Stars: The Golden Years*. Hill & Wang, 1970.
Shipman, David, *The Story of Cinema*. St. Martin's, 1982.
Stone, Robert, *Children of Light*. Knopf, 1986.
Swanson, Gloria, *Swanson on Swanson*. Random House, 1980.
Temkin, Owsei, *The Falling Sickness: A History of Epilepsy from the Greeks to the Beginnings of Modern Neurology*. Johns Hopkins Press, 1971.
Thayer, Tiffany, *Call Her Savage*. Claude Kendall, 1931.
Tuttle, Frank, *They Started Talking*. Unpublished manuscript.
Walker, Alexander, *The Shattered Silents: How the Talkies Came to Stay*. Morrow, 1978.
Wellman, William, *A Short Time for Insanity, an Autobiography*. Hawthorn, 1974.
Yallop, David A., *The Day the Laughter Stopped: The True Story of Fatty Arbuckle*. Dutton, 1983.
Zukor, Adolph, with Kramer, Dale, *The Public Is Never Wrong*. Putnam, 1953.

# NOTES

---

"To DS" denotes interview with author. Abbreviations of sources most frequently cited:

RAB  =  Rex A. Bell
TLB  =  Tui Lorraine Bow
TC   =  Teet Carle
DD   =  Daisy DeVoe
AJ   =  Arthur Jacobson

## PROLOGUE

Page
1   "I'm runnin' wild": *Runnin' Wild,* music by A. Harrington Gibbs, lyrics by Joe Grey and Leo Wood. All rights reserved. Used by permission.

"She was the girl": F. Scott Fitzgerald, "A Patriotic Short," *The Pat Hobby Stories.* Fitzgerald refers to a fictitious successor of Clara's; by definition his description applies to her, too.

"Just a working girl": William Kaplan to DS.

"Jest a woikin' goil": Some written accounts retain Clara's dialect; others refine it. All who knew her stress it, so it appears throughout the text. Her words and their meaning remain the same.

"It's one of the great": David Shipman, *The Great Movie Stars: The Golden Years.*

"I smile": "The Real Clara Bow," *Motion Picture,* September 1930.

2   "I wish I were": Ibid.

"All the time the flapper": Ibid.

## PART ONE: BROOKLYN GOTHIC

4   "Even now": Clara Bow as told to Adela Rogers St. Johns, "My Life Story," *Photoplay,* February, March, and April 1928. Unless otherwise noted, all statements in this section come from this series (see Chapter 15).

Page

### Chapter One

5   his mother died: Catherine Gaylor Bow (1838–77). Her thirteenth child, Harris Bow, lived four days.

"a stupid, ugly little guy": Sam Jaffe to DS. Also, DD to DS; William Kaplan to DS; Gertrude Cohn to DS; etc.

"a modern Gomorrah": Herbert Asbury, *The Gangs of New York.*

more whores than Methodists: Needless to say, the outraged reformer was a Methodist Bishop.

6   emotionally unstable mother: Sarah Hatton Gordon (b. 1849).

"serious anemia": Letter from Clara Bow to Rudy Behlmer, June 14, 1963.

7   Apparently . . . she was already pregnant: Sarah Bow conceived her second daughter ten months after her marriage. It is possible but improbable that her first was also conceived within this period.

"hell on earth": Jacob Riis, *How the Other Half Lives.*

### Chapter Two

10   Frederick Gordon committed: Sarah Hatton Gordon was committed to the Long Island State Hospital for the Insane in Brooklyn on August 22, 1906. On October 30, she was transferred to King's Park State asylum in Suffolk County, where she died on November 9, 1907.

"very much a dream existence": Letter from Dr. Frederick Moersch to Dr. John Doyle, January 13, 1940.

11   "I have known hunger": Letter from Clara Bow to Rudy Behlmer, June 14, 1963.

ghetto nomads: An incomplete list of Clara's childhood residences:

| | |
|---|---|
| 1905 | 697 Bergen Street |
| 1906 | 766 Bergen Street |
| 1909 | 746 Dean Street |
| 1912 | 436 Prospect Place |
| 1913 | 428 Prospect Place |
| 1915 | 436 Prospect Place |
| 1916 | 33 Prospect Place |
| 1917 | 2215 Emmons Avenue |

Page

1919   33 Prospect Place
1921   887 73rd Street
1922   347 Ridgewood Avenue
1923   9 Prospect Place
1923   44 Church Street

11   "Don't look at me": RAB to DS.
     whipped her: Ibid.

12   Johnny: last name unknown.
     a B+ average: P.S. 111, P.S. 9, P.S. 98 records, 1911–19.
     a cousin: Nell Baker.

13   "We'd go to the Carlton": John Bennett to DS.
     "You ain't goin' ": DD to DS.

14   "ugliest little mutt": Dallas *Morning News,* June 17, 1930.

15   abortionist: "The reason I quit this job would make a small book
     . . . tragic, too." Letter from Clara Bow to Rudy Behlmer, June
     14, 1963.

16   "Called in person": "A Dream Come True," *Motion Picture Classic,*
     January 1922.

18   "The trouble was": "She Wants To Succeed," *Motion Picture Clas-
     sic,* June 1926.
     "The rapidity of her improvement": *Shadowland,* January 1922.


*Chapter Three*

20   "made a 'still' ": "A Dream Come True," *Motion Picture Classic,*
     January 1922.

21   Clara Bow, her wealthy aunt: Clara Hart Bow (1861–1937),
     widow of Edward Bow (1856–1915), Robert's eldest brother.
     a cousin: David Decker (1894–1928), son of Robert Bow's sister
     Eurilla (1874–1944).
     "Find out for yourself": "She Wants To Succeed," *Motion Picture
     Classic,* June 1926.

22   Then she fainted: Original manuscript by Rudy Behlmer, cor-
     rected by Clara Bow, May 1963.

23   committed Sarah to an asylum: King's County Asylum in Brook-
     lyn. The name had been changed since her mother's 1906 com-
     mitment to the same facility.
     intensive psychotherapy: See Chapter 28.

24   "Recovered": King's County asylum records.
     she told him that her mother: John Bennett to DS.

Page
26    "temporal lobe epilepsy": Dietrich Blumer, *Psychiatric Aspects of Epilepsy.*

epilepsy was classified: Isaac G. Briggs, *Epilepsy, Hysteria and Neurasthenia.*

masturbation and sunstroke . . . enemas or emetics: Ibid.

**Chapter Four**

27    Osgood Perkins: Father of actor Anthony Perkins.

was paid $2,000: Gene D. Phillips, *Fiction, Film and F. Scott Fitzgerald.*

"horrible": AJ to DS.

28    "just looking at each other": Ibid.

"There's no describing him": Ibid.

29    "This dynamic and erratic whirlwind": Frank Tuttle, *They Started Talking.* All rights reserved. Published with permission of Fredrika Tuttle and Helen Tuttle.

"Oh, that happened": AJ to DS.

"Christ!": Letter from F. Scott Fitzgerald to John Peale Bishop, undated [April 1925]. All rights reserved. Published with permission of the Princeton University Library and Fitzgerald estate.

"the whole picture is sordid": Letter from New York Motion Picture Commission to W. W. Hodkinson Corp., January 21, 1924.

"Glenn Hunter gives an interpretation": *Variety,* February 29, 1924.

"Money never meant much": AJ to DS.

30    Bachman appointed Maxine Alton: Later Alton would try to take credit for bringing Clara to Bachman's attention. Events at the time refute this. (AJ to DS. Also, see Chapter 5).

"Clara was going": Maxine Alton, "Clara's First Train Ride," *Photoplay,* January 1930.

"By the time": Ibid.

31    "Howda they stay fresh": Ibid.

"She wore the same sweater": Ibid.

PART TWO: HOLLYWOOD FLAPPER

34    Oh, come my love: Dorothy Parker in *The Hollywood Book of Quotes.*

Page

### Chapter Five

35   Reid died: January 18, 1923. Sarah Bow had died on January 5.
36   Paramount: The titular "Paramoun." appears throughout the
     text, though the studio was actually known as Famous Players–
     Lasky from 1916 until 1927, when it was retitled Paramount
     Famous–Lasky Corporation. In 1930 its name was changed again
     to Paramount Publix, then in 1935 to Paramount Pictures, Inc.
     "The Artist agrees": Five-year contract between Famous Players–
     Lasky Corporation and Clara Bow, August 16, 1926. The clause
     was omitted before she signed it (see Chapter 9).
     five years later: See Chapter 18.
     "What happened?": Alton, op. cit.
     "You'll understand": Ibid.
37   "Is this a joke?": Ibid.
     "state-righted": AJ to DS.
     "pleaded and cajoled": Alton, op. cit.
     "It was the most brutal": Ibid.
     "She was an emotional machine": Ibid.
38   "the longest weeks": AJ to DS.
     "I'd try to pay": Ibid.
39   "He didn't try": Bow, op. cit.
     quadrupled her salary: AJ to DS.
40   "Two days": Colleen Moore to DS.
     "You don't need that close-up": AJ to DS.
     "You're a big star": Ibid.
     "She'd gone straight to a doctor": Ibid.
41   "would make the bosses sore": Bow, op. cit.
     she accidentally discovered Schulberg and Alton: Institute of
     Living records.
     "The first Christmas": AJ to DS.
     She insisted: Ibid.
     "Clara was the sweetest": Ibid.

### Chapter Six

42   "She ran away with it": AJ to DS.
     "A horrid little flapper": *Variety,* January 10, 1924.

Page
42      "quite well played": New York *Times,* January 7, 1924.

"impossible": Alton, op. cit.

thirteen Baby Stars: 1924 WAMPAS Baby Stars, in alphabetical order: Clara Bow, Elinor Fair, Carmelita Geraghty, Gloria Grey, Ruth Hiatt, Julanne Johnston, Hazel Keener, Dorothy Mackaill, Blanche Mehaffey, Margaret Morris, Marian Nixon, Lucille Ricksen, Alberta Vaughn.

"who during the past year": Roi A. Uselton, "The Wampas Baby Stars," *Films in Review,* January 1970.

"He was a drunk": Ruth Hiatt to DS.

43      "Clara clung to my mother": Ibid.

"She was peppy and vivacious": Ibid.

"I liked her": Dorothy Mackaill to DS.

"Clara was an awfully sweet girl": Ruth Hiatt to DS.

"Clare Bow": New York *Times,* October 21, 1924.

44      "She'd change her hairstyle": Diana Serra Cary (Baby Peggy) to DS.

"She had somebody come in": AJ to DS.

Grace Kingsley arrived: Ibid.

45      "I'm Clara Bow's father!": Ibid.

One night Jacobson casually mentioned: Ibid. Jacobson refuses to identify the director by name.

Robert went down the block: At the time the Bows lived at 1714 North Kingsley Drive and Ella Mowery at 1740. They moved to 7576 Hollywood Boulevard shortly thereafter.

a twenty-three-year-old orphan: "Marital Ties Cut by Father of Clara Bow," Los Angeles *Examiner,* December 22, 1927.

"about an hour and a half": AJ to DS.

"kissless romance": *Examiner,* op. cit.

46      he spanked her: "Spanking Hurt," *Variety,* August 13, 1924.

"wild harum-scarum child": *Examiner,* op. cit.

"the most colossal golddigger": Ibid.

the couple planned: AJ to DS.

"The pivotal idea": New York *Times,* February 5, 1925.

47      "a damned fresh kid": "The Kid Who Sassed Lubitsch," *Motion Picture Classic,* June 1925.

"a godsend": "She Wants To Succeed," *Motion Picture Classic,* June 1926.

"Clara Bow absolutely triumphs": *Variety,* August 1, 1925.

"Joseph P. Kennedy Presents": The trailer for *The Keeper of the Bees* is all that survives of the film.

Page
47    "Clara Bow acts all over the lot": *Variety,* October 25, 1925.

"When a man spends too much time": American Film Institute, *Index of Feature Films,* 1921–30.

48    "daily changes": *Variety,* June 12, 1925.

"wrap it up": AJ to DS.

"She was wearing": Budd Schulberg, *Moving Pictures: Memories of a Hollywood Prince.*

49    "the assistant director": Ibid.

50    "She could cry": William Kaplan to DS.

"We all loved her": Ibid.

"As long as she was working": Ibid.

"Bar Mitzvah suit": Gertrude Cohn to DS.

"alerting her to the B.P.-Bow situation": Schulberg, op. cit.

"His organization was the cheapest": Letter from Louise Brooks to Kevin Brownlow, November 22, 1977.

51    "My impression of my father and Clara": Budd Schulberg to DS.

"He wanted her": AJ to DS.

"She was scared": Sam Jaffe to DS.

*"meshuganah shiksa":* Schulberg, op. cit.

### Chapter Seven

53    actors and technicians from neighboring productions: William Bakewell to DS. Bakewell was acting in *The Last Edition* on an adjoining stage.

"They all bristled up": David Butler, Director's Guild Oral History by Irene Kahn Atkins.

"Am I doing all right?": William Kaplan to DS.

"steady fella": Schulberg, op. cit.

"my first really big love experience": "The Love Life of Clara Bow," *Motion Picture Classic,* November 1928.

"I don't know what was in the note": Schulberg, op. cit.

54    "We was real happy": Bow, op. cit.

"greasy Mexican": RAB to DS.

Audiences jeered: *Variety,* January 20, 1926.

"B. P. Schulberg is probably getting the best break": *Variety,* October 21, 1925.

55    "She has eyes": New York *Times,* July 19, 1926.

56    "When she tried to be sexy": William Wellman in Richard Schickel, *The Men Who Made the Movies.*

56    "the inadvisability of having Miss Bronson": *Variety,* November 18, 1925.

"If I read this in a paper once more": "A Comedy of Errors," *Photoplay,* March 1926.

57    lacks a comforting resolution: When *Dancing Mothers* opened in New York, Paramount provided audiences with "coupons" to evaluate its ending *(Variety,* February 26, 1926).

"I saw that the girl got no sympathy": "She Wants to Succeed," *Motion Picture Classic,* June 1926.

"languidly patrician"; "alarmingly active": Pauline Kael, *5001 Nights at the Movies.*

58    "She was absolutely a sensation": Louise Brooks in *Hollywood: The Pioneers,* a Thames Television production. Interview transcript courtesy of Kevin Brownlow and David Gill.

bought a chow dog the same shade: AJ to DS.

## *Chapter Eight*

59    "Every dame": John Kobal, *People Will Talk.*

"Oh, honey": Helene Rosson to DS.

"A tough guy": Edward Sutherland, Columbia University Oral History.

"Oh, yeah, he was a tough guy": AJ to DS.

"Gable owes everything": Kobal, op. cit.

61    " 'on' all day and alone at night": Kobal, op. cit.

62    "knew that there was something going on": William Kaplan to DS.

"A temperament that responded": Adela Rogers St. Johns, *Love, Laughter and Tears: My Hollywood Story.*

"the most undereducated aspirant": Richard Griffith.

Schulberg suggested that Paramount executives trick Clara: Memo from Henry Herzbrun to B. P. Schulberg, July 8, 1926.

the studio contacted Robert Bow: Letter from Henry Herzbrun to Bernard Campe, July 16, 1926 (see Chapter 9).

To add treachery to trickery: Letter from Louis E. Swarts to Henry Herzbrun, April 27, 1926. "Thanks for yours of April 21st about the Clara Bow option. I see no reason for advising Jack Bachman on the subject," Paramount's East Coast attorney wrote his West Coast counterpart.

63    "I'd been in show business": TLB to DS.

unbilled roles: These included a few Stan Laurel comedy shorts

Page

and *The Great Circus Mystery,* a 1924 Universal serial. Tui also had a featured role in a 1926 low-budget quickie called *Sunshine of Paradise Alley,* the only movie in which she was ever billed.

63    "I couldn't believe": TLB, *The Mourning After: Memories of a Star-Crossed Spirit.*

64    "Where is he?": Ibid.

"and they came, my dear": TLB to DS.

"people who'd never paid no attention": Bow, op. cit.

"Victor Fleming steered me straight": Ibid.


**Chapter Nine**

65    "and said he hadda friend": "Ego Complex Defined by Clara Bow," Los Angeles *Examiner,* June [9?], 1926.

"We talked": Ibid.

"poet lover": Ibid.

"Never mind my fiancé": Ibid.

"She bit his lips": Ibid.

"I didn't bite his lip": "The Love Life of Clara Bow," *Motion Picture Classic,* November 1928.

66    "Don't worry": Ibid.

"He said, 'I'm gonna marry ya' ": "Clara Bow's Not Married to Mr. Savage," Los Angeles *Examiner,* June 5, 1926.

" 'Don't be sill' ": Ibid.

"If we get a license": Ibid.

"Take me home": Ibid.

"I am engaged to Gilbert Roland": Ibid.

"I thought she returned my love": "Savage Just Episode in My Young Life, Declares Clara Bow," Los Angeles *Examiner,* June 6, 1926.

A haunting voice comes in the twilight: Ibid.

67    "to end it all": "Actress' Beau Cuts Wrists," Los Angeles *Times,* June 6, 1926.

"Lunacy Commission": Comprised of members of the L.A. County Medical Association and General Hospital's Psychopathic Department.

"Say, listen, Judge": " 'Never Meant to Die,' Savage Tells Court," Los Angeles *Examiner,* June 8, 1926.

blush "the color of her hair": "Ego Complex Defined By Clara Bow," op. cit.

Page
68 "Mr. Savage is just an episode": "Savage Just Episode in My Young Life, Declares Clara Bow," op. cit.

the Savage clan: Nicholas Savage to DS. Also, Helen Savage Cummings to DS; Alice Savage to DS.

69 "She took Larry Gray home": Gertrude Cohn to DS.

"She told me, 'Be yourself' ": Eddie Cantor as told to David Freedman, *My Life Is in Your Hands.*

"captivating, heart-snatching heroine": New York *Times,* October 11, 1926.

Manhattan police were needed: *Variety,* October 13, 1926.

"Clara Bow! And how!": *Variety,* July 14, 1926.

70 "Clara Bow has taken everyone": *Motion Picture,* October 1926.

"She danced even when": Adolph Zukor with Dale Kramer, *The Public Is Never Wrong.*

Clara stalled negotiations: Unsigned letter [from B. P. Schulberg?] to Adolph Zukor, August 20, 1926.

revised version of Clara's contract: Ibid.

71 Neil McCarthy, who informed: Ibid.

"She could flirt": New York *Times,* July 12, 1926.

Paramount would establish: Five-year contract between Famous Players–Lasky Corporation and Clara Bow, August 16, 1926. Also, letter from Henry Herzbrun to California Trust Company, September 7, 1926.

72 Two years later: See Chapter 18.


*Chapter Ten*


73 "Wild Bill": AJ to DS.

"San Antonio became": William Wellman, *A Short Time for Insanity.*

74 "Vickie": TLB to DS.

"She was so cute": Charles "Buddy" Rogers to DS.

"Aw, jeez": TLB to DS.

"She wasn't fooling around": TLB to DS.

75 "the weather was so hot": Dallas Morning *News,* June 17, 1930.

"She slit his necklines": Letter from Louise Brooks to Kevin and Virginia Brownlow, December 12, 1970. Also, David Chierichetti, *Hollywood Costume Design.*

"Clara loathed the uniform": Edith Head and Paddy Calistro, *Edith Head's Hollywood.*

Page
75    FOR EDITH: Photograph property of Academy of Motion Picture Arts and Sciences, Edith Head Collection.

76    "I saw more of Clara": "Wings Star at Showing of the '27 Oscar Winner," New York *Times,* October 31, 1987.


### PART THREE: THE "IT" GIRL

78    "I was seventeen": Kobal, op. cit.


***Chapter Eleven***

79    "If Hollywood hadn't existed": Meredith Etherington-Smith and Jeremy Pilcher, *The "It" Girls: Lucy, Lady Duff Gordon, the Couturière 'Lucile,' and Elinor Glyn, Romantic Novelist.*
      Would you like to sin: Ibid.

80    "You don't realize": Gloria Swanson, *Swanson on Swanson.*

81    "Her British dignity": Ibid.
      "It is a pity": Etherington-Smith and Pilcher, op. cit.
      "I believe she plans": Ibid.
      Elinor's latest novelette: *It* first appeared in serialized form in *Cosmopolitan* magazine.
      " 'It', hell": Dorothy Parker, November 26, 1927. Reprinted in *The Constant Reader.*
      "Of all the lovely young ladies": Etherington-Smith and Pilcher, op. cit.
      "When I got back": "The Love Life of Clara Bow," *Motion Picture Classic,* November 1928.

82    "So this is Clara Bow": "Who's IT Defines What's 'IT,' " *Photoplay* [month unknown], 1927.
      "I was awful confused": Letter from Clara Bow to Anthony Glyn, January 28, 1961. Published with permission of Sir Anthony Glyn.

83    director Clarence Badger: Josef von Sternberg is often credited with directing at least one scene of *It.* He denied this, as do others involved with the movie. (Kevin Brownlow to DS. Also, Priscilla Bonner to DS; DD to DS.)
      "Santa": TLB to DS.
      "Following my directions": Letter from Clarence Badger to Louise Brooks and James Card, date unknown. Also, *Image,* October 1957.

84    "set up the camera": Louise Brooks in *Hollywood: The Pioneers*.
      "When I start to direct": Ibid.
85    "She was difficult to follow": AJ to DS.
86    "Clara always 'gave' ": Priscilla Bonner to DS.
      "Look!": "Who's IT Defines What's 'IT,' " *Photoplay*, op. cit.
      "that shithead": King Vidor to Leatrice Gilbert Fountain. Also,
      Leatrice Gilbert Fountain with John R. Maxim, *Dark Star: The
      Untold Story of the Meteoric Rise and Fall of the Legendary John Gilbert*.
      Opening-week grosses doubled: *Variety*, February 16, 1927.
87    "This Bow girl": *Variety*, February 9, 1927.
      "Clara Bow is the quintessence": "Has the Flapper Changed?",
      *Motion Picture*, July 1927.
88    $15,000: Grant Deed to 512 Bedford Drive, October 27, 1926.
      "a swell guy": TLB, op. cit.
89    "Once Elinor Glyn": Charles "Buddy" Rogers to DS.


      *Chapter Twelve*


90    "He was never a flamboyant swordsman": Budd Schulberg, op.
      cit.
      "He had many girlfriends": Veronica Cooper to DS.
      "lean clear through": William Kaplan to DS.
      "Women were so crazy": Kobal, op. cit.
      "I came to Hollywood": AJ to DS. Jacobson witnessed
      Bankhead's assault on Cooper during the shooting of *The Devil
      and the Deep* (1932).
91    "one-night stand": TC to DS.
      "that peculiar personality": Colleen Moore to DS.
      "Before *Wings*": Charles "Buddy" Rogers to DS.
92    "the secret dream": Schulberg, op. cit.
      "I always liketa help": Bow, op. cit.
      "grunting and pointing": Esther Ralston to DS.
93    "and chatted with him": Esther Ralston, *Some Day We'll Laugh*.
      "While we was doin' ": Bow, op. cit.
      "temporary": "Clara Bow Breaks Troth 'Temporarily,' " Los An-
      geles *Examiner*, December 2, 1926.
      "That was the last of Gilbert Roland": "The Love Life of Clara
      Bow," *Motion Picture Classic*, November 1928.
      "I will always love Clarita": Ibid.
94    "Gary's such a big boy": Ibid.

Page
94   "Clara would regale me": Ralston, op. cit.

"All I can say": Hector Arce, *Gary Cooper: An Intimate Biography.*

"I wouldn't put it past Clara": Esther Ralston to DS.

"Oh, yeah": Lina Basquette to DS.

"Oh, she'd say": TLB to DS.

95   "How many scenes," etc.: "Suffering to Stardom, *Photoplay,* April 1927.

emergency resuscitation: AJ to DS.

James Wong Howe: At the time of *Children of Divorce,* Howe (who also shot *Mantrap*) did not yet use the middle name by which he became known. It appears in the text to avoid confusion.

96   "To this minute": Rudy Behlmer, "Clara Bow," *Films in Review,* October 1963.

"If Clara Bow ever makes": "Give Clara Bow a Break," *Motion Picture Classic,* April 1931.

### Chapter Thirteen

97   "Clara Bow's return": *Variety,* May 25, 1927.

alcoholic male model: AJ to DS.

98   Clara gave Cooper a shiner: St. Johns, op. cit.

"The public likes me": "Evoking Emotions Is No Child's Play," *Theater,* November 1927.

"Give me the maximum number": Memo from B. P. Schulberg to Henry Herzbrun, January 11, 1927.

"and you can still use her": Memo from Henry Herzbrun to B. P. Schulberg, January 12, 1927.

"Gary was big and strong": "The Love Life of Clara Bow," *Motion Picture Classic,* November 1928.

"I adored Vickie": TLB to DS.

"The big 'strong man' ": *Theater,* op. cit.

99   her vacillation between Cooper and Fleming: At the time of Clara's collapse, Cooper was on location in Arizona. DARLING CLARITA, he wired her, VERY UNHAPPY TO HEAR YOU ARE ILL. I MISS YOU. I LOVE YOU. PLEASE INFORM ME OF YOUR CONDITION. HAVE SOMEONE WIRE ME [at] ARIZONA HOTEL. TAKE CARE OF YOURSELF. LOVE, GARY. (Telegram from Gary Cooper to Clara Bow, February 26, 1927.)

"ridiculous": Manuscript by Rudy Behlmer, corrected by Clara Bow, May 1963.

"There was no 'nervous breakdown' ": TLB to DS.

Page
99    sample invoice: April 9, 1927.

"Clara has not got this": Note from Robert Bow to Henry Herz-brun on invoice dated April 25, 1927.

"Disneyland": Louise Brooks in *Hollywood: The Pioneers*.

"It is just an ordinary": "The Playgirl of Hollywood," *Liberty*, August 3, 1929.

100    "the greatest actor": "That Awful 'It'!", *Photoplay*, July 1930.

"And facing you": AJ to DS.

CLARA, wrote Mix: Photograph property of RAB.

TO CLARITA: Ibid.

"Clara said it was a *loving* room": TLB, op. cit.

"Gary just gulped": Ibid.

101    cost Clara over $10,000: "Clara Out $10,000 on Pop's 'It' Restaurant," *Variety*, May 15, 1929.

"Judge Cooper was a dignified old man": TC to DS.

"His mother didn't like me": RAB to DS.

"a silly fight": Manuscript by Rudy Behlmer, corrected by Clara Bow, May 1963.

"if Gary had tried": TLB to DS.

"Gary, why don't you marry Clara?": TLB, op. cit.

"Too late": Ibid.

102    "made light": RAB to DS.

"Poor Gary": Jon Bradshaw, *Dreams That Money Can Buy: The Tragic Life of Libby Holman*.

on-the-sly sex for another two years: Dorothy Colbert to DS. Also, DD to DS. (See Chapter 21.)

"Clive wasn't nearly": *Variety*, August 31, 1927.

banned by New York censors: Letter from [New York] Motion Picture Division to Paramount, August 20, 1927.

103    religious reference that was also banned: Ibid.

"cringed for *Hula*": Schulberg, op. cit.

"blonde Clara Bow": Ibid.

"one of the feeblest": New York *Post*, August [29?], 1927.

"Paramount has the right idea": *Variety*, August 31, 1927.

104    "Miss Bow is now getting": "Par. Buys Bow Contract; Schulberg Gets $100,000," New York *Times*, August 18, 1927.

"Vic was fascinated": William Kaplan to DS.

"Vickie knew everythin' ": Bow, op. cit.

"Vickie wanted to marry her": TLB to DS.

"I believe the great love": TC to DS.

Page
105    "I really don't care": *Theater,* op. cit.

"Marriage ain't woman's only job": Dorothy Manners, "What Do Men Want?" [magazine and month unknown], 1927.

"She was her *own* man": Dorothy Mackaill to DS.

John Gilbert: Fountain and Maxin, op. cit.

Norman Kerry: Lita Grey Chaplin to DS.

Warren Burke: William Bakewell to DS.


### Chapter Fourteen

107    "If a book such as this": New York *Times,* August 31, 1975.

108    "Get on your feet!": TC to DS.

the Noblest Trojan": "Noblest Trojan," Los Angeles *Times,* February 6, 1980.

109    finale to Drury's Trojan career: Joel McCrea to DS.

"What's all this fuss?": TC to DS.

"a Greek god": Ibid.

110    "Where've these boys *been"*: Ibid.

"Captain Morley Drury's marvelous exhibition": Los Angeles *Times,* October 30, 1927.

"How d'ya get in touch": TC to DS.

"I wanna talk t'Morley Drury," etc.: Ibid. Also, Morley Drury to DS.

111    "I was amazed": Morley Drury to DS.

"Bring a fella for Tui": Ibid.

"Relax": Harry Edelson to DS.

"Nothing happened": Morley Drury to DS.

112    "We had a good time": Lowry McCaslin to DS.

"individually and collectively": "The Playgirl of Hollywood," op. cit.

"Howard Jones had nothing": Lowry McCaslin to DS.

"Okay, but hold the noise down": TLB, op. cit.

"in record time": Ibid.

"Why can't you act": Ibid.

113    "We just wanted to have some fun": TLB to DS.

tell Robert Bow they were going to Joan Crawford's: Ibid.

"the sort of place": Alexander Woollcott in *The Hollywood Book of Quotes.*

Page
113   "I loved to dance": "Noblest Trojan," Los Angeles *Times,* February 6, 1980.
      "Imagine wanting": TLB, op. cit.
114   "muscles being flexed": Ibid.
      "Jeez!": TLB to DS.
      "If you don't shut up": TLB, op. cit.
      "Fine with me!": Ibid.


*Chapter Fifteen*

116   "She dislikes gossip": "That Awful 'IT'!", *Photoplay,* July 1930.
      "there was one subject": Schulberg,. op. cit.
      "Her Brooklyn accent": Letter from Louise Brooks to Kevin Brownlow, November 22, 1977.
      "Eddie recoiled in horror": Louise Brooks in *Hollywood: The Pioneers.*
      she and Tui traveled to Yosemite: TLB to DS.
      "Clara wasn't well liked": Lina Basquette to DS.
117   "The women in the film colony": Ibid.
      "It was a shocker": Fredrika Tuttle to DS.
      used their towels as makeup rags: Helen Tuttle to DS.
118   "the apostle of unmarried sex": Schulberg, op. cit.
      "Hiya, Judge!": Ibid.
      "beginning with the judge's top jacket button": Ibid.
      "Well gee whiz": Ibid.
119   "This country got into trouble": Adela Rogers St. Johns in *American Biography,* August 1976.
      "half-witted": "Adela Hyland Tells Mate's 'Half-Witted' Rebuke, Gets Decree," *Hollywood Citizen,* October 31, 1934.
      "number one": TC to DS.
      "an omen": "The Playgirl of Hollywood," op cit. The ensuing account of Adela's interview with Clara comes from this profile.
122   "I think wildly gay people": Bow, op cit.
      accompanied her to U.S.C. games: "The Playgirl of Hollywood," op cit.
123   "agreed with us": St. Johns, op. cit.
      "I was as shocked": Colleen Moore to DS. Also, Colleen Moore, *Silent Star.*
      "She was so warm": Elaine St. Johns to DS.
      "I'm crazy t'see": St. Johns, op. cit.

Page
123   "dragged down": Elaine St. Johns to DS.
124   "amid tears and recriminations": St. Johns, op. cit.
      "Why do they always": Ibid.
      "Mosta my friends're": "How They Manage Their Homes," *Photoplay*, September 1929.


*Chapter Sixteen*

126   Schulberg assigned *Get Your Man:* The movie was Dorothy Arzner's third as director.
      Rogers replied: Charles "Buddy" Rogers to DS.
      "She bitched to me": TLB, op. cit.
      "I told her": Dorothy Arzner in *Hollywood: The Pioneers.*
      "She was just automatically": Ibid.
127   "Now you come together": Ibid.
      $100,000 bonus: "Par. Buys Bow Contract; Schulberg Gets $100,000," New York *Times,* August 18, 1927. Clara heard Schulberg received $250,000 but could not verify this "since I never got a penny from it." (Manuscript by Rudy Behlmer, corrected by Clara Bow, May 1963.)
      "Clara Bow and myself": *Red Hair* treatment by Elinor Glyn, March 17, 1927.
      a theme song called "Red Hair": "Red Hair" by Alfred Bryan, Francis Wheeler, and Ted Snyder.
128   "Billy" Bow: William Addison Bow, son of William S. Bow (1865–1954).
      "Sure, Billy's my cousin": Los Angeles *Times,* January [day unknown], 1928.
129   An inadvertent problem: AJ to DS.
      "Freddie ain't no mind-reader": Ibid.
      "She raised such hell": Ibid.
130   "Bow plus Glyn": *Variety,* March 28, 1928.
      "This Bow girl": *Variety,* March 21, 1928.
      "exceeded even the fondest": Ibid.
      "Clara Bow is the best bet": *Variety,* May 23, 1928.
      "well above normal": *Variety,* March 14, 1928.
      a $10,000 bonus: Letter from B. P. Schulberg to Clara Bow, April 9, 1928.
131   "particularly tragic parts": Elinor Glyn, *Romantic Adventure.*
      Paul Bern was urging Clara: TLB to DS.

Page
132  "Dr. Toland is very anxious": Letter from Clara Bow to Ben Schulberg. February 10, 1928.

"pale and interesting": TLB, op. cit.

133  "I wasn't used to": TLB to DS.

"I think he's *gorgeous*", etc.: Ibid.

134  "Okay, sweetie": TLB, op. cit.

"that sonofabitch": Ibid.

"He told me": "Clara Bow Love Suit Settlement of $30,000 Bared," Los Angeles *Examiner,* June 18, 1930.

*Chapter Seventeen*

135  Fan Mail Department: A subsidiary of the studio's Publicity Department, the Fan Mail Department was run by Marion Brooks. It was discontinued during the Depression.

33,727 fan letters: *Variety,* June 27, 1928.

"The 'It' Girl, Hollywood, U.S.A.": Miscellaneous fan mail to Clara Bow. Property of RAB.

the favorite star herself: *Motion Picture* announced that its "Answer Man" received more inquires about Clara than any other star (August 1928).

"Maybe youse guys": TC to DS.

fan letter from a boy: sixteen-year-old Lyman Scott.

"She would have gone": TC to DS.

136  two studio photographers: Otto Dyar and Don English.

"they stormed her": TC to DS. Clara made 240 sales in five minutes.

"Of course I know": Clinton Anderson, *Beverly Hills Is My Beat.*

a high-speed chase: TLB to DS. Also, "Clara Bow's Home Guarded, Plot Hinted," Los Angeles *Examiner,* August 30, 1927.

"An inmate of the Illinois State Hospital for the Insane": Letter from "Mr. Rand" to Clara Bow, October 2, 1928.

137  "I am sorry": Letter from B. P. Schulberg to Clara Bow, March 14, 1928.

"I could see it": TLB to DS.

"fans who come to see Clara": *Variety,* June 20, 1928.

"We don't want to see you suffer": "How to Tell Clara from Sue," *Motion Picture Classic,* August 1928.

"Poorest vehicle": *Variety,* July 4, 1928.

"Bow drew": *Variety,* July 11, 1928.

☆ 312                                                          NOTES

Page
137  *"Ladies of the Mob* seemed"*: Ibid.

138  "She wanted terribly": TLB to DS.

"Clara was making money": Kobal, op. cit.

"The world expects": Los Angeles *Examiner,* August 16, 1929.

139  "the ignorant": Schulberg, op. cit.

"Watch this", etc.: Jack Oakie, *Jack Oakie's Double Takes.*

140  "Get that boy": Ibid.

silly songs about Clara and Tui: "Clara Bow and Tui Lorraine / They are two girls I can't quite explain" are the only lyrics Tui recalls. (TLB to DS. Also, TLB, op. cit.)

"C'mon, everybody!": Oakie, op. cit.

"How d'ya know": Ibid.

"I'm lonely": TLB to DS.

"You better watch it", etc.: TLB, op. cit.

142  "Clara needed a mother": TLB to DS.

"disenchanted with what marriage was all about": Ibid.

"It came as a complete surprise": "Step-Mother of Clara Bow Ordered to Leave Country," Los Angeles *Times,* September 27, 1928.

"was pretty crazy": Solly Baiano to DS. Baiano was Clara's favorite on-the-set musician.

"on the lavender side": Ibid.

"that way": DD to DS.

"t'be real buddies": TLB, op. cit.

143  Bela Lugosi visited: Ibid.

"knowing, wicked grin": Ibid.

"Clara adores men only": Ibid.

"We became a sort of family group": TLB to DS.

"shockingly jealous": Ibid.

"a number of little dears," etc.: TLB, op. cit.

144  "I don't see why": Ibid.

"We're through": Ibid.

Tui defaced it: TLB to DS.


*Chapter Eighteen*


145  "because Miss Bow": New York *Herald Tribune,* date unknown.

"The final scene is so utterly": Memo from Vivian Moses to Ben

Page

Zeidman, May 16, 1928. Moses ran Paramount's Writing Department.

146  "a friend": William Earl Pearson, Jr., to DS.

"I have found the one man": "The Love Life of Clara Bow," *Motion Picture Classic,* November 1928.

147  "The wife was gonna sue me": "Clara Bow Airs Love Suit," Dallas *Morning News,* June 18, 1930. Also, "Clara Bow Love Suit Settlement of $30,000 Bared," Los Angeles *Examiner,* June 18, 1930.

"I don't want no publicity": TLB to DS.

"in any action or proceeding": Letter from Clara Bow to W. I. Gilbert, October 13, 1928.

GIVE BILL: Telegram from Henry Herzbrun to Clara Bow, October 14, 1928.

"I was a patient": Signed statement by Clara Bow.

148  dissolving Clara's studio-controlled trust fund: "I am awaiting your check for $25,000.00 . . . pursuant to agreement entered into between this corporation and Miss Clara Bow at your office yesterday." Letter from Henry Herzbrun to California Trust Company, October 17, 1928.

149  "the longest cablegrams": "Clara Bow Airs Love Suit," op. cit.

DARLING, wired Pearson: Cablegram from William Earl Pearson to Clara Bow, January 7, 1929.

his wife was also in Germany: William Earl Pearson, Jr., to DS.

Dear Ben: Note from Clara Bow to B. P. Schulberg, undated [December 1928].

150  "silent because the boys": *Variety,* December 12, 1928.

"See that man": Ralston, op. cit.

151  "I heard a deep, strange voice": New York *Times,* September [day unknown], 1928.

"pass" his voice test: Charles "Buddy" Rogers to DS.

"titles": Tuttle, op. cit.

"How can I be in pictures": William Kaplan to DS. A prop man at Preferred (on *My Lady's Lips* and *The Plastic Age*) and Paramount (on *Mantrap* and *Hula*), then assistant director of *Three Weekends,* Kaplan had just been promoted to Dorothy Arzner's assistant. He helped prepare Clara's filmed voice test and witnessed her reaction to it.

## PART FOUR: TALKIES

154   "Talkies are spoiling": *Motion Picture,* March 1929.


### Chapter Nineteen

155   *Kid Boots:* See Chapter 9.
     "beyond comparison": *Fortune,* October 1930.
     "overnight": AJ to DS; William Kaplan to DS; Albert S. Rogell to DS; etc.

157   'Little Bo Peep': Colleen Moore to DS.
     "Eeet is all foolishness": Alexander Walker, *The Shattered Silents.*
     "hang up": Institute of Living records.
     "an excited little girl": Charles 'Buddy' Rogers to DS.
     "whiny": Sam Jaffe to DS.
     "We were at fault": Ibid.

158   "wearing her usual sweater and skirt": Louise Brooks in *Hollywood: The Pioneers.*
     "in absolute ignorance": Letter from Louise Brooks to Kevin Brownlow, November 23, 1977.
     "just began to talk": Louise Brooks in *Hollywood: The Pioneers.*
     "so damn beautiful": TLB, op. cit.
     "stunned and helpless": Letter from Louise Brooks to Kevin Brownlow, November 23, 1977.
     "They make me feel": Louise Brooks in *Hollywood: The Pioneers.*
     musical contralto: Letter from Louise Brooks to Kevin Brownlow, November 9, 1970.
     "She was Hollywood's top female": Letter from Louise Brooks to Kevin Brownlow, November 23, 1977.
     "But she already knew": Louise Brooks in *Hollywood: The Pioneers.*
     The day after *The Wild Party:* January 3, 1929.
     a national survey: "Cinema's Crown for Popularity Awarded Clara," Los Angeles *Examiner,* April 6, 1929.

159   first annual AMPAS awards ceremony: May 16, 1929.
     "What the hell is this, Ben?": Kobal, op. cit.
     "We had quite a time": Dorothy Arzner in *Hollywood: The Pioneers.*

160   "constant fear": William Kaplan to DS.
     a deal was made: AJ to DS.

Page
160 a dangerous habit: Ibid.
161 "niggers": Ibid.
"Laughing, crying or condemning": *Variety,* April 3, 1929.
"Miss Bow Talks!": New York *Times,* April 2, 1929.
162 "skyrocketing": *Variety,* April 10, 1929.
"hot": Ibid.
"packing 'em in": *Variety,* April 17, 1929.
"one of its big weeks": *Variety,* May 1, 1929.
"started off with a bang": Ibid.
"Will accept Bow": *Variety,* April 17, 1929.
163 "Hours for seats!", etc.: "Clara Bow 'Breezes In' and Says Hello to Old Brooklyn Neighbors," Brooklyn *Daily Eagle,* March 1, 1929.
Jimmy Dundee: AJ to DS. Also, TC to DS.
164 A client suggested: DD to DS.
Tui Lorraine (who hated Daisy): TLB to DS.
"secret recipe": DD to DS.
165 her red hair look pink: Barbara Leaming to DS. Leaming is Hayworth's biographer.
"You don't have to live", etc.: DD to DS.

*Chapter Twenty*

167 home was a shambles: DD to DS.
"There's no reason", etc.: Ibid.
168 "Daisy DeVoe was a pain": TC to DS.
"If you're planning to retire": DD to DS.
"I know what a hundred dollars is": Bow, op. cit.
169 Trust PR-875: Declaration of Trust between Clara Bow and California Trust Company, May 29, 1929.
170 "wavishing Kay Fwancis": Shipman, op. cit.
she swore violently: Joseph L. Mankiewicz to DS.
"New chapter in the Clara Bow career": *Variety,* July 13, 1929.
171 *A Hell of a Life:* Unless otherwise noted, Richman's words come from his memoirs.
"May God bless and keep you": "The Richman Era," *Show,* June, 1962.
"Jesus, what a woman!": Ibid.

Page
173    "A ham who exploited her": Letter from Louise Brooks to Kevin Brownlow, November 23, 1977.

"a scumbum": DD to DS.

174    MY DEAREST . . . TO MY NAPOLEON . . . TO MY GORGEOUS LOVER: Photographs property of Dorothy Colbert.

"The very moment I laid eyes on you": "You Can't Stop Me from Falling in Love with You," music by J. Fred Coots, lyrics by Benny Davis. All rights reserved. Used by permission.

175    "Clara's engagements": *Coast Reporter,* April 4, 1931.

176    a side trip to Brooklyn, etc.: DD to DS.

"my aunts": Jean Gordon and Gertrude Gordon.


### Chapter Twenty-one

178    *"The Saturday Night Kid":* Joseph L. Mankiewicz to DS.

replacing Mankiewicz: Mankiewicz did receive a "Titles" credit for the silent version of *The Saturday Night Kid.*

"Selecting a moderately good program": *Variety,* November 15, 1929.

wife Louise Brooks: Coincidentally, Brooks had been featured in *Love 'Em and Leave 'Em,* the silent movie which provided *The Saturday Night Kid*'s plot.

"Arthur was so good": Edward Sutherland, Columbia University Oral History.

179    "I loved her": Jean Arthur to DS.

"The closer she came": AJ to DS.

"Who the hell is *that?",* etc.: Ibid.

"She was simply fascinated": Head and Calistro, op. cit.

180    "See if ya can help": TC to DS.

"The shopgirl lingo": *Variety,* November 15, 1929.

"A horrible picture": Manuscript by Rudy Behlmer, corrected by Clara Bow, May, 1963.

"A lousy no-good bastard": Richman, op. cit.

"This is from the Club Richman?": AJ to DS.

"She reverted": Ibid.

181    Gary Cooper's house: Dorothy Colbert to DS. In *A Hell of a Life,* Richman refers to his rival as "one of the best-known stars . . . a bachelor." Cooper married in 1933.

"Cheap sonofabitch": Richman, op. cit.

182    "I hope t'Christ": Joseph L. Mankiewicz to DS.

Page
183   "I always wanna cry", etc.: "Empty Hearted," *Photoplay*, October 1929.

184   GRIEF STRICKEN BY MESSAGE: Cablegram from William Earl Pearson to Clara Bow, November 20, 1929.

      "Believe we should take every advantage": Memo from M. C. Levee to Henry Herzbrun, November 29, 1929.

185   she said she was having a hysterectomy: DD to DS.

      Daisy heard about it: *Ibid.*

      house doctor at Madame Frances's: George Eells, *Hedda and Louella.*

      "clap doctor": *Ibid.*

      he was sterile: Dorothy Colbert to DS.

186   a Christmas gift from Clara: Arthur Jacobson still cherishes an elegant onyx and gold cigarette case engraved, "To Artie Jacobson, Merry Christmas, Clara Bow, 1929."

      "That was the way she liked to spend": TC to DS.

      Guinn Williams: RAB to DS.

      her arrival, etc.: "A Film Star Arrives," New York *Times,* February 2, 1930.

187   center of attention at . . . the Cotton Club: Cab Calloway to DS.

      twelve Broadway plays, etc.: "Rest in Dallas to Clara Bow Is Going to Bed at 5 in the Morning," Dallas *Evening Journal,* June 17, 1930.

      Isotta-Franschini: *Show,* op. cit.

      She drove straight to Sheepshead Bay: Millicent Bow to DS.

188   "in the proper surroundings": Los Angeles *Examiner,* January 25, 1930.

      "I sorta half-sing, half-talk": "The Real Clara Bow," *Motion Picture,* September 1930.

      cheered louder for "True to the Navy": William Kaplan to DS.


      *Chapter Twenty-two*


189   "Even then it was a terrific bargain": Joel McCrea to DS.

      "A darling boy": Sally Blane to DS.

      "The epitome of decency": Patsy Ruth Miller to DS.

190   "I'm not going to hang on forever": "Clara's New Beau," *Motion Picture Classic,* November 1930.

191   "She's the first girl": "Give Clara Bow a Break," *Motion Picture Classic,* April 1931.

Page
191    Robert Bow's hatred of Rex: RAB to DS.

"Slow in tempo": *Variety,* May 23, 1930.

"the biggest bitch": TC to DS.

192    "it will call for a lot of faith": *Variety,* May 9, 1930.

"cater-cornered": Walker, op. cit., paraphrases Jolson's joke as "sleeping crossways."

a Grinnell College newspaper's gossip column: *Grinnell Scarlet and Black,* April 16, 1930. The item read: "Word was flying around the city during vacation that Clara Bow was the proud mother of triplets. The proper thing to do is to offer congratulations which we shall hold until Clara answers our wire. Her delay in this is inexplicable after our warm friendship last summer."

"Miss Bow has not seen": Letter from Henry Herzbrun to John H. T. Main, April 30, 1930.

all three parties apologized: Letter from Edward D. Allen to Henry Herzbrun, May 6, 1930; letter from Zaneta Eager to Henry Herzbrun, May 7, 1930; letter from Frank Furbush to Henry Herzbrun, May 6, 1930.

"Paramount opened its doors": TC to DS.

193    "Gilbert Roland was the first," etc.: Harry Brundidge, *Twinkle, Twinkle, Movie Star!*

194    Anatomy of a scandal: DD to DS; TC to DS; William Earl Pearson, Jr. to DS. Also, accounts in the Dallas *Evening Journal,* Dallas *Morning News,* Los Angeles *Examiner,* Los Angeles *Herald,* and Los Angeles *Times,* June 16–25, 1930.

196    calling the film *Oh, Doctor!:* "In view of tremendous publicity now being given Bow's latest outburst, we feel *Oh, Doctor!* [a] cleanup title for her next picture. If you concur, we can make lead of *Hula* [a] young doctor . . ." Paramount West Coast Night Letter, June 19, 1930.

197    DEAREST DADDY: Telegram from Clara Bow to Robert Bow, June 19, 1930.

198    a stunning publicity portrait of Clara in a bridal gown: see Photographs. Property of RAB.

in a nun's habit: John Engstead, *Star Shots: Fifty Years of Pictures and Stories by One of Hollywood's Greatest Photographers.* Photograph property of Academy of Motion Picture Arts and Sciences.

"She disregards all laws of convention": *Photoplay,* August 1930.

Page

**Chapter Twenty-three**

200   "Yeah, I'm crazy about her": "Rex Claims Key to Heart of 'It' Girl," Los Angeles *Examiner*, January 18, 1931.

DEAREST SWEETHEART: Telegram from Rex Bell to Clara Bow, September 8, 1930.

told Daisy to pack their bags: DD to DS.

"Aw, pull in your neck": Ibid.

"You'd better get over there": Ibid.

201   "Either you make that check good": Schulberg, op. cit. Daisy DeVoe was also threatened (DD to DS).

"Miss 'It' won't be worth shit": Ibid.

202   "at that time": TC to DS.

"We agonized about what to do": Ibid.

"no story to make with Clara": Memo from David O. Selznick to B. P. Schulberg, February 2, 1931 (Rudy Behlmer, *Memo from David O. Selznick*).

"Crisis-a-Day-Clara": Schulberg, op. cit.

203   "The trouble with me is": " 'Quit Pickin' on Me!' Says Clara Bow," *Photoplay*, January 1931.

he announced . . . accepted by Lina Basquette: "Richman Says He'll Wed Lina Basquette," Los Angeles *Examiner*, November 25, 1930.

"Harry Richman would do anything": Lina Basquette to DS. Also, "Wed Richman? No, Says Lina," Los Angeles *Examiner*, November 26, 1930.

"a mistake": *Photoplay*, op. cit.

204   "I can't make no sense", etc.: Tuttle, op. cit.

the most infamous man in America appeared: "Capone Watches Work on Latest Picture," Los Angeles *Examiner*, November 15, 1930. Capone had just been branded "Public Enemy #1" by the Chicago Crime Commission.

205   "Jeez!": Tuttle, op. cit.


PART FIVE: "THIS AIN'T NO LIFE"


208   Miss Humpty Dumpty: *Photoplay*, December 1929.

"She has a way": Robert Stone, *Children of Light*.

Page

### Chapter Twenty-four

Source materials, unless otherwise noted: DD to DS; *People vs. DeVoe* transcripts and trial records; and coverage in the Los Angeles *Evening-Express,* Los Angeles *Examiner,* Los Angeles *Herald,* Los Angeles *Times, Motion Picture Classic,* New York *Times.*

210 her lover . . . James Wong Howe: AJ to DS.

213 "If she flaps her yap," etc.: AJ to DS.

215 an indictment for thirty-seven counts: Prior to the trial, Buron Fitts dropped two counts of the indictment.

218 had Clara revealed that her nemesis: Later Louella Parsons disclosed the truth but withheld Howe's name and race ("Daisy Affair Not Revealed by Film Star," Los Angeles *Examiner,* May 31, 1931). During the trial, however, Parsons offered Clara no support.

220 CLARA BOW'S SPENDING ORGIES: Headline of Los Angeles *Evening-Express,* January 19, 1931.

"If the producers": *Variety,* January 16, 1931.

towns in Texas and California: San Angelo and Riverside, respectively.

"Bow in hysterical condition": Paramount West Coast Night Letter, January 16, 1931.

221 his mistress: Schulberg, op. cit. Also, Kobal, op. cit.; TC to DS; AJ to DS.

222 "the thing she likes best": "The Playgirl of Hollywood," op cit.

"my wonderful fan friends": Letter from Clara Bow to Rudy Behlmer, June 14, 1963.

### Chapter Twenty-five

224 "extracting the last ounce": Memo from David O. Selznick to B. P. Schulberg, June 3, 1931 (Behlmer, op. cit.).

"She had a reputation": Regis Toomey to DS.

225 "I talked to her": Ibid.

"Forget it": Ibid.

"She couldn't keep her eyes off it": AJ to DS.

"Clara blew her top": Ibid.

226 "This ain't no life": Ibid.

Page
226   "the brazen mistress", etc.: *Coast Reporter,* March 28, 1931; April
4, 1931; April 11, 1931; April 18, 1931.

227   she . . . vomited: Manuscript by Rudy Behlmer, corrected by
Clara Bow, May 1963.

Libby Holman bought a Great Dane: Bradshaw, op. cit.

a new rumor: Mary Anita Loos to DS. Also, AJ to DS.

228   "We are opposed to blackmail": *Coast Reporter,* April 4, 1931.

"I modified it": "Girnau Jailed on Bow Series," Los Angeles
*Examiner,* April 23, 1931.

"morally unfit": *Coast Reporter,* March 28, 1931.

WE HAVE TRIED: Telegram from B. P. Schulberg to Clara Bow,
April 24, 1931.

229   Dear Ben: Letter from Clara Bow to B. P. Schulberg, April 24,
1931.

231   WE ARE ABOUT TO DISBAND: Telegram from Henry Herzbrun to
Clara Bow, April 27, 1931.

"We have prevailed upon Bow": Paramount West Coast Night
Letter, April 28, 1931.

"I can't do it": "Clara's Microphone Fright," *Photoplay,* July 1931.

"shattered nerves": "Clara Bow in Hospital—Picture Is Postponed," Brooklyn *Daily Eagle,* May 6, 1931.

232   "With wretched showing": Paramount West Coast Night Letter,
May 22, 1931.

"to negotiate a settlement": Paramount West Coast Night Letter,
May 27, 1931.

"there is a big chance": "Clara Bow Seeks to Quit the Screen,"
New York *Times,* May 31, 1931.

233   "I don't wanna hold Paramount": Louella Parsons, "Star Frees
Paramount from Contract," Los Angeles *Examiner,* June 3, 1931.

"I euchred her": Letter from B. P. Schulberg to Henry Herzbrun,
June 3, 1931.

"Dear Clara": Letter from B. P. Schulberg to Clara Bow, June 6,
1931.

"That's for all ya done": TC to DS.


*Chapter Twenty-six*

235   "We have an announcement": AJ to DS.

"Do you agree": *Ibid.*

300,000 acres: Three hundred acres was deeded land; the rest
was leased from the government.

Page
236    "Rex was afraid": "Clara Bow's First Interview Since Her Mar-
       riage," *Movie Classic,* April 1932.

       "I'll never announce": "Rex Bell Denies Wedding Clara Bow,"
       New York *Times,* December 5, 1931.

       "Gosh, how I could put away": " 'Rest Cure' Aid to Clara Bow
       'Comeback,' " Los Angeles *Examiner,* December 15, 1931.

237    "I never seen her": Ibid.

       "To the Greatest Actress": Letter from Allen R. Cooper to Clara
       Bow, May 31, 1931.

       Clara burst into tears: " 'Rest Cure' Aid to Clara Bow 'Come-
       back,' " op. cit.

238    "I don't know": "Roughing It With Clara," *Photoplay,* September
       1931.

       "For the first time": Ibid.

       Frederic Girnau's trial, etc.: *United States vs. Frederic Girnau* trial
       records.

239    first trans-Atlantic telephone call: "London Phones Clara Bow
       Bell in Las Vegas," Las Vegas *Age,* December 5, 1931.

       "Give us a break": "Clara Bow Becomes Bride of Rex Bell,"
       *Movie Classic,* February 1932.

       "I didn't know how": "Clara Bow's First Interview Since Her
       Marriage," op cit.

       "He's given me": Ibid.

       "No Nevada divorces": "Wedded Bliss Is Told by Clara Bow,"
       Los Angeles *Examiner,* December 19, 1931.

       "Where Now, Clara?": *Photoplay,* August 1931.

       "too good t'pass up": "Clara Bow Out to Wilds," Los Angeles
       *Examiner,* June 15, 1931.

240    platinum blonde Jean Harlow: A year later Harlow starred in
       *Bombshell,* a superb comedy whose movie star heroine, Lola
       Burns, bears more than a passing resemblance to Clara. Labeled
       "The 'If' Girl," Lola is devoted to her drunken father and corrupt
       secretary (played by Una Merkel, a dead-ringer for Daisy DeVoe).
       One of Lola's lovers, a tough and talented director, wants to
       marry her and put her life in order. It is no coincidence that
       *Bombshell's* director was Victor Fleming.

       "sensational vehicle": Teletype from David O. Selznick to RKO,
       March 4, 1932 (Behlmer, op. cit.).

241    "Rex taught me": "The Return of Clara Bow," *Variety,* November
       1932.

242    "hardly a thought": David Shipman, *The Story of Cinema.*

       "Turning Clara Bow loose": *Variety,* November 29, 1932.

Page
242   highest-grossing week: Ibid.

243   Clara visited him: Schulberg, op. cit.

TO ELINOR GLYN: Anthony Glyn, *Elinor Glyn.*

"I wanna write down": "Clara Bow Will Study Writing While Abroad," Los Angeles *Herald,* November 30, 1932.

"Can't ya understand": "So Clara Did Paris," *Photoplay,* June 1933.

244   *Mein Kampf:* Book property of RAB.

"Madness": Letter from Clara Bow to Hedda Hopper, December 26, 1959.

244   "The one thing": "Clara's European Diary," *Photoplay,* May 1933.

Bel-Air mansion: 10010 Stone Canyon Road.

"Clara had a great sense," etc.: Marion Lewyn to DS.

245   "A more mature": *Variety,* November 30, 1933.

"I've had enough": *Hollywood: The Pioneers.*

"I don't wanna be remembered": "Clara Bow Will Study Writing While Abroad," op. cit.

## PART SIX: MRS. BELDAM

248   "Marriage means": "Must Clara Bow Choose Between Marriage and Career?", *Movie Classic,* April 1933.

"She has been exceedingly unhappy": Letter from Dr. Frederick Moersch to Dr. John Doyle, January 13, 1940.

*Chapter Twenty-seven*

249   "My desert paradise": "Desert 'Shack' Gives Hope to Clara Bow," Los Angeles *Examiner,* December 17, 1931.

rented a house: 530 June Street.

two hundred pounds: AJ to DS. Jacobson visited Clara once during this period and did not recognize her.

250   playing bridge: Lew Ayres to DS.

spontaneous miscarriage: September 1936.

"the 'It' Cafe": Opened on August 31, 1937.

251   Clara had wanted a daughter: "I always wanted at least one girl . . ." Letter from Clara Bow to Rudy Behlmer, June 14, 1963.

"You're lucky": RAB to DS.

Page

  "sassin' ": Ibid.

  "HIYA, BETTY!": Ibid.

252 shot out his tires: Marion Lewyn to DS.

252 marital rift: Mayo Clinic records. Also, Institute of Living records.

  "a stupid cowboy": Report of Dr. Frederick Moersch, January 4, 1940.

253 "She now despises the ranch": Ibid.

  various ailments: Mayo Clinic records. Also, Institute of Living records.

  severe claustrophobia: Ibid.

  "Needless to say": Moersch, op. cit.

254 King Bow's favorite chores: Marge Marshall to DS.

  "You're just like your father": RAB to DS.

255 "Somethin's wrong": Ibid.

256 "Who d'ya like best", etc.: Ibid.

  "Mom?": Ibid.

  "Do you know how to read," etc.: Marge Marshall to DS.

  Tony showed her a note: Ibid. Also, RAB to DS.

  "She'll live": Ibid.

258 he would walk uptown: RAB to DS.

  "Had enough, Daddy?" Ibid.

259 Clara had consented: Manuscript by Rudy Behlmer, corrected by Clara Bow, May 1963.

  raising $550,000: Ralph Edwards Productions to DS.

  she stayed drunk: Institute of Living records.

  Karl von Hagen advised: Dr. Karl von Hagen to DS. Also, Institute of Living records.

  "I'm gonna get shock treatment": RAB to DS.


*Chapter Twenty-eight*

Source materials, unless otherwise noted: Institute of Living records; Dr. John Donnelly to DS; Francis J. Braceland, M.D., *The Institute of Living: The Hartford Retreat, 1822–1972.*

261 "Nocturnal Visitor": Story by Clara Bow. All rights reserved. Published with permission of RAB.

  "Off the screen": Letter from Louise Brooks to Kevin Brownlow, March 25, 1980.

  "The only thing": Toronto *Telegram,* September 8, 1968.

Page
263  "Of all the movie stars": Schulberg, op. cit.

264  The first memory: Twenty years earlier Clara told this to Daisy DeVoe (DD to DS).

265  "shockingly jealous": TLB to DS (see Chapter 17).

Robert Bow raped her: Institute of Living records do not state conclusively whether Clara acknowledged this. It may be that she told Rex, who informed doctors. Since Clara never mentioned it to Dr. von Hagen, this sequence seems most likely. The duration of the abuse is also speculative. Clara's romance with Artie Jacobson probably put an end to it, though her insistence on having Jacobson live with her and Robert in Hollywood may have been motivated in part by fear of its resumption.

266  "The problem of chronic insomnia": Letter from Clara Bow to Hedda Hopper, June 25, 1950.

"I found no evidence": Dr. Karl von Hagen to DS.

267  "I can't let her come back": RAB to DS.

"He won't let me": Ibid.


*Chapter Twenty-nine*

268  committed her to the Southern California Sanitarium: May 1952.

"worshipped": RAB to DS.

Doris Day: A. E. Hotchner, *Doris Day: Her Own Story.*

269  "Upset to no end": Letter from Clara Bow to Hedda Hopper, July 23, 1962.

"Rumors of me": Ibid.

"She was totally current": RAB to DS.

270  "I don't want you boys": Ibid.

"We knew the rules": Ibid.

a postcard of an obese woman: Marion Lewyn to DS.

"Why, you're Clara Bow!": RAB to DS.

"Remember me?": TC to DS.

271  a facelift: "I do hope by now that the swelling has subsided in your face," Clara wrote the deposed King of Broadway. "Again, let me say that the plastic surgery you had done is superb." Letter from Clara Bow to Harry Richman, August 25, 1956.

She refused his offer, then his visits: "Clara, do you suppose I would bother with any story in pictures if I wasn't badly in need of money," Richman pleaded after Clara had made her position clear. "You never at any time let me believe I was bothering you. I will swear on my Mother's Grave [sic] that I wouldn't do one blessed thing to cause you any worry or unhappiness." Letter from Harry Richman to Clara Bow, June 29, 1957. Also, RAB to DS.

271    "Still handsome": Letter from Clara Bow to Jack Oakie, December 10, 1961 (Oakie, op. cit.).

Hello Clarita Girl: Letter from Gilbert Roland to Clara Bow, December 19, [1949]. Constance Bennett, Roland's ex-wife and the mother of his two daughters, had replaced Clara in *What Price Hollywood?* in 1932.

272    invited him to her home: RAB to DS.

FOR CLARA BOW BELL: Photograph property of RAB.

Monroe as Clara: *Life,* April 20, 1959.

would not permit a "biopic": RAB to DS.

"I slip my old crown": Christmas cards from Clara Bow to Hedda Hopper and Louella Parsons, 1960. Her statement was handwritten in each.

inauguration: Invitation from the Inaugural Committee to Mr. and Mrs. Rex Bell, January 20, 1953.

"I needed no reminder": Letter from Rod Serling to Clara Bow, January 15, 1964.

273    "I was in a hospital": Letter from Clara Bow to Anthony Glyn, January 28, 1961.

"If, God forbid": Letter from Clara Bow to Lyston Jaco, May 5, 1952.

"You really showed up Agnes DeMille": Letter from Clara Bow to Hedda Hopper, December 26, 1959.

274    "The old saying": Letter from Clara Bow to Lyston Jaco, February 2, 1962.

"He had a universal appeal": "The Cowboy and the 'It' Girl," *Nevada,* July–August, 1985.

"The emotional strain": "Clara Bow's Career Exacted a Heavy Toll," Los Angeles *Mirror,* May 28, 1956.

275    "I am going to make this letter short": Letter from Clara Bow to Rex Bell, April 23, 1961.

"lovely": Letter from Clara Bow to Rudy Behlmer, June 14, 1963.

"wonderful": Ibid.

"I'm a grandma now!", etc.: Marion Lewyn to DS.

277    "I was stunned": Hedda Hopper, "Rex Bell's Will Stuns Clara Bow," Los Angeles *Examiner,* July 16, 1962.

"I'm gettin' everythin' together": RAB to DS.

Page

"the lining", etc.: Letter from Clara Bow to Lyston Jaco, August 13, 1960.

278    Marilyn Monroe committed suicide: In 1960 Rex made an un-billed cameo appearance in the Reno rodeo sequence of *The Misfits,* starring Monroe and his old buddy Clark Gable. Two years later all three were dead. (Rex also appeared in *Lone Star,* a 1952 western starring Gable and Ava Gardner.)

278    "She was so lovely," etc.: Letter from Clara Bow to Rudy Behlmer, June 14, 1963.

"the most neglected and underrated": James Card to DS.

Clara was furious at Paramount: "I am not naive and I know sponsors pay good money for films," she wrote the studio's president, "so I shall expect at least 30% of what you take in for any films of mine sold to a T.V. sponsor, this is only fair. If we can't agree on this there are always courts of law to settle matters." Letter from Clara Bow to Y. Frank Freeman, June 22, 1960.

the studio had informed her: "The fact is," its attorney stated, "that there were no limitations whatsoever on these photoplays or on their exhibition and exploitation." Letter from Sidney Justin to Clara Bow, July 8, 1960.

279    "I cannot understand": Manuscript by Rudy Behlmer, corrected by Clara Bow, May 1963.

1963 encounter with Clara: Rudy Behlmer to DS.

"I never paid any woman," etc.: Manuscript by Rudy Behlmer, corrected by Clara Bow, May, 1963.

"I've had many offers": Letter from Clara Bow to Rudy Behlmer, June 14, 1963.

280    On Sunday evening, etc.: "Clara Bow Dies," Los Angeles *Times,* September 28, 1965.


## EPILOGUE

281    autopsy report: Final report of W. Arterberry, M.D., October 19, 1965.

"You brush off Clara Bow": Letter from Louise Brooks to Kevin Brownlow, October 26, 1968.

282    an obligatory stop: "Babylon Revisited," *New York,* May 5, 1986.

283    "The 'It' Girl of the '80s": "These Big Girls Don't Cry," *Time,* March 4, 1985.

"the Material Girl" announced: Hollywood *Reporter,* September 11, 1985.

Page

"If I ever saw Mother": RAB to DS.


### AFTERMATH

284    "I had a ball": DD to DS.

"You two are railroading": Ibid.

285    $600 million: "Barry Diller and the Killer Dillers," *Manhattan, inc.,* February 1988.

morals clauses: Currently Paramount's reads: "If Artist should . . . fail, refuse or neglect to govern Artist's conduct with due regard to social conventions and public morals and decency, or commit any act which brings Artist into public disrepute, scandal, contempt or ridicule or which shocks, insults or offends a substantial portion or group of the community or reflects unfavorably on Artist or Employer, then Employer may . . . terminate this agreement at any time . . ."

286    in bed with two prostitutes: John Bright in Lee Server, *Screenwriter.*

# INDEX